Interior design and identity

Published in our
centenary year
~ **2004** ~

MANCHESTER
UNIVERSITY
PRESS

STUDIES IN
DESIGN

general editor:
Christopher Breward

founding editor:
Paul Greenhalgh

Interior design and identity

edited by
Susie McKellar and Penny Sparke

Manchester University Press

Manchester and New York

distributed exclusively in the USA by Palgrave

Published by Manchester University Press
Oxford Road, Manchester M13 9NR, UK
and Room 400, 175 Fifth Avenue, New York, NY 10010, USA
www.manchesteruniversitypress.co.uk

Distributed exclusively in the USA by
Palgrave, 175 Fifth Avenue, New York NY 10010, USA

Distributed exclusively in Canada by
UBC Press, University of British Columbia, 2029 West Mall,
Vancouver, BC, Canada V6T 1Z2

British Library Cataloguing-in-Publication Data
A catalogue record for this book is available from the British Library

Library of Congress Cataloging-in-Publication Data
A catalog record for this book is available from the Library of Congress

ISBN 978 0 7190 6728 0 *hardback*
ISBN 978 0 7190 6729 7 *paperback*

First published by Manchester University Press 2004
First digital paperback edition published 2012

Printed by Lightning Source

Contents

Illustrations

Contributors

Quintin Colville graduated from the RCA/V&A History of Design MA Course in 1998. He is currently completing a PhD thesis on the role of material culture in constructing notions of class among royal naval personnel, 1930–60. He is a junior research fellow at Linacre College, Oxford, and Caird senior research fellow at the National Maritime Museum. In 1999 he was awarded the Julian Corbett Memorial Prize in Modern Naval History by the Institute of Historical Research for an essay on *HMS Belfast*, and in 2002 the Alexander Prize by the Royal Historical Society for an essay on naval uniform.

Emma Gieben-Gamal graduated from the V&A/RCA History of Design MA Course in 1999. She has taught the history of design at the Surrey Institute of Art and Design and was a research fellow at the Open University working on the GLAADH project. She also co-founded gieben & wulf CULTURAL RESEARCH Ltd, and has written for magazines such as *Frieze* and *The Art Book*. She is co-author, together with her partner, Andrea Wulf, of a forthcoming cultural history of English gardens to be published by Little, Brown in 2004.

Amanda Girling-Budd graduated from the V&A/RCA History of Design MA Course in 1998. She teaches the history of design and is a part-time researcher at the Centre for the Study of the Domestic Interior. She is currently researching the production and consumption of elite furnishings in Victorian Britain for a PhD thesis on the archive of the nineteenth-century cabinet-making firm Holland & Sons.

Mary Guyatt's interest in mental asylums began while a student on the V&A/RCA History of Design MA Course, from which she graduated in 1999. She has since had work published on artificial limbs and on the medallion produced by Wedgwood for the Society of the Abolition of the Slave Trade. She works as a curator of designs at the Victoria and Albert Museum.

Susie McKellar graduated from the V&A/RCA History of Design MA Course in 1993. Since then she has taught widely in the subject area. Her publications include contributions to *The Gendered Object*, edited by Pat Kirkham and published by Manchester University Press; *Utility Re-Assessed*, edited by Judy Attfield and published by Manchester University Press; and the *Journal of Design History*. She is currently working as a research assistant at the RCA where she is also completing her PhD thesis of 'Sensible consumption, sanctified consumption or subversive consumption? Consuming through consumer guides'.

Jeremy Myerson is Professor of Design Studies and Co-Director of the Helen Hamlyn Research Centre at the RCA. A writer, editor and researcher specialising in design and architecture in relation to social change, he is author of a number of books on office design, including *The Creative Office* (with Philip Ross), *Home Office* (with Sylvia Katz), and *New Workspace; New Culture* (with Gavin Turner).

Scott Oram graduated, with distinction, from the RCA/V&A History of Design MA Course in 1994 and is currently a senior lecturer in Contextual Studies at Liverpool School of Art and Design, Liverpool John Moore's University. His paper '"Five miles of liquid fire": making sense of spectacle, looking at illuminated art in Blackpool (1879–1998)', was presented at the Ninth International Symposium of Electronic arts (ISEA98 Revolution), September 1998.

Katherine Sharp graduated from the V&A/RCA History of Design MA Course in 1995. She is a curator for the National Trust.

Penny Sparke is a Professor of Design History, and Dean of the Faculty of Art, Design & Music at Kingston University. Between 1982 and 1999 she worked at the RCA where she was a tutor on, and later the course director of, the V&A/RCA History of Design MA Course. She has published widely in the area of design history and is currently researching the relationship between gender and interior design in the USA in the early twentieth century.

Fiona Walmesley graduated from the RCA/V&A History of Design MA Course in 1991. She is currently directing and producing her first documentary, *Family Ties*, for Granada North West Television.

Louise Ward graduated from the RCA/V&A History of Design MA Course in 1996. She currently works as a freelance consultant on arts events and exhibitions. Recent projects have included London Underground's 'Platform for Art' programme and the National Art Collection Fund's centenary celebrations.

STUDIES IN DESIGN anthologies

General editor's foreword

When the Manchester University Press Series 'Studies in Design' was launched under the editorship of Paul Greenhalgh in 1990 its aim was to provide a much needed forum for work that was developing internationally in the relatively new field of the history and theory of design and material culture, setting design in all its forms within a wider intellectual framework. More than a decade later the series has demonstrated its commitment to this mission through the publication of an expanding list of monographs, edited collections and introductory text books by established and younger scholars whose work has made a real impact on the development of the discipline of design history at home and abroad. A major strength of the series has been its close relationship, through the professional backgrounds of its authors, to the teaching of design history and theory in universities and colleges, in departments of history, cultural studies, art and design history and particularly in the area of design education. It seems fitting then that this new sub-series of 'Studies in Design' offers a space in which the work of graduates who have benefited from the development of scholarship noted above can find a broader circulation.

In some ways informing and running in parallel with the series, the post-graduate course in the History of Design, founded in 1983 and run by the Royal College of Art and the Victoria and Albert Museum, has also played a pioneering role in defining the territory of design history on an international stage. It has produced many graduates who have since been highly influential in the worlds of lecturing, museum work, retailing, design consultancy and journalism (indeed several have gone on to publish in this series). The V&A/RCA Studies in Design Anthologies offer a valuable overview of the original work that this community has produced. The selected contributions for the anthologies have been sourced from the extensive student archive of the V&A/RCA course and have been selected on the grounds of their quality and innovative academic content. Each volume has been edited by prominent scholars associated with the course, and through its introductory essay and range of case studies aims to provide a variety of themed approaches to the historical study of objects as powerful mediators of design, production and consumption in significant fields of material and popular culture including interior design, popular entertainment and the magazine. These anthologies are a vivid demonstration of the maturing of a discipline and offer a unique insight into the potential uses of design historical approaches as a means of unpacking the material nature of the past.

Christopher Breward

Acknowledgements

For their assistance in the preparation of this book we wish to thank Jeremy Aynsley, Stephen Calloway, Rosemary and Brian Campbell, Helen Clifford, John Cornforth, Robert Harling, Jane Harrold, Ruth Hayden, Gillian Naylor, Dr Richard Porter, Stephen Sartin, Charles Saumarez Smith, John Styles, Peter Thornton, the late Clive Wainwright, Colefax and Fowler, the staff of Britannia Royal Naval College, Dartmouth and the staff of the Lancaster County Record Office. We would also like to extend our thanks to Alison Welsby, Jonathan Bevan and the staff at Manchester University Press.

Introduction

Penny Sparke

U NLIKE THE HISTORY OF ARCHITECTURE, which has an extensive
literature attached to it, significant studies of the history of the
design and decoration of the interior are few and far between.
With the exception of a handful of texts which have taken a scholarly and
analytical approach to the subject – these include, for example, Leora
Auslander's *Taste and Power: Furnishing Modern France* (1996), as well as
more recent studies such as those which form the basis of the essays compiled by Inga Bryden and Janet Floyd in their 1999 publication *Domestic
Space: Reading the Nineteenth-Century Interior* – many of the books on the
subject are disappointingly superficial.[1] The fact that they tend to emphasise the attractiveness and social cachet of the *ideal* interior, as opposed to
providing accounts of real lived-in spaces, and that they depict a narrow
world of gloss and glamour that tells us little about how human beings
have interacted with their interiors over the years, can leave the reader
feeling less than satisfied.

This book, written by ten design historians (all of them, at some
time, either staff members or students on the joint Royal College of Art
and Victoria & Albert Museum [henceforth, respectively, RCA and V&A]
postgraduate programme in the history of design), has a different
objective from many of the publications with which it will inevitably
share the shelves. At its heart lies a desire to penetrate the complex aesthetic and symbolic world of the interior as it has been constructed by
professionals and amateurs both inside and outside the home, in Britain
and the USA, from the eighteenth century to the present day. In line with
that broad aim, the contributions focus on ways in which individual and

collective identities have been formed through the constructed spaces they have made and/or inhabited. The relationship is not a simple one, however, as the chapters of this book explain. It is, rather, a dynamic process whereby individuals have created spaces through which to express themselves and/or others, while those individuals have, in turn, formed their own identities in response to the spaces in which they have found themselves. The relationship between people and their interiors is not a static one: the constantly transforming nature of the domestic interior is such that neither it, nor the identities it represents, can ever be stable.

This subject is not an easy one to chart. Unlike histories of product, graphic or fashion design, the object of these studies is constantly in flux and, to make it even more of a moving target, is composed of a multitude of variables, both material and immaterial – the latter represented by the space into which furniture, furnishing and other interior objects are placed. The multiplicity and variability of the interior renders it a difficult object for analysis. Combine this with the disjunction between the heavily documented idealised interiors and ephemeral, and poorly documented, *lived-in* interiors, especially those inhabited by the less wealthy, and the difficulty of the task in hand becomes apparent. This complexity in the interior is intensified by its ambiguous relationship with architecture, which has both 'owned' it and 'disowned' it at different historical moments. While the eighteenth-century interior decorator paid close attention to ornamental elaboration, the architectural modernists sought to reduce the symbolic significance of the interior to a functional space within the built structure, populated by a minimal amount of furniture and furnishings. For all these reasons, and more, it is not surprising that an analytical study of the interior has been so long in coming.

Central to the scholarly endeavour that fills these pages lies an interest in the relationship between gender and material culture. Much of the current enthusiasm for the interior has grown from work undertaken by social and cultural historians on the problematical nineteenth-century notion of the 'separate spheres', the idea, that is, that with the advent of industrialisation middle-class men and women came to inhabit distinct environments – the public sphere of work and the private sphere of the home. These spheres, in turn, were imbued with

different, gendered, value systems which extended to the aesthetic languages used within them. The strict polarity of these worlds has been
rightly questioned, but it remains the case that discussions of the domestic interior retain a strongly gendered (primarily feminine) dimension to
them. It is no coincidence, therefore, that a number of the chapters of
this book, including Katherine Sharp's study of women's decorative work
in the eighteenth century (chapter 1), and Penny Sparke's and Louise
Ward's accounts (chapters 4 and 5) of the work of early members of
the twentieth-century interior decorating profession, focus on so-called
'feminine culture'. The identities in question in these studies are those of
creative women, both amateur and professional. Woman have dominated the realm of the domestic interior, however, not only as producers
but also as consumers, as is demonstrated by Amanda Girling-Budd in
her study (chapter 2) of the nineteenth-century British firm Gillows,
which uncovers the extent of the role of women in the consumption
choices of articles that formed part of the domestic interiors of middle-
and upper-middle-class homes. Interestingly, also, in nineteenth-century
mental asylums, the interiors of which form the subject of chapter 3 by
Mary Guyatt, men and women were strictly segregated, echoing the idea
of the separate spheres.

   In spite of this strong emphasis on feminine culture men also have
inhabited interiors, as is demonstrated by Quintin Colville's study
(chapter 6) of the Britannia Royal Naval College, Dartmouth, which
concentrates on the formation of a masculine culture within a space
which is ambivalently both domestic and anti-domestic at the same time.
The gendering of the interior and the complex cultural issues arising
from this process provides, not surprisingly, therefore a recurrent *leitmotif*
of the book.

   While gender is one of the driving themes behind the work presented here, it does not totally eclipse the important discussion of the
relationship between class and the domestic interior. On the contrary, if
gender is the first, most obvious, port of call, class is not far behind it,
and, in several instances, constitutes the dominant socio-cultural force
behind the formation of the domestic interior. A number of case studies
are presented for which class is all-important. Amanda Girling-Budd's
account of particular projects undertaken by Gillows, for example,
emphasises the importance of rank and the role of the traditional interior

in confirming the level of propriety of its upper middle-class clients. The importance of social emulation for British middle-class clients is emphasised, as is the need for those customers to embrace a highly conventional aesthetic which had strong social connotations. Emerging from Girling-Budd's work, but also from that of Mary Guyatt and Quintin Colville, is the proposition that the model of the domestic interior that derived from the homes of the eighteenth-century aristocracy (both British and French) – the 'mansions' as they are frequently referred to – provided *the* aspirational style for middle-class consumers throughout the nineteenth and twentieth centuries. It also provided the ideological backcloth against which modernist architects and designers struggled in the early twentieth century in their efforts to create a democratic, classless society through design. The abhorrence expressed by figures such as Adolf Loos and Le Corbusier in the face of the 'bourgeois' interior had built into it anxieties about both class and gender. The fact that so much design historical writing to date is rooted in modernist thought contributes to the paucity of material dedicated to the interior and makes the task this book has set itself both important and compelling.

The significance of the historical model for the aspirational middle-class interior at a time of social turbulence, in this instance as manifested in the early twentieth-century USA, is a theme which emerges strongly from Penny Sparke's chapter on the work of the American interior decorator Elsie de Wolfe. The familiar language of eighteenth-century France provided a starting point for the development of a language of interior decoration which denoted social standing and upward mobility. It was a subtle language which decorators like de Wolfe used knowingly and with great sophistication. Later on in the same century, across the Atlantic, as demonstrated by Louise Ward (chapter 5), the same level of stylistic conservatism was an essential ingredient of the inter-war interior created by an American decorator who worked on British soil, Nancy Lancaster, for upper-middle-class clients. Half a century on, however, as Ward explains, that visual language had become transformed, unhooked from its origins and hence capable of being used freely by an upwardly mobile market in the USA. Tantalisingly, while both de Wolfe and Lancaster utilised established models in their work they also skilfully transformed them to include modern inflections.

In sharp contrast to the elite work of de Wolfe and Lancaster, the interiors described by Scott Oram (chapter 9) demonstrate how it was possible, in 1950s' Britain, for a working- and lower-middle-class grouping to embrace the modern (or, as it was referred to then, 'contemporary') style without fear of declassifying themselves. Indeed, new to the luxury of interior embellishment, which they created in their own homes, the couples of this social grouping had nothing to lose and everything to gain. Through its Scandinavia-inspired teak coffee-tables and G-plan sofas, the modernist dream had finally found an outlet. (It is, incidentally, a dream that still underpins the aspirations of consumers of IKEA furniture seeking to transform their lives and their positions in society.)

Not until we reach the world of work and the modern office of the late twentieth century, however, as Jeremy Myerson shows us in chapter 10, does the modern interior become a fully fledged reality, its traces of historicism and class aspiration having been totally eradicated and replaced by the classlessness of the modern work ethic which naturalises everything. Or does it? As the notion of the 'home office' hovers in the wings, the possibility, as Myerson explains, of a link between personal identity and the interior returns once again. Myerson's study takes us farther into the public world of work than the other chapters of the book. As do most interiors linked to the commercial sphere, the office illustrates the appropriateness of the modern style in this context. Even in this working arena, though, the power of tradition has tended to reassert itself as a strategy for reinforcing hierarchical differences as evidenced, for example, by the gentlemen's club-inspired, dark wood and leather interior of the chairman's room in Richard Rogers's high-tech Lloyd's Building constructed in the City of London in the late 1980s.

The tension between the traditional and the modern interior lies at the heart of most of the chapters. It is a tension which has huge gender and class implications. A complete commitment to the modern idiom was apparent only in spaces which had a technological starting point, as evidenced, for example, by the interiors of the *Queen Mary*, described here by Fiona Walmsley (chapter 8), or by the cubicles of the inter-war British hairdressing salon, documented by Emma Gieben-Gamal (chapter 7). This is safe, classless, modern territory where conventional identities can be put at risk and reformed as part of a modernity which, through the promise of technology, offers the same level of quality to everyone. In the home, however, where identity values are largely formed, the link between identity and interior decoration is more sensitive. The conservative aesthetic provided by de Wolfe and Lancaster is one which the middle classes found it hard to forego. The officer class in the British Navy, described by Colville, also clung firmly to that aesthetic and to the social kudos that came with it.

A key theme in this book, however, is the emulation of the language of the domestic interior within the public or near-public sphere. Several discussions focus on the way in which the design and decoration of the domestic interior have provided a locus for a dialogue between class and gender identities, material culture and the languages of interior decoration. They position the domestic interior as a key factor in the formation of personal and collective identities. Other chapters focus on interiors which are not, first and foremost, homes – those of nineteenth-century lunatic asylums, of inter-war hairdressing salons, of an inter-war ocean liner, of a naval training school and, finally, of the late twentieth-century office. All are instances of the vast number of 'public' spaces (the book could have included many others – among them libraries, department stores, hotels, railway trains, etc.) which, to a greater or lesser extent, depend on an extant language of the domestic interior.

While these latter interiors are seemingly located in the public rather than the private arena, this apparently strict binary opposition, once examined in detail, is quickly eroded. Indeed many of the spaces are not accessible to the public at large but rather to select groups only. What is more, many of them function as 'homes from home', providing residential opportunities, outside of the home, for short or extended periods. The distinction between 'home' and 'non-home', it turns out, is not necessarily an easy one to make. What we are, in fact, dealing with here is a series of *hybrid* interiors which contain vestiges of the domestic but perform other functions as well. All combine private and public spaces – the mental asylum, for example, has corridors as well as private bedrooms; there are decks, restaurants *and* bedrooms on the *Queen Mary*; the hairdressing salon has a public reception area in addition to more private cubicles for individual clients in the rear. The great divide between *public* and *private* proves more ambivalent than it may have seemed on a first encounter.

The model deriving from comfortable domesticity co-exists with an anti-domesticity, the aesthetic of which owes more to the open spaces of the railway station, and of other sites of modernity, than it does to the traditional arena of the home, with its signifiers of social status. Several of the case studies presented here reveal to us that the aesthetic model of the domestic interior that exists in this hybrid environment is, once again, that of the nineteenth-century bourgeois home, itself dependent on an earlier aristocratic model of domesticity. Both the naval college and the lunatic asylum aspired to be conventional homes-from-home that did not challenge existing class structures. The level of comfort provided both through personal touches, and the furniture and furnishings, is also the same. Indeed the creators of the interiors of the nineteenth-century lunatic asylum, we are told by Guyatt, went as far as to use them self-consciously in an affective way to produce a level of calm and contentment in its residents. This understanding of the power of the known and remembered interior to create a desired psychological state helps explain both the wishes of many to use the domestic interior as a stabilising force within society as well as the modernists' determination to eradicate it.

It was not only the traditional bourgeois living space that provided a model for these hybrid interiors, however. While the pursuit of comfort and status led to an adoption of the historical aristocratic idiom, especially that associated with the living area of the home, the more functional parts of these interiors looked elsewhere for inspiration. The cubicles of inter-war hairdressing salons, for instance, took their lead from the utilitarian spaces located 'below stairs' in the home. Ironically the language of utility subsequently crept back into the home under the influence of the 'scientific management' movement. These 'anti-aesthetic' spaces of the home, and those of the hybrid interior, have been largely overlooked to date, and they merit greater attention. These studies provide insights to the continuous dialogue between the domestic and the non-domestic, the symbolic and the utilitarian faces, of the interior.

The chapters of this book touch on the relationships of both consumers and producers with the interior. In the case of lunatic asylums, for instance, we learn not only that residents inhabited domesticated spaces but that the furniture was supplied by the same companies which furnished private homes. The distinction between consumer and producer is problematised to a considerable extent in several of the chapters, however, due to the fact that some consumers were also producers, and vice versa. From Katherine Sharp's eighteenth-century creative ladies to Scott Oram's residents of Lincoln it is clear that many people could, and did, aestheticise their own living spaces, as indeed they continue so to do. What is significant here is not so much how the results either did or did not relate to general stylistic trends but rather what they meant for individual creators and users. In the case of the latter some of the methods of the ethnographer have been wedded to those of the art historian, the social psychologist and the socio-economic historian to help provide as full a picture as possible. It is a daunting interdisciplinary task, but one which cannot be avoided in an analysis of the historical domestic interior.

While on an amateur basis consumers can be their own producers, so the professional designer and decorator can consume their own work. The chapter on Elsie de Wolfe shows how, as with all the other seemingly clear-cut divisions here outlined – those separating the public from the private, the domestic from the non-domestic, etc. – in the context of the domestic interior the line demarcating amateur and professional work is decidedly blurred. De Wolfe is a case in point. Untrained, she gained her reputation as a decorator through undertaking unpaid work on her own home in New York; 'turning professional' did not stop her decorating her own homes, and it was in undertaking those projects that, arguably, she expressed herself most fully.

The motives underpinning people's renovation (or non-renovation) of their interiors have been many, and they have changed over time. While the mid-nineteenth-century client (as Girling-Budd explains) was often in pursuit of an expression of propriety, reasons for redecorating subsequently included the desire for enhanced social status by appearing to be tasteful or fashionable or, most recently, the need to express *self*. Styles have varied accordingly, and decorators, designers or, most commonly, householders themselves have selected the appropriate aesthetic idiom from those on offer at any given moment.

All these thoughts and themes, and others besides, populate the pages of this book. Rather than attempt a full-blown history of the interior this book has opted for the 'micro' approach, believing that rich insights and telling tensions may be found in the details and specificities of the case-studies presented here. Only by recounting those details – and by avoiding generalisation – can the fascinating complexities of the interior emerge. The generalising will come later, built up from the kind of detailed analyses found in this book.

All of the chapters presented here locate themselves within specific historical moments and are based on research from primary sources. The book offers a wide-ranging set of case studies which address these key themes from a number of distinct perspectives. It is up to the reader, ultimately, to decide whether or not the whole is greater than the sum of the parts.

Note

1 See L. Auslander, *Taste and Power: Furnishing Modern France* (Berkeley: University of California Press, 1996), and I. Bryden and J. Floyd (eds), *Domestic Space: Reading the Nineteenth-Century Interior* (Manchester and New York: Manchester University Press, 1999). In addition to art, design and architectural historians, geographers and anthropologists are also beginning to look at the domestic interior – see A. Busch, *Geography of Home: Writings on Where We Live* (Princeton, NJ: Princeton Architectural Press, 1999) and I. Cieerad (ed.), *An Anthropology of Domestic Space* (Syracuse, NY: Syracuse University Press, 1999). The AHRB Centre for the Study of the Domestic Interior – managed by the Royal College of Art, the Victoria and Albert Museum and the Bedford Centre, Royal Holloway, University of London – is currently creating a database of source material relating to the domestic interior from the sixteenth century onwards, which will include a bibliographical overview of the subject.

1 ✧ Women's creativity and display in the eighteenth-century British domestic interior

Katherine Sharp

IN EIGHTEENTH-CENTURY Britain women became involved in a range of creative and decorative activities to an extent that was unprecedented. These activities can be seen as formative elements of the aesthetic practice later known as 'interior decoration'. Rather than relating to the whole interior space and its material components, however, some of these early artistic ventures – among them shell work, cut-paper work, embroidery, feather work, drawing, painting, japanning, carving, gilding and displaying collections – were smaller in scale. Nonetheless they all took place within the domestic sphere, contributing to its decoration in what was often a highly personal way. In addition they played a key role in refining women's 'taste', a concept which was to remain central to the art of interior decoration. Like that later activity also, these early creative practices played a significant part in helping women to establish their social and personal identities.

In 1736 Miss Anne Granville visited her sister, Mrs Pendarves, in Little Brook Street, London. Anne was delighted with her sister's home. Mrs Pendarves (better known to posterity as Mrs Delany) was of noble birth, witty, beautiful and sought after. Throughout her life her overriding enthusiasm was for decorative handiwork in all the many different forms fashionable during her time, and particularly embroidery, shell work and cut-paper work.[1] 'Indeed', Anne wrote to her mother, 'the house may be called the cabinet of curiosities, for it is full of prettiness and ingenuity.'[2] Mrs Delany was a prolific exponent of the numerous 'home' arts pursued by women in the eighteenth century (see figure 1). Hers was a period in which circumstances were unusually favourable to privileged women who wished to express themselves visually in the domestic environment. While some began to direct architects and craftsmen with an authority that would once have belonged solely to their husbands, others engaged in the creation of ornamental features in their houses. This chapter focuses on the latter practice, which had a significant influence on the way in which women evolved as homemakers as well as housekeepers. As it became more widespread, it lost the creative edge and energy exuded by its early enthusiasts; but at its height an unprecedented degree of freedom was manifested by women in influencing the appearance of the domestic sphere.

It was a phenomenon nurtured by a process in which men had gradually allowed their wives to make aesthetic decisions relating to the household. Towards the end of the seventeenth century, for example, Mrs Pepys, encouraged by her status-conscious and successful husband, the diarist Samuel Pepys, had begun to acquire some of the interests and skills that were becoming desirable accomplishments for an ambitious man's wife. Samuel Pepys himself indulged publicly in the eminent pursuits of astronomy, drawing, mechanical invention and collecting. At this early period, and typical of many men of his time, it was he, rather than his wife, who took responsibility for display within his London home. There are several references in his diary to thoughtfully made purchases of furniture and other decorative goods, only some of which he undertook with Mrs Pepys.[3]

Pepys was evidently aware of the need to keep in with the fashion and took pains to assure himself that he was making the right choices. In 1668 he was contemplating the purchase of tapestries. He and his wife spent a whole afternoon deliberating over them at upholsterers' shops, but did not buy any until the following day, after he had 'shown her Mr Wren's hangings and bed at St. James's and Sir W. Coventry's in the Pell-Mell, for our satisfaction in what we are going to buy'.[4] It seems that this self-conscious concern (and probably his watchfulness with money) sometimes made it difficult for him to trust his not quite accomplished wife to make decisions on her own. In 1660, she was allowed to buy 'a bed and furniture for her chamber' without Pepys's intervention;[5] but, significantly, in 1663, the selection of 'a paynted Indian Callico for her to line her new Study'[6] was made jointly.

The appearance of his wife's closet seems to have been a serious matter to Pepys. A 'closet' or 'cabinet' was a small room intended primarily for study, reflection and prayer. It usually contained prized personal possessions such as books, paintings and collections of curiosities. In the seventeenth century, as the closet's significance as a private reception room increased, it became more elaborately decorated and, by the time of Anne Granville's visit to her sister seventy-six years later, ladies' cabinets in particular were 'full of prettiness and ingenuity'. In 1660, Pepys had been impressed by a visit to the house of Sir William Batten, 'where he lives like a prince' and where 'among other things, he showed us my Lady's closet, where there was a great store of rarities'.[7] Pepys probably wanted his own wife's closet to create an impression. He

1 Flower mosaic by Mrs Delaney

certainly spent considerable time and effort trying to get it right. On 9 October 1663, he and Mrs Pepys spent 'most of this day and afternoon … setting things now up and in order in her closet, which endeed is and will be, when I can get her some more things to put in it, a very pleasant place'.[8] It seems likely that this project was undertaken in honour of Mrs Pepys's growing shell collection

In the ensuing decades activities such as painting, studying from nature and all manner of decorative work were to flourish among educated women. Mrs Delany revelled in the novelty and variety of her modish pursuits and operated at the very height of their fashion;[9] and although the young elite of the following generation tended to embrace

2 Shell work from 'A la Ronde'

new ideals and interests, the popularity of ladies' 'amusements', as these creative occupations had become known, became well established in a wider social context. For example, Mrs Philip Lybbe Powys,[10] genteel but not aristocratic, was an eager practitioner in domestic art in the mid-to-late eighteenth century; and sixty years after her visit to Little Brook Street, Miss Granville's description could as easily be applied to another house, 'A la Ronde', in Devon, where Miss Jane and Miss Mary Parminter were lavishing time, devotion, shells and feathers on the decoration of a little sixteen-sided cottage orné [11] (see figure 2).

The roots of this transformation in the scope of women's activities were embedded in the 'New Learning' [12] and, in England, in the changes in political life that had followed the restoration of Charles II. While London grew as the centre of power and influence in England, the wives and daughters of men of business, women whose lives had hitherto been devoted to housekeeping and child-rearing, and little else, began to find the demands on their time changing. They came to London and started to occupy a world of jostling political contenders and patrons. An ambitious man needed his wife to aspire to the *beau monde*, to fit in gracefully with exalted society and to generate admiration that would reflect well on himself. Like his carriage and his house, a woman was part of her husband's visible wealth. In London she was more visible than elsewhere, with her accomplishments and achievements, as well as her bearing, on display to the circle of his peers. This situation had some positive effects for women, and many seized the opportunity to follow fashionable pastimes that would provide them with both a social life and intellectual stimulation.

Women were largely excluded from the more established fields of academic study; but, because it was empirical, and therefore eminently accessible to anyone with the time to observe the natural world, they found they were able to participate in the 'New Learning'. As had their husbands and fathers, women began to study mathematics, science and natural history, collecting and arranging specimens to assist their observations. As a result, a cabinet of curiosities [13] was found in most fashionable houses at this date. This was sometimes augmented by collections of rare and exotic living plants, making the garden effectively an extension of the cabinet. For some women, the pastime of collecting, and the knowledge acquired in its pursuit, provided a new impetus. Already accustomed to the close examination of colour, design and thread by virtue of their almost compulsory early training in needlework, women could now transfer their study of minute detail to the patterns of nature and transcribe them on to paper, canvas or silk.

Embroidery, which had long been confined to stylised forms and figures, entered what might be called a renaissance in this period, for by the early eighteenth century it was shedding its robustly repetitive and narrational characteristics to demonstrate greater realism. As the century progressed, the trend towards naturalism increased, paralleling the proliferation of published botanical material and reflecting a greater emphasis on direct observation. Like embroidery, sketching directly from nature became more popular; and later in the century Mrs Delany began working on a collection of nearly 1,000 botanically correct illustrations made from cut paper. The source material for these paper mosaics, or what she called her *'hortus siccus'*, came from prominent plant collectors, who were only too pleased to have their specimens recorded in such a way. For Mrs Delany, in 1768 widowed for the second time, this occupation was the solace of her increasingly lonely life.[14]

Collecting was a source of creativity. The inspiration for designs in embroidery, painting, drawing and work in other media came largely from the study and understanding of nature. Even decorative designs for shell work reflected the order in which shells were displayed in the collector's cabinet. All women sewed; most fashionable women collected; and a great many of them broadened the scope of their pursuits to reflect their interests in the natural world. Making things for the home was now infused with scientific knowledge as well as with fashion. For many generations women had been expected to show diligence with the needle. Now they were demonstrating their abilities in a much wider range of creative ways to enhance the domestic space.

Seventeenth-century handbooks published in Britain for women (and usually written by women) had been confined largely to recipes for cooking and preserving, and to medicinal applications. By 1673, however, Hannah Woolley was breaking the mould with her *Gentlewoman's Companion*. In this book she vigorously defended the rights of women to intellectual pursuits and listed among her own accomplishments several that suggest her interest in the cabinet of curiosities and in the making of ingenious objects with which to furnish and decorate the home:

The things I pretend the greatest skill in, are all works wrought with a Needle, all Transparent works, Shell-work, Moss-work, also cutting of Prints, and adorning Rooms, or Cabinets, or Stands with them. All kinds of Beugle-works [bead work] upon Wyers, or otherwise. All manner of pretty toyes for closets. Rocks made with Shells, or in Sweets. Frames for Looking-glasses, pictures, or the like. Feathers of Crewel for the corner of Beds.[15]

Mrs Delany's inclinations, evident at an early age, were given full reign in her adulthood, assisted by her educational and social background. She spent her childhood in London being groomed for a life at court. This plan foundered for political reasons, so she was married off at 18 to the ageing and repulsive Alexander Pendarves, who took her to Cornwall and made her life a misery until he died six years later. From a young age she had been taught to sew and to read in English and French; she learned history and could play the harpsichord; and it is known that she was cutting paper into intricate designs from the age of 8.[16] Her background ensured that she moved easily in society and was received in some of the most fashionable drawing rooms of her day, while her young womanhood coincided with a period in which the study of natural history was diminishing in serious academic circles. When she made her famous comment that she was 'running wild after shells'[17] she was expressing the new spirit in which many collections were made. She flourished during a brief period in which elite women were free to pursue their wide-ranging interests, from botany to book learning and from drawing to domestic decoration. For a while the world seemed to be opening up to them, and the newly widowed, childless and financially independent Mrs Pendarves (later Mrs Delany) was extremely well placed to take advantage of it. In the words of her ardent admirer Jonathan Swift, the Irish satirist and author of *Gulliver's Travels*, she had 'nothing to do but be happy'.[18]

Mrs Pendarves was happy, but she would not have agreed that she had 'nothing to do'. Like many of her generation, she regarded needlework as the duty of women. She rarely relinquished it, except perhaps when required to do so by her husband. When decorating the chapel at 'Delville',[19] the house near Dublin which she shared with her second husband, Dr Patrick Delany, dean of Down, she explained: 'D.D. employs me every hour of the day for his chapel. I make the [shell] flowers and other ornaments by candle-light, and by daylight, when I don't paint, put together the festoons that are for the ceiling'.[20] At other times the needle-work continued, so that Dr Delany noted: 'she works even between the coolings of her tea'.[21] She had an ingrained horror of idleness, stimulated by a combination of religious belief and the patrician principle that she should lead by example. Needlework and reading were clearly at the top of the hierarchy of her activities, nourishing to both soul and mind, while the rest, which she called her 'amusements', were fun; and while needlework and reading were quiet, contemplative activities, others, such as shell work, gilding or cutting paper, were rather messy ones. Thus, when planning a new closet in which to store her various tools, she told her sister: 'my own room is now so clean and pretty that I cannot suffer it to be strewed with litter, only books and work'.[22]

Mrs Delany decked the chapel at Delville with 'flowers' made from shells, 'grapes' made out of nuts and branches and 'vines' cut out of cards, all painted 'in imitation of stucco'. It must have been spectacular, set on a crimson background with silver bells among the shell flowers, gothic arches made out of shells, and the oak-branches and vines around the window demonstrating her skill with the scissors.[23] For this creative woman, there was a religious dimension to the appreciation of shells and flowers, the two main academic interests in her life. She wrote: 'The beauties of shells are as infinite as of flowers, and to consider how they are inhabited enlarges a field of wonder that leads one insensibly to the great Director and Author of these wonders.'[24] Fittingly, the shell 'flowers' at Delville were naturalistic imitations of real flowers.

These varied activities occupied a somewhat ambiguous position in the opinion of the public. On the one hand, they were seen as non-intellectual, and did not upset the received opinion that women should not try to look or be clever. On the other, they were considered frivolous, were often costly, and were treated with suspicion by those who felt that women should devote all their time to domestic duties. This notion occasionally troubled even the confident Mrs Delany. As she revealed to her sister: 'Your mind is ever turned to help, relieve, and bless your neighbours and acquaintance; whilst mine I fear ... is too much filled with amusements of no real estimation; and when people commend any of my performances I feel a consciousness that my time might have been better employed.'[25]

Some people, like the Reverend Griffith Hughes, author of *The Natural History of Barbados*, evidently thought things could be worse: 'How many Ladies do we see fashionably murdering their time in Gaming! A Diversion attended with some of the most abject Vices, and shocking Consequences ... Whereas the Joys of this our Pursuit [in this case, shell work] are pure, and intirely founded on a contemplative Turn of Mind.' [26] This debate was to have deeper consequences for subsequent generations of creative women.

The charge of frivolity became increasingly significant in England as the century progressed. The apparent addiction of females to fripperies and decorative things ran the risk of being regarded not only as too trivial and too irrational but also a little too French. Wary English males regarded French manners as foppish and degenerate, and what was regarded as excessive ornamentation, emanating from France, and reminiscent of the salons over which intellectual French women had control, could be considered effeminate by association. [27]

Although the eighteenth century was characterised by greater integration of the sexes, it was, paradoxically, marked also by a deeper and more profound separation. As men began again to distance themselves culturally from women, or, more precisely, from the process of feminisation, they also began to abandon the interests they had shared with women, including the collecting and study of natural curiosities. Gentlemen going on the Grand Tour collected sculpture and fine art in large quantities, but women were excluded from the discourse surrounding this activity. Although a growing number of them made tours of Europe, women could not participate in male coteries such as the Society of Dilettanti, which practised a particularly sexualised brand of erudition and connoisseurship. [28] As a result, women's decorative work was undertaken increasingly in an isolated culture. Activities such as carving, shell work, feather work and the naturalistic representation of nature in handiwork ceased to align themselves with the interests of fashionable men. Once they had been stamped as inherently feminine, the sort of occupations Mrs Delany loved so much, and which were enjoyed by an ever-increasing number of women, were heaped together under the epithet 'ladies' amusements', a label from which they have suffered ever since. Simultaneously the momentum surrounding the making of these ornaments began to slacken among their elite first constructers; but as long as prominent collectors, such as Sir Joseph Banks, were welcomed into society drawing rooms, well-connected women like Mrs Delany, and her friend the dowager duchess of Portland, were able to maintain their interest in natural history and from it continued to draw their creative inspiration.

The activities enjoyed by Mrs Delany and her friends may have started to become less prevalent in the more fashionable circles, but by the time Mrs Powys was writing her travel journals, in the second half of the eighteenth century, they were becoming increasingly popular among the lower gentry and the rising middle classes. Tourism was also rapidly attracting people from a widening range of social and economic groups. Mrs Powys was an indefatigable traveller. She went all over the country, writing down in a series of journals what she had seen. Just as Samuel Pepys had done a century earlier, she observed what was happening in other people's houses, then went home and made changes in her own. Unlike tourists of lesser means, Mrs Powys could readily relate to the interiors she viewed, as they would be in many respects comparable with what she could achieve herself. She frequently employed the word 'taste' in her journals. By the 1770s she was speaking of the 'present taste' as if she knew exactly what that was – indeed, only an informed person, and a visitor of houses, like herself, would be in a position to form such an idea. Wealth no longer being a reliable measure of social superiority, *taste* became the watchword and the new mechanism of display. For Mrs Powys, a member of the well-off professional classes, exercising taste was a means of advancing herself socially.

Taste was a language common to men and women. Although the lack of a classical education often prevented their involvement in, for instance, the creation of a classical landscape or learned discussions about ancient art, women were perfectly capable of appreciating and understanding the principles of contemporary taste. While it is hard to imagine that a sophisticated and image-conscious man would open his doors to the scrutiny of his peers should he consider his house to be full of his wife's frills and fancies, it is equally hard to imagine that she would put them there unless they fell in with the taste of the day. Mrs Powys, in her journals, rarely noted anything women had made unless it formed part of an overall scheme of decoration, such as a set of chair covers, paintings or bed hangings. Of women's handiwork, only embroideries, paintings and collections were noted in her visits to houses, suggesting that evidence of other 'amusements' was kept to a minimum in the display of the main rooms or confined to the intimate spaces the ordinary tourist was not shown, such as closets or cabinets. It is possibly because of this that Mrs Powys did not comment on the remarkable shell room at Mereworth Castle, Colen Campbell's Palladian villa in Kent, which she visited in 1772.

Though Mrs Powys made no mention of shells on her travels, she frequently commented on collections of china, which were evidently prominently positioned within the interiors of the great houses she visited. The exclusion of women from the inner circle of fine-art collecting meant that the collecting of china was, perhaps, the only area in which women were allowed to enjoy some degree of unchallenged expertise. A classical education, after all, was of no use when assessing the Oriental ceramics that lined the walls of a lady's closet. As might be expected, Mrs Powys collected china. At Kirklington Park in 1778 she visited Lady Dashwood's china closet and demurely recorded a small triumph for female connoisseurship: 'Her ladyship said she must try my judgment in china, as she ever did all the visitors of that closet, as there was one piece there so much superior to the others. I thought myself fortunate that a prodigious fine old Japan dish almost at once struck my eye.' [29]

Like shells, china found its way into the decoration of grotto rooms. The placing of broken pieces of curved ceramic – to catch the light – between the crusty exteriors of the rocks and shells around them was a common device. China was also displayed in ornamental dairies, another female domain. Mrs Powys noted, for example, that Mrs Freeman's dairy at Fawley Court was 'ornamented with a profusion of fine Old China'.[30] There was an erroneous and ancient association between the composition of shells and that of porcelain, and a mutual association with luxury, which historically allied the two and accounted for their established partnership both in the cabinet of curiosities and in forms of decoration.

The association of collecting with decorative work went beyond the simple bounds of the materials used and the forms created. There was a rather more profound link between them, particularly in the case of shell work. In the cabinet of curiosities, shell and other collections were arranged in such a way as to reflect a divine order. Symmetry was a key quality of order, and it was a habit hard to break, even as science revealed an increasingly complex world and as the order of society was itself changing. Disorder was irrational, however, and therefore disturbing, so shells in the cabinet were often arranged in neat geometric designs, graded according to size and shape, and sometimes combined with 'pyramids' or 'rocks' made in shell. The geometric aesthetic remained in shell work throughout most of the eighteenth century; it was adhered to by traditionalists who preferred it to the 'irrational' arrangements occasionally found in grottoes.

The arrangement of a collection had a significant visual impact in the presentation of the domestic interior. Collections were not invariably confined to closets. Mr Freeman's collection, for instance, was displayed in the breakfast parlour at Fawley Court, 'in recesses on each side of the chimney', where there were 'two elegant cases of English woods inlaid, glazed so as to show all the curiosities they contain of fossils, shells, ores, &c, &c'.[31] It was not enough merely to possess a collection: it was important to show ingenuity and, increasingly, taste in its display. In 1784, Thomas Martyn, author of *The Universal Conchologist*, complimented several women, one of them the dowager duchess of Portland, well-known as a passionate collector of natural history specimens, for the knowledge they displayed in the layout of their cabinets. One of the ladies singled out for praise, Mrs Fordyce, seems to have got the balance between science and art exactly right. Her collection was described as being 'classed and arranged with the most critical judgment and elegant taste, according at the same time instruction and delight'.[32]

It was, of course, impolite for a tourist to linger in front of any one item for very long, and smaller items, such as those in the cabinet, could be overlooked. An allowed exception to this was at Strawberry Hill, where Mrs Powys noted 'a curious picture of flowers done in feathers'.[33] It was only in 1769, after a visit to Bulstrode, home of the dowager duchess of Portland, that Mrs Powys made a reference to what must have been a range of ladies' handiwork. There she noticed 'numberless other curiosities and works of taste in which the Duchess has displayed her well-known ingenuity'.[34] It is perhaps significant that the widowed duchess was a great friend of Mrs Delany.

Throughout her journals, it is apparent that Mrs Powys was particularly interested in the work of women. It is clear, also, that women themselves set a personal value on the things they made, as demonstrated by their frequent exchange as gifts. A century of increased sociability and tender friendships, combined with daunting physical distances, placed extra meaning on the possession of a knotted purse or a decorated box made by a friend. Mrs Powys recounted an occasion when Queen Charlotte and her party were conversing about some chair covers and how recollection of Mrs Powys's own painted silk gown gave the queen a conversational *entrée*. The queen, with the king, two of the princesses, Lady Louisa Clayton and 'two gentlemen', had been visiting Henley Park, home of the dowager Mrs Freeman. In a letter to a friend, Mrs Powys wrote: 'The ladies, you know, are great workers, and admired some beautiful chairs Mrs Freeman is now working. The Queen too, I'll assure you, asked what work her neighbour, Mrs Powys, was about, as she knew she was very ingenious by some painting she had seen some years ago of hers.'[35]

There was no notion, in the eighteenth century, that amateur production should be judged differently from or more leniently than that of professionals. Professionals were seen simply as artisans whose technique had been perfected by years of practice. Evidence, according to eighteenth-century definitions, of genius, taste and sensibility in an amateur painting, for instance, tended to be prized more highly than the quality of execution, since a very high degree of the latter would suggest that more time than was considered seemly had been spent acquiring it.[36] Public exhibitions of paintings, needlework, cut paper, shell work and other media often included amateur as well as professional work, the two sometimes displayed side by side, as was so often the case in the home. In fact, the quality of some women's decorative work was very high indeed, and probably compared well, technically, with professionals' examples. In Mrs Delany's case, for example, her two- and three-dimensional depictions of flowers in embroidery, cut paper and shell work were extremely sophisticated, and although amateurs were usually praised for their 'ingenuity' rather than their technique, her paper flowers were highly commended for cutting, colouring and accuracy.[37]

By the early 1800s the varied occupations that had absorbed and amused privileged women throughout the eighteenth century had generally fallen from favour with the nucleus of the fashionable elite. For instance, decorated grottoes – widely believed to have been popularised in England by Alexander Pope at Twickenham, and once almost obligatory in any pleasure garden – were soon reviled by those with pretensions to the latest taste. Always skirting the edges of the irrational, grottoes and other items of decorative fancy would become victims of their own whimsy in a process that was feminising the work of their creation. The gradual alienation of women from a self-consciously masculine culture would have a profound effect on the handiwork they produced. Their pursuits would continue throughout the nineteenth century, but they would become marginalised and lack the creative drive that had characterised the work of their eighteenth-century pioneers.

Notes

1 Mrs Delany, born Mary Granville in 1700, was associated with Handel, Swift and Sir Joseph Banks. Her first husband, Alexander Pendarves, died in 1724. She married Dr Patrick Delany, dean of Downpatrick, in 1743.

2 *The Autobiography and Correspondence of Mary Granville, Mrs Delany*, ed. Lady Llanover (London: Richard Bentley, 1861), vol. 1, p. 590.

3 Most of the time he went without her to buy furniture. He was very cost-conscious, which might have made him more cautious. For instance, in July 1661 he recorded that 'this morning I went up and down into the City to [buy] several things (as I have lately done for my house): among other things, a fair chest of drawers for my own chamber and an Indian gown for myself. The first cost me 33s, the other 34s': *The Diary of Samuel Pepys*, ed. R. Latham and W. Matthews (London: Bell & Hyman, 1970–83), vol. 2, p. 130. On another occasion, in 1664, he 'walked home, calling among the Joyners in Woodstreete to buy a table, and bade in many places but did not buy till I came home to see the place where it is to stand, to judge how big it must be': *ibid.*, vol. 5. p. 251.

4 *Ibid.*, vol. 9, p. 330.

5 On 2 October 1660, Pepys noted: 'So home again, where my wife tells me what she hath bought today; viz, a bed and furniture for her chamber, with which, very well pleased, I went to bed': *ibid.*, vol. 1, p. 257.

6 *Ibid.*, vol. 4, p. 299.

7 *Ibid.*, vol. 1, p. 280.

8 *Ibid.*, vol. 4, p. 328.

9 Mrs Delany was decorating shell grottos from the earliest days of their new-found popularity in the eighteenth century and may have been influential in promoting the take-up of this and other decorative pursuits. She enthused others with her cut-paper work and taught Princess Elizabeth how to cut silhouettes during her years of intimacy with the royal family at

Windsor. Her flower collages, also known as paper mosaics, her 'herbal', or her '*hortus siccus*', enjoyed considerable celebrity, attracting the admiration of Sir Joshua Reynolds, Sir Joseph Banks, Erasmus Darwin and Horace Walpole.

10 Caroline Girle (1739–1817) was the kind of woman perhaps most affected by the social changes that occurred during the eighteenth century. She came from the prosperous middle class: her father was a surgeon in Lincoln's Inn Fields and both her parents, of whom she was the only child, owned property. In 1763, she married Philip Lybbe Powys of Hardwick Hall in Oxfordshire. She kept a journal of her travels around the country and of her visits to great houses, and seems to have followed most of the female pursuits made fashionable by women like Mrs Delany. According to the editor of her journals, she 'was a skilled needlewoman … she embroidered, worked in cloth, straw plaited, feather worked, made pillow lace, paper mosaic work, &c., dried flowers and ferns, painted on paper and silk, collected shells, fossils, coins, and was a connoisseur in china, &c.': *Diaries of Mrs Philip Lybbe Powys*, ed. E. J. Climenson (London: Longman's, Green & Co., 1899), p. 159.

11 'A La Ronde' was built in 1796, by two cousins, Jane and Mary Parminter, following a ten-year tour of the Continent. Its sixteen-sided form is said to have been inspired by the octagonal basilica of San Vitale at Ravenna, which they had seen on their travels. The cousins dedicated the next few years to embellishing their unusual house. It remained in the same family, with decoration and contents more or less intact, until 1991. It now belongs to the National Trust.

12 The 'New Learning' constituted the foundation of the Enlightenment. From the end of the sixteenth century, led by such figures as Galileo (1564–1642), Francis Bacon (1561–1626) and René Descartes (1596–1650), the basis of philosophy and political reasoning began to shift from the supposed first principles laid out in Christian scripture and in the teachings of the ancient philosophers towards those of mathematics and scientific discovery. For the first time, the study of nature was regarded as a route by which it was possible to achieve both worldly and spiritual understanding. For some it revealed the divine method; for others it confounded established religious teaching and radically challenged received political and social wisdom. It therefore remained controversial throughout the seventeenth century before popularly gaining ground in the eighteenth.

13 A cabinet of curiosities was a room containing a collection. The collection usually consisted of a wide range of natural phenomena, shown with objects produced by human skill, and the tools and machines of their manufacture. From the middle of the seventeenth century, cabinets of curiosities started to proliferate among gentlemen scholars. These cabinets were arranged to demonstrate the world in microcosm, as those men understood

it. In fact, the cabinets were also an outward sign of personal accomplishment and were used to show off the academic and practical skills – from science and languages to drawing and mechanical invention – of their owners. The strong link between collecting, erudition and handiwork was thus well established. In the eighteenth century collections tended to become less academic in orientation. Carved cherry stones seem to have been popular from an early date, and were evidently still to be found in ladies' cabinets in the late eighteenth century. In 1798, Mrs Powys visited an exhibition of ivory work and made a note of '[A]ny device carved for lockets, bracelets, rings, or toothpick cases in as small pieces as I did the cherry-stone baskets, and with something like the same knives': *Diaries*, p. 298.

14 Mrs Delany produced nearly 1,000 botanical illustrations in cut paper over a period of ten years. They were laid out in ten volumes, and all were indexed in her own hand. Most of the examples were cut at Bulstrode, the home of the dowager duchess of Portland, where Mrs Delany was a frequent guest, and many of the specimens she copied also came from there. In 1782, failing eyesight forced her to abandon the project. Her work was widely admired at the time for its accuracy, as well as for its delicacy and vivid colouring. The intensity of colour is afforded by dyed paper laid on to a black background. The volumes are held at the British Museum.

15 Hannah Woolley, *The Gentlewoman's Companion; or a Guide to the Female Sex* (London: Dorman Newman, 1673), pp. 10–11.

16 Ruth Hayden, *Mrs Delany, Her Life and Her Flowers* (London: British Museum Press, 2000), p. 15.

17 Mrs Delany, *Autobiography*, vol. 1, p. 484.

18 Hayden, *Mrs Delany*, p. 49.

19 She lived at Delville (now demolished), 1743–68.

20 *Letters from Georgian Ireland: The Correspondence of Mary Delany 1731–68*, ed. Angélique Day (Belfast: Friar's Bush Press, 1991), p. 166.

21 Hayden, *Mrs Delany*, p. 91.

22 *Ibid.*, p. 95.

23 *Ibid.*, p. 101.

24 Mrs Delany, *Autobiography*, vol. 1, p. 14.

25 Mary Delany, *Letters from Georgian Ireland*, p. 165.

26 Rev. Griffith Hughes, *The Natural History of Barbados* (London: 1750), pp. 267–8.

27 See arguments in Michèle B. Cohen, 'A genealogy of conversation: gender subjectivation and learning French in England', PhD thesis, Institute of Education, London, 1992.

28 The Society of Dilettanti was formed in 1734. It was initially a young men's club with rumbustious tendencies, its aim to discuss *virtu* and experiences picked up on the Grand Tour. Its aristocratic membership gradually expanded to include some of the leading antiquaries of the day. The club shaped the character of fine-art connoisseurship during the eighteenth century and became extremely influential outside its own circle. Women featured in the business of the society only in that they were accorded the status of works of art and pursued in the same way.

29 Mrs Powys, *Diaries*, p. 198.

30 *Ibid.*, p. 36.

31 *Ibid.*, p. 147.

32 Thomas Martyn, *The Universal Conchologist* (London: 1784), vol. 1, p. 14.

33 Mrs Powys, *Diaries*, p. 227.

34 *Ibid.*, p. 120.

35 *Ibid.*, pp. 218–19.

36 See arguments in relation to drawing and painting in Kim Sloan, *A Noble Art: Amateur Artists and Drawing Masters c. 1600–1800* (London: British Museum Press, 2000), p. 216.

37 See notes 9 and 14.

2 ✧ Comfort and gentility: furnishings by Gillows, Lancaster, 1840–55

Amanda Girling-Budd

URNITURE AND FURNISHINGS represent key consumption choices that reflect not only personal preferences, but also the value systems that underlie the wider culture. This chapter uses the example of the furniture and furnishings supplied by Gillows of Lancaster to local clients in the middle of the nineteenth century to examine the motivations for purchasing preferences.

Historians of consumption have assumed that emulation is the driving force behind consumption. The economic historian Neil McKendrick drew on ideas developed in America in the last years of the nineteenth century by Thorstein Veblen who maintained that objects were used competitively in struggles for social oneupmanship, and the greater the amount spent on useless, or purely decorative, objects the more conspicuous the wealth of the purchaser. Veblen's work was a critique of the mores of wealthy east coast American families, but his aspirational model has been watered down into the less value-laden one of emulation which assumes that taste is established at the highest social level, is copied by those further down the scale and so filters down in attenuated forms through the social strata.

Actual motivations for consumption choices are less straightforward, reflecting the complexity of social structures and value systems. Although emulation is certainly one motivation for consumer behaviour, ascribing all purchasing choices to a desire to copy one's social superiors is too simplistic, and the model does not take account of geographical, social and cultural particularities. A broader explanation of consumption is offered by Mary Douglas and Baron Isherwood in *The World of Goods:*

Towards an Anthropology of Consumption. Consumption for Douglas and Isherwood is 'the very arena where culture is fought over and licked into shape'. The choices a consumer makes

> say something about himself, his family, his locality, whether in town or country, on vacation or at home, the kind of statements he makes are about the kind of universe he is in, affirmatory or defiant, perhaps competitive but not necessarily so. He can proceed, through consumption activities, to get agreement from fellow consumers to redefine some traditional events as major that used to be minor, and to allow others to lapse completely ... Consumption is an active process in which all the social categories are being continually redefined.[1]

This anthropological approach, in which the process of consumption is one of the means by which culture is established and constantly re-established, is comprehensive enough to take account of geographical, social and cultural particularities and allows for many motivations for consumption choices, including those of competition and emulation. The consumption choices of Gillows's clients in the 1840s and 1850s are examined to see the extent to which emulation can be ascribed as a motivating principle, and Gillows's records and other contemporary material are used to suggest other possible motives for purchases. In particular the notion of *propriety* is explored as an alternative guiding principle behind consumption choices.

Gillows in the middle of the nineteenth century was an important cabinet-making firm with a base in Lancaster and an outpost in London. The Gillows family left the business in the 1820s and the firm was taken over by Leonard Redmayne, a former book-keeper with the firm. Gillows maintained the reputation it had established in the eighteenth century for quality work for well-to-do clients, although the decline of Lancaster as a maritime port and the economic depression that the town suffered during and after the Napoleonic Wars had severely affected Gillows's business. Its London branch had been established in the 1770s, and by the middle of the nineteenth century it had eclipsed the original base in Lancaster, which by that time was little more than a factory for London. Nevertheless, there was a loyal local clientele, comprising gentry from the rural hinterland and families whose wealth derived from trade and who were based in Liverpool, Lancaster and other Lancashire towns.

Gillows's surviving sales ledgers allow sales at mid-century to be analysed in terms of destination. Table 1 represents sales from the Lancaster branch for 1852, the year in which the first tranche of furniture for the new Palace of Westminster was supplied by Lancaster, but otherwise a typical year. The invoices direct to London from Lancaster represented stock for the London shop. Invoices to clients of the London operation were for clients who ordered from the London branch but who lived closer to the Lancaster branch and so were supplied from there. Together with furniture for Westminster these London-generated orders amounted to 88 per cent of Lancaster's income. There is little doubt that London demand enabled Gillows in Lancaster to survive the local depression: there were only eighty local clients in 1852, and they generated £2,234 for the firm.

Table 1 *Gillows, Lancaster: value of invoices 1852*

Invoices: total value, Lancaster 1852	*Invoices to clients of Gillows, Lancaster*	*Invoices to clients of Gillows, London*	*Invoices direct to Gillows, London*	*Invoices to Gillows, London, for furniture for new Palace of Westminster*
£10,437	£2,234	£591	£6,076	£1,536

Source: Gillows archive: Account Book 1846–57 and Ledger 1839–62.[2]

The Gillows material and other contemporary sources reveal patterns of consumption particular to the rural gentry and wealthy traders, the social grouping which formed the clientele of the Lancaster firm. Several key features emerge from the material and mark this client group out as distinctive, both in the pattern of its purchasing and in the values which inform its consumption choices. Areas examined in detail include the level of service offered by the firm, and its relationship with its clients; the scales of value attached to different goods in the Gillows stock and the way in which these were used to denote status in the domestic interior; the control of purchasing according to gender; and, lastly, the relative importance of motivations for purchasing preferences such as emulation, fashion, the desire for conformity and the idea of propriety. This last feature, which concerns the significance ascribed to objects in the home, will draw on clients' family histories and material such as diaries to augment the Gillows material.

Two sets of Gillows's invoices in particular will serve to illustrate most of the distinguishing features identified from the firm's account book: invoices to John Bond, a Lancaster gentleman, whose income came from land but whose wealth came originally from the slave trade; and those to James Addison Clarke, who lived in the countryside outside Lancaster, again a landowner and an inheritor of wealth gained through the slave trade. James Addison Clarke had married Margaret Oates Bond, John and Elizabeth Bond's daughter. Bond and Clarke can be considered members of the Lancaster county elite as both served as deputy-lieutenant, an honorary position reserved for members of the gentry. Both men were relatively new landed proprietors and both had connections with trade. One of John Bond's sons, Edward, was a partner in Gillows and there was a connection by marriage to Leonard Redmayne, another Gillows partner. Bond and Clarke therefore straddled the divide between town and county society, or trade and land ownership, and in this they were typical of the elite of north-west England at that time. Typical also is the fact that the source of family wealth was in trade and in particular the Atlantic maritime trade. The two families were connected by marriage, and in this relatively small social group connections of trade, marriage or friendship were common.

An analysis of a Gillows's account book covering the period 1846–57 shows that the provision of services, as opposed to the supply of goods, was a significant if minor element of the firm's operation. The figures in table 2 relate to itemised sales to Lancaster clients in 1852.

Table 2 *Sales to local clients of Gillows, Lancaster, 1852*

	Supply		Service		
Type of sale	*Furniture*	*Soft furnishings*	*Furniture repairs and alterations*	*Soft furnishings alterations*	*Other household services*
Value	£531	£292	£14	£23	£38
% value	91.65		8.35		

Source: Gillows archive: Account Book 1847–56 [3]

A high level of service to clients was the norm for top-flight London furnishers at the time. It was a way of encouraging continued patronage, and was facilitated by the proximity of the firms to their clients, around

Oxford Street and Mayfair. Much of this work reflected the London season, with workmen from firms such as Holland & Sons in Mayfair effectively cleaning and packing up town houses while their clients retired to the country. Analysis of Holland & Sons' records shows that in 1853 services provided for clients in their own homes constituted around 40 per cent of total sales.[4] Although there are no surviving records for comparison, it seems likely that Gillows's Oxford Street branch would have carried out a similar level of service for its London clients. But for Gillows, Lancaster, this kind of service was on a much smaller scale, representing less than 10 per cent of sales. An analysis of invoices for 1852 reveals only five clients who received the level of service considered routine for London clients.

John Bond is the most significant of these clients. Invoices to him in the account book reflect the special relationship between the Bonds and the firm. Gillows's workmen were constantly in John Bond's house in Dalton Square, Lancaster, undertaking routine maintenance tasks. Furniture was regularly French polished, the front door oiled, pictures cleaned and roller blinds washed and remounted. Although John Bond's son Edward was a partner in the firm, the family relationship did not warrant a discount. All of these services were charged at normal rates. Margaret Oates Clarke's diary reveals that John and Elizabeth Bond entertained frequently in Dalton Square. The relationship with Gillows enabled them to maintain the house in a manner which would have withstood the scrutiny of visitors.

The only other client to have regularly received this kind of service was Richard Spooner Bond, Edward Bond's younger brother, who lived at Hindley, near Wigan. Despite the distance, Gillows's workers travelled to perform tasks at his house. In May 1852 Betsy Marr spent nine days there turning window curtains into drapes for a bed and performing other sundry tasks, for which she was paid 2s a day. The cost of her rail ticket, 16s, was almost as much as her wages. In the same month George Ingall was there for nearly three days fixing curtains, laying carpets, wallpapering and doing sundry jobs, and was paid 3s 6d a day. Travelling expenses and the cost of board and lodging were always met by the client, to whom no discounts were allowed.

An obvious explanation for restricting service of a high level to just a few clients was that most of Gillows's clients lived at too great a distance from Lancaster. Only a handful of its clients were resident in Lancaster in the period covered by the account book, and it seems likely that the kind of relationship that developed between firms and clients in London seldom developed in Lancaster and that this level of service remained a special privilege for family members and was not expected by most clients.

There is a single exception to this rule. In 1852, the year analysed in detail, Oliver Farrer of Ingleborough Hall, paid £3 11s 6d to have his furniture French polished by a Gillows's workman. Mr Bruton spent thirteen days at the Hall polishing furniture. The bill came to £4 6s 6d, of which £2 6s 6d was for Bruton's wages at 3s 6d a day, 15s was for materials and the remaining 35s was for Bruton's board and lodging. The Farrers were the largest landowners in the Western Dales, and in 1814–16 had spent £1, 694 on furniture and furnishings from Gillows, not far short of the sum that all Gillows's north-western clients spent with the firm in 1852. This may be the one example of a customer enjoying a special relationship with the firm because of longstanding patronage.

Although Gillows performed relatively few tasks in clients' homes, repairs and alterations to existing furniture and furnishings were an important element of the business. Most of this work was carried out at Gillows's factory in Lancaster.

Of the £70 for which Gillows invoiced John Bond in 1852, just £15 was spent on furniture; his purchases included various mahogany pieces for a bedroom. Most of his bills, none of which was at cost price, were for repairs and alterations to soft furnishings. It was customary to re-use soft furnishings where possible, even among wealthier clients of the top London firms. In August Bond was charged £3 10s for, among other things, 'washing the outsides of bed furnitures & dyeing the linings, and additional pink lining', and just before the new year he spent 10s on 'ripping the work of your two ottomans, cleaning the needlework, turning the silk & gimp'.[5] Several other clients had similar work carried out, including dyeing and remaking curtains and recutting and remaking carpets.

This reflects how material goods were valued relative to labour. Silk and other fabrics were expensive compared with the labour required to turn them into finished goods. In 1852 a yard of chintz cost the equivalent of a day's wage for the Gillows's seamstress Betsy Marr. It was cost effective to re-use fabrics, to have furniture repolished and to remove fixed covers from seating, and to clean and re-attach them. In the 1850s Britain was on the cusp of a new era in which the price of finished goods was pushed down by a combination of the application of machinery and increased competition in retailing; but in Lancaster, at mid-century, finished goods were still highly valued, reflecting what they cost to consumers and the logistical difficulties of obtaining them. The careful use and re-use of goods is a key aspect of household management and was re-inforced by the prevailing moral code which equated the efficient and economical running of a household with moral probity.

Purchasing decisions that related to the household came within the sphere of the woman of the house. This was not reflected in Gillows's invoices, which were always directed to the household's male head, where one existed. All invoices for goods and services for Swarthdale House, the home in their early married life of James Addison Clarke and Margaret Oates Clarke, one of John Bond's daughters, were addressed to James Clarke, Esq. The Clarkes exemplified the prevailing ideology in which men and women inhabited separate and equally important spheres, each with its own duties, responsibilities and rewards. Evidence from Margaret's diary suggests that she was responsible for decisions relating to the domestic sphere.[6] James was frequently away from home, visiting his ailing father in Cockerham or riding to Ulverston to look after his family's property interests there. Margaret had two young children who were largely in the care of a nurse, and she recorded days spent either on social visits or busy with domestic affairs such as preparing oranges for marmalade or working in the greenhouse.

Margaret also had purchasing power. On 27 March 1844 she recorded: 'My husband returned just as I was settling down to an early dinner. In the afternoon he put up the pictures which I purchased at Colonel Parker's and after that we took a long walk.'[7] There is no mention in the diary of furniture or furnishings, nor any suggestion of a special relationship with Gillows, though the family were clients of the firm during this period. However, the diary does make it clear that Margaret supervised work in the house, such as the visit from the clockmaker: 'January 22nd ... James went to Lancaster. Mr Halton came to put up the hand of the clock and set it to rights.'[8] Margaret was also closely involved in the purchase of a new carriage in 1845, accompanying her husband to inspect it when it was near to completion, though it is not clear whose opinion carried more weight in this and other household decisions. It seems likely that Margaret's influence on larger purchases, such as the carriage and the furnishing of their home, was considerable, though ultimately James Addison Clarke was in control of the family's finances and the final decision on any expenditure would probably have been his.

Gillows's invoices show that the firm offered goods of varying quality or elaborateness, or with particular characteristics that could be used by clients to different effect, including the display of social position, the flagging up of the rank of members of the household and as markers of a room's function. Invoices to James Addison Clarke show these different uses of furnishings to interesting effect. Following the death of his father in 1845 and James's inheritance of part of the lordship of the manor of Cockerham and of other properties, the Clarke family moved from Swarthdale to a house called 'Summerhill', near Ulverston (see figure 3). It was a late eighteenth-century property, larger than Swarthdale House, set on a hill with commanding views of the sands of Barrow in Furness, with Morecambe Bay and Lancaster beyond. The surviving Gillows account book covers the refurbishment and furnishing of, and the move to, 'Summerhill'. The total bill over a period of three years came to around £1,300 and was Gillows's largest individual private commission in the period 1846–53. Much of the furniture and furnishings for 'Summerhill' was new and is fully described in Gillows's records, though the invoices also listed furniture and furnishings which had been altered or repaired. Although the invoices do not record the contents of the house as would an inventory, they do allow a broad picture to emerge of the interior furnishings.

The levels of conspicuous consumption expressed by the Clarkes in their furnishing of the principal reception rooms are dealt with later. Here the way in which conventional associations of timber or colour with particular rooms and the reinforcing of domestic hierarchies through furnishings are examined.

There is a surprising uniformity in the colour schemes used throughout the house. Crimson and green were the dominant colours on the ground floor. Crimson moreen curtains from Swarthdale House were altered to fit the dining room windows and the new seat furniture was covered in crimson morocco leather.[9] For the library, curtains brought from Swarthdale House were dyed. The colour was not noted but they

3 'Summerhill' in the
late nineteenth century

probably matched the 'Dantzic oak chaise longue', which was also covered in crimson morocco and had loose covers of 'crimson Monteith
calico print'. The drawing room had a new suite of curtains of 'green
twilled chintz lined and fringed', with 'a portion of your own chintz'
which was probably some of the 'green twill chintz' supplied to Swarthdale House in 1847, described at the time as the 'same as the drawing
room furniture'. A new rosewood commode had green morocco falls
attached to the shelves and two sets of covers were made for the two new
rosewood 'Marquise' sofas, one in crimson silk and worsted damask and
another in print overall, the colour not specified. The entrance hall also
had crimson curtains, in merino damask. Colour was not used here as a
marker of function or status, but it did conform to prevailing standards.
Green and crimson were standard furnishing colours in the middle of the
nineteenth century: surviving card tables almost invariably have green –
or more rarely crimson – inserts; green and crimson predominate in seating where original leather covers survive; and the most notable
application of green and crimson was in the furnishing of the newly
rebuilt Palace of Westminster where the House of Lords and the House of
Commons were differentiated by their respective predominant colours of
crimson and green . The Clarkes' choice of red and green furnishings
offered them the opportunity to incorporate their existing furniture into
the new scheme; it also reflected a concern for convention.

Their choice of timber for individual rooms was governed by similar
motives. It was conventional at the time for particular timbers to be

associated with particular rooms. So, the new furniture installed in the dining room was mahogany. Gillows supplied a set of mahogany imperial dining tables on reeded legs and twelve mahogany chairs with carved stay rails and seats upholstered in crimson morocco leather, edged with silk braid. Fitted furniture in the room, such as a cornice pole and a rack for the leaves of the dining table and a cupboard to fit a recess, was made from oak. Both timbers would have been considered suitable for dining rooms. Furniture in the drawing room was probably exclusively rosewood, and it would have matched the rosewood furniture that we know the Clarkes possessed – earlier invoices refer to the cleaning and repair of a rosewood table and box.[10] Rosewood had been considered appropriate for drawing room furniture since the beginning of the 1840s, so it represented not simply conventional but by this time slightly old-fashioned taste. An alternative timber for the drawing room might have been walnut or perhaps mahogany.

Furnishings provided a means of making tangible differences in rank within the household, and that so much was bought new on the acquisition of 'Summerhill' allows this material differentiation to be clearly read today. It was most obvious in servants' rooms but was clear also within the family itself. The family's rooms and guest rooms had Frenchpolished wooden beds with chintz drapes, while the servants' rooms had iron bedsteads and their drapes were in 'Manchester stripe', a utilitarian material.[11] All the beds had a hair mattress topped with a feather mattress, but the master bedroom's feather mattress had 'best seasoned and dressed feathers' at £10 12s; the children's bedroom had 'best feathers' at £8 4s; the night nursery (the nursemaid's room) had 'common feathers' at £7 3s, while the housemaid's feather mattress, also made of common feathers, was the smallest and the cheapest at £4 12s. Beds in the housemaid's room and a servant's spare room were allocated only one pillow, while all the others had two. Carpets demonstrated a similar pattern of differentiation. The master bedroom had the most luxurious and most expensive option, a fitted Brussels carpet; the other family rooms had fitted Kidderminster, a slightly less expensive, good quality carpet; the spare room had a fitted Dutch carpet which was coarse, hard-wearing and inexpensive; and the housemaid's and cook's rooms had a much smaller, unfitted, square of Dutch carpet. The room described in the Gillows's records as 'No 1 Spare' must have been occupied by a housekeeper, listed in the 1851 census as Isabella Fawcett, a widow aged 67. Her position as respected family servant, closer in status to the Clarke family than other servants, was reflected in the fitted carpet and the furniture which was painted to simulate maple, the same as the furniture in the principal bedrooms, while the furniture in the rest of the servants' rooms was uniformly painted 'drab'.

David Cannadine has stressed the importance of hierarchy, or rank, as an ideological structure in nineteenth century society, and one which prevailed despite new ways of thinking about society in terms of distinct classes.[12] Referring to the Palace of Westminster, Cannadine examines how hierarchies were maintained through ritual and theatrical display, and reinforced by architecture and art. A clear example of this phenomenon is the way in which Pugin's designs for the Palace's furnishings used different levels of elaboration, most clearly visible in carved decoration on oak furniture, to denote the rank of a room's principal occupier.[13] Gillows's invoices show that similar processes were at work on a domestic scale in their clients' homes. Down to the last detail furnishings were both a manifestation of rank and a reinforcement of social hierarchies.

Emulation and its concomitant, Veblen's 'invidious comparison', are usually identified as the main motivators for conspicuous consumption. But neither competitive consumption nor simple copying of styles made fashionable by the elite are convincing as explanations for the purchasing behaviour of individuals such as the Clarkes and their neighbours. In this locality and for this group of consumers the desire to conform to current social mores may have been at least as powerful a motivator, and propriety may be the key factor in purchasing choices.

The blurred boundaries of Lancashire society at mid-century may begin to explain the apparent influence on the minor gentry in the area of the Evangelical movement. *Family Fortunes*, Leonore Davidoff and Catherine Hall's examination of the middle classes from a gendered perspective, identifies the Evangelical movement as a powerful moral influence on the middle classes, out of which grew the ideology of separate spheres of influence for men and for women.[14] Women had a crucial role as the nurturers of virtue in children, and, as a parallel development, the home became an idealised repository of virtue. As Davidoff and Hall have pointed out, this 'democratisation of domesticity was solidly rooted in the homes of the middle class and not in the country estates of the minor gentry'.[15] They maintain that writers like Sarah Stickney Ellis were

> particularly concerned with those families of traders, manufacturers and professionals where there were one to four servants, where there had been some kind of liberal education and where there was no family rank. 'False notions of refinement' were rendering their women, 'less influential, less useful and less happy than they were'. This was a moral crisis for the nation and her concern was to find ways of improving, 'the minor morals of domestic life'.[16]

The tension between the demands of gentility and those of virtue identified by Davidoff and Hall in the 1830s' writings of Sarah Stickney Ellis seem to be evident still in the late 1840s among both the middle classes and those members of the minor gentry who formed Gillows's clientele in and around Lancaster. Their purchasing choices for the most part were modest, conservative, not overly influenced by fashion and governed by the notion of propriety as much as by a desire to copy the style of social superiors.

The way in which the Clarkes furnished 'Summerhill' exemplifies the tension between demands of gentility and those of virtue, and there are clues in Margaret Clarke's diary to the value system which informed the Clarkes' choices. The exercise of propriety, or appropriate behaviour, was important to her. Nineteenth-century society was highly stratified and there was widespread concern that social hierarchies should be maintained as a bulwark against the threat of riot or revolution – or even of reform. Knowing one's place was crucial to the maintenance of the system and behaviour that was inappropriate to one's social position was frowned upon. The need to conform to social norms may have been particularly pressing in a social milieu like Lancaster, where social divisions were not always clear. An entry in Margaret Clarke's diary illuminates her attitude to offences against propriety:

> Took a walk with Mamma on the Green and I went to see Mr Simpson's new house, saw the gentleman himself and congratulated him on his engagement with Miss Atkinson. I should think it were indeed a matter of congratulation to him. Is it as much to the lady? His house is very handsome and the view from it very fine, but it is totally ruined by being so near the town and it is too large for the land he possesses.[17]

Not only was Mr Simpson's house too big for his land, but his choice of bride was inappropriate.

Margaret was not critical of building in the grand style *per se*. Her diary records the Clarkes' growing friendship with Mr and Mrs George Marton who lived at nearby Capernwray. George Marton, a member of an old landowning family, was MP for Lancaster. In 1844 he and his wife lived at Capernwray Old Hall, a modest farmhouse, but nearby they were building a vast new mansion in the Gothic style, designed by Edmund Sharpe, a Lancaster architect who specialised in Gothic. 'A splendid day. Went to dine at Capernwray. No-one but ourselves. After dinner we walked round the new building. When completed it will be very handsome and spacious.'[18] The size and grandeur of Capernwray were considered appropriate to the status of the Martons in the county, and were commended by Margaret. Mr Simpson, on the other hand, had offended against propriety, and in so doing threatened the underlying hierarchical social system, the codes of which were written into the architecture of early nineteenth-century Lancashire.

Margaret was also critical of pretentiousness and disparaging of too keen an interest in fashion. A young man she met at her father's house in Lancaster came in for withering comment: 'stayed all night in Dalton Square, met a young man Rawlins whose father I well remember. He seemed agreeable, but evidently appeared to wish to be thought a man of fashion.'[19]

Margaret's comments on Capernwray and Mr Simpson's house are rare in that they refer to appearances. Her diary betrays no interest in fashion or in the appearance of her possessions, as if an interest in the surface appearance of things might have been thought vulgar or trivial. Her comments on objects whose display might be thought just as important as their function were limited to their practicality. For instance her diary entry for 7 December 1844 reads: 'a new cloak arrived from London. I think it will be comfortable.' Similarly in March 1846 she recorded that the previous month she and James 'went to Liverpool to look at a new carriage that we have had built'. On 4 March 'James went to L'pool and returned the next day bringing the new carriage ... went to see Mrs C[larke] ... Returned home in the new carriage which is very comfortable and easy'.

This denial of surface appearances has a moral quality. Just as individuals were judged not on appearance but on character, so the look of clothes and household possessions was studiously ignored by Margaret in favour of their practical qualities. Comfort was compatible with virtue. In fact, the pursuit of comfort in order that the home should be a physical as well as a moral haven was an important aspect of the prevailing domestic ideology. Pride in one's possessions, on the other hand, was morally suspect, and the active display by others of their possessions seems to have evoked Margaret's distaste: 'Went to Lancaster to spend the day at the Green Area. Mrs C and Jane very kind but I wish they would not take every one over the house that calls on them.' [20]

So how does the furnishing of 'Summerhill' correspond with what her diary reveals about Margaret Oates Clarke? To what extent is the tension between the respective demands for gentility and modesty played out in the choices the Clarkes made?

Although the expenditure on 'Summerhill' was considerable the house was not a country seat, and although larger than the Clarkes' previous home it was not grand. The large drawing room was probably the showiest of the principal rooms, combining new and older elements. In March 1847, when they were still at Swarthdale House, the Clarkes bought 25 yards of green twill calico to match their drawing room furniture. This fabric was later used to make the drawing room curtains for 'Summerhill' and it had fringing added. The Clarkes were evidently concerned to re-use costly materials and adapt furniture and furnishings to new uses. This not only made economic sense but conformed to the morally weighted strictures of household management.

New furniture for the drawing room included an expensive rosewood commode with marble top and two rosewood 'marquise' sofas with sprung seats, finished in canvas with two sets of covers – one in crimson silk and worsted damask, the other in printed cotton – and six inexpensive 'light chairs' with 'carved backs and willow seats'.[21] This would have matched existing rosewood drawing room furniture which came from Swarthdale House. A surviving table from the Clarkes' drawing room is in a style which was variously described in commentaries at the time as 'modern' or 'Grecian' and is a curvilinear development of the Greek revival style fashionable during the Regency period [22] (see figure 4). This style predominates in Gillows's estimate sketch books of the 1840s. Rosewood had been considered appropriate

4 Detail of a tilt-top
table made by Gillows
for J. Clarke between
1837 and 1846

for drawing room furniture since the Regency period, although by the
1840s it was beginning to be eclipsed by walnut, and the 'modern' style
was well established as appropriate for genteel households. An alternative might have been an eighteenth-century French style. This has been
identified as a *nouveau-riche* style, but it was popular among landed proprietors and those with relatively new wealth, and there were collectors
of original French *ancièn regime* furniture from both groups.[23] Most well-
to-do families made do with English nineteenth-century copies or
furniture based loosely on the style, and it was a popular style for the
boudoirs and drawing rooms of London's town houses. It was not so
popular in the north west of England. None of the sketches in Gillows's
estimate sketch books has a discernible French influence. There are existing examples of furniture in the French style with a Gillows's stamp, but
these were probably made in London for London clients. Even an ambitious client such as Colonel T. R. G. Braddyll, who overreached himself

financially with the building of Conishead Priory, was reluctant to go for the grand French style despite persuasion by Gillows:

> Hayward [Bradyll's steward] also writes me word that you have given up the plan of finishing the second drawing room in the French style and that you wish the furniture the same character as the house. Though this will be more strictly in keeping I cannot but regret the pleasing variety which the adoption of the Louis XIV style would have made.[24]

The Clarkes' choice of rosewood furniture in the more conventional modified Greek revival style reflects a preference for conformity over individuality. It may reflect the Clarkes' desire to consolidate their social position rather than an attempt at aggrandisement.

The Clarkes' position within their local community was emphasised materially in the local parish church. The Clarkes had their own pew and another for their servants. These pews were dressed by Gillows in an appropriate manner. The Clarkes' family pew was lined with crimson cloth, trimmed with silk gimp, and a bronze rail was put up from which hung crimson moreen curtains. A lockable oak-drawer box was fixed to the pew. The servants' pew was lined with green baize and fitted with a green canvas blind. A pine drawer without a lock was fixed to the servants' pew.[25] As a place of worship which was open to all, the church was a locus of social cohesiveness, but it also provided ample opportunity for marking out social divisions. The expression of hierarchical structures through furnishings that was clear within the Clarkes' home was repeated in a more public setting for a wider audience. We do not know the number of pews that were decorated in this way or whether the Clarkes' furnishings conformed to an accepted standard, but we can assume that the church would have offered a visual expression of the relative social positions of the congregation. It is interesting that crimson and green were again used, signifying both tradition and relative status, just as in the House of Lords and the House of Commons.

To what extent the Clarkes were emulating their social superiors is a question yet to be answered. There is no doubt that Gillows used the emulative principle in their marketing strategy. They named particular models of furniture after aristocratic patrons: so, for instance, the two easy chairs that the Clarkes brought from Swarthdale House and had re-upholstered for the dining room at 'Summerhill' were the 'Wescombe' and 'Lucan' chairs, both named after aristocratic families who, presumably, were former clients. It seems unlikely that those names, which seem always to be associated with nobility, simply refer to the first client whose chair was of that design. It suggests that Gillows was aware of the usefulness of harnessing its clients' social aspirations. Interestingly, by the 1870s models in the sketch books were associated not with members of the aristocracy but with professional designers; so chairs were described, for example, as 'Edis Pattern' or 'Talbert Pattern'. This reflects both the broadening of the market for domestic furniture and the new importance of design both as a profession and as a marketing tool. Gillows also used the emulative principle as part of the design process, and a surviving tilt-top table that was part of the Clarkes' original drawing room furniture at Swarthdale House provides an example (see figure 4). The table is now at the Judges' Lodgings Museum in Lancaster. It conforms closely to a loo table illustrated in one of Gillows's estimate sketch books. An entry was made in an estimate sketch book when a design was made for the first time, and these entries were used in two ways: they function as templates, with a drawing as a visual record and notes on materials, measurements and costings, and usually the name of the maker included so that the pieces could be remade to the same specifications; and they were used in pattern books for clients. A representative of the firm, probably one of the partners, would visit a client at home to discuss designs and the estimate sketch book would be a key aid to communicating design ideas. The Clarkes' loo table differs from the one made in 1840 for J. Y. P. Michaelson, Esq., only in its principal timber, albuera wood, and in some additional carving at the top of the pillar[26] (see figure 5). The opportunity for emulation offered by this process is clear; but if the process is to be described as aspirational the objects copied have to belong to a social superior. Although several aristocrats are named in the estimate sketch books, by far the majority were ordinary clients, that is, members of the county élite, landowners and well-off tradesmen, people like the Clarkes. J. Y. P. Michaelson was probably a member of the Michaelsons of Greenbank, Cartmel, a landowning family very similar in status to the Clarkes. The motivation for adopting a design similar to that of another Gillows's client seems to have been a desire to exhibit a sharing of taste with their peers, and so to reinforce a sense of propriety.

There is no evidence that the Clarkes were aiming at a grand style.

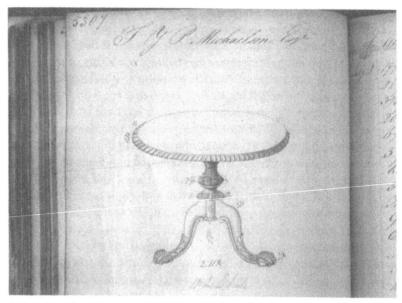

5 Drawing of a table made for J. Y. P. Michaelson by Gillows in 1840: detail from
a page of Gillows's Estimate Sketch Books, 1837–49

Gilding was an obvious marker of both wealth and status, with its long
association with each, but evidence in the invoices suggests that gilding
at 'Summerhill' was limited to architectural mouldings in the drawing
rooms and dining room, and a gilt frame for the looking glass above the
new rosewood commode in the drawing room. This modest use of
gilding contrasts with that evidenced in another set of invoices in
Gillows's account book. These were for the Bibby brothers, the Liverpool
shipping magnates.

John Bibby spent just over £750 on furnishings for the drawing
room and breakfast room at Hart Hill in 1851. The order included rosewood chairs, a 'marquese' sofa and a 'marquese' couch, all covered in
crimson silk brocatelle with matching curtains and 'a reeded and gilt cornice and lath with wreaths and carved & gilt ends'. One of the grander
pieces for the drawing room was a rosewood commode with statuary
(marble) top, described in the invoice as being six feet in length, having 'a
door in the centre with crimson silk and metal trellis panel sunk pilasters

with carved foliage droppers on a plinth a metal rim on the top'. It cost £46 15s and is one of the most expensive items in the account book. Some element of its design must be new because it is illustrated in the sketch book. More expensive still was 'a Console table with statuary marble top 6ft long shaped front and ends molded edge on carved and gilt legs', with 'a glass frame to surmount it, carved and gilt to suit the window cornice for his glass plate', at £60.

In 1852 James Bibby was invoiced for goods worth £358, which makes his the largest order for a client billed by the Lancaster branch in that year. The items listed are strikingly similar to those bought by his brother. Again the principal room being refurnished was the drawing room, and the predominating textile was silk brocatelle. He, too, ordered a 'marquese' sofa and rosewood chairs, and two music stools. James outdid his brother slightly with 'a gilt console table with shaped statuary marble top, moulded edge surmounted with a gilt glass frame richly ornamented with blind frames for his glass plates'. At £63, this was the most expensive piece of furniture sold by Gillows in 1852 and the purchase was comparable with the Clarkes' expenditure of £53 10s on their commode with glass above. Theirs is rosewood, though, and only the frame is gilt, while the fabric of the curtains and seat furniture at Summerhill was chintz, not silk. The level of display recorded in the Bibbys' invoices is unusual in interiors supplied by Gillows and suggests the kind of furnishings that prompted Veblen to coin the phrase 'conspicuous consumption'. It is notable that the Bibby brothers were metropolitan clients, and there may be a distinction between the preferences of city and country clients. The Clarkes' commission, although it was substantial in sales' terms, was modest by comparison. The understatement of their furnishings may again have reflected a desire for conformity rather than social advancement.

The desire for propriety was a more convincing motivation for consumption than was social aspiration both for the Clarkes and for the majority of Gillows's Lancaster clients. They were marked out by their conservatism, reflecting their need for continuity, their acknowledgement of tradition and the drive to maintain the status quo in a world whose social lines were blurred and its social structures constantly threatened by change. The Clarkes' furnishing choices, like those of many of their friends and acquaintances, reflected the tension between the desire to be seen to be morally circumspect and the need to be recognised as people of gentility. This tension underpinned the notion of propriety. Fine judgement would have been required to achieve decorative schemes which displayed thrift without appearing shabby, and which signalled gentility without appearing ostentatious.

The ritual quality of the creation of the domestic interiors at 'Summerhill' is inescapable. The furnishings were pointless unless seen by their peers. Just as Margaret Clarke was able to comment on the inappropriate behaviour of Mr Simpson, whose large house had excited her derision during her social round, so visitors to 'Summerhill' would have made their own private judgements on the propriety of the Clarkes' home and the fitness of the furnishings. This endless round of judgements is what forms and reforms their culture. Emulation has a part to play in consumption preferences; but, for this group of individuals, to copy the tastes of their social superiors was to risk alienating their peers and a desire for the respect and approval of social equals was their guiding principle.

Notes

1 Mary Douglas and Baron Isherwood, *The World of Goods: Towards an Anthropology of Consumption* (New York: Norton, 1979), p. 45.

2 Westminster Archive Centre, 344/59 Ledger 1839–62, 344/157 Account Book 1846–57. In Gillows's records the London branch is referred to as Ferguson & Co. The Lancaster end is referred to as Redmayne & Co. The two branches operated as separate entities in terms of financial control.

3 Westminster Archive Centre, 344/157.

4 A. Girling-Budd, 'Holland & Sons of London and Gillows of London and Lancaster: a comparison of two nineteenth century furnishing firms', unpublished MA thesis, RCA/V&A, London, 1998.

5 Westminster Archive Centre, 344/157, Account Book 1846–57, fo. 336.

6 County Record Office, Lancaster, DDX 1622, Acc. 5692, Box 2: Margaret Oates Clarke's diary (1844–46).

7 *Ibid.*, entry for 27 March 1844.

8 *Ibid.*, entry for 22 January 1844.

9 Westminster Archive Centre, 344/157, Account Book 1846–57, fo. 336.

10 *Ibid.*, fo. 14.

11 All the information on furnishings for the bedrooms at 'Summerhill' is from Westminster Archive Centre, 344/157, Account Book 1846–57: James Clarke's invoice for August 1848, fos 83–104.

12 David Cannadine, *Class in Britain* (New Haven, CT, and London: Yale University Press, 1998); and 'The Palace of Westminster as a palace of varieties', in C. Riding and J. Riding (eds), *The Houses of Parliament, History, Art, Architecture* (London: Merrell, 2000).

13 Girling-Budd, 'Holland & Sons', pp. 96–102.

14 Leonore Davidoff and Catherine Hall, *Family Fortunes: Men and Women of the English Middle Class 1780–1850* (Chicago, IL: University of Chicago Press, 1987).

15 *Ibid.*, p. 184.

16 *Ibid.*, p. 183.

17 County Record Office, Lancaster, DDX 1622, Acc. 5692, Box 2: Margaret Oates Clarke's diary (1844–46), 20 January 1844.

18 *Ibid.*, 22 June 1844.

19 *Ibid.*, 8 May 1844.

20 *Ibid.*, 11 April 1846.

21 Westminster Archive Centre, 344/157, Account Book 1846–57, fo. 87.

22 For instance J. C. Loudon, *An Encyclopaedia of Cottage, Farm and Villa Architecture and Furniture* (London, 1839).

23 Marc Girouard, *The Victorian Country House* (New Haven, CT, and London: Yale University Press, 1979), chapter 22: 'The nouveau riche style'; J. Mordant Crook, *The Rise of the Nouveaux Riches* (London: John Murray, 2000).

24 Westminster Archive Centre, 344/175, Letter Book 1829–42, p. 218: Letter from Edward Bond to Colonel T. R. G. Braddyll about the furnishing of Conishead Priory, 17 March 1841.

25 Westminster Archive Centre, 344/157, Account Book 1846–57, fos 103–4.

26 Westminster Archive Centre, 344/104, Estimate Sketch Book 1837–55, fo. 5307.

3 ✧ A semblance of home: mental asylum interiors, 1880–1914

Mary Guyatt

Wonders may be done in improving a bare, cold, unhappy-looking room; by a good table-cover here or there; or a nicely embroidered sofa-pillow of cloth or satin, or better still, one of those lovely new low screens, with the tall tufts of grass or lilies which we owe to Walter Crane's skilful pencil ... I confess I like a room to look as if it were inhabited ... litter [is] a powerful weapon in the hands of a person who knows how to make a room look comfortable.[1]

So WROTE Lady Barker in her 1878 design manual *The Bed Room and the Boudoir*. Although aimed at the owners of suburban villas, these sentiments found equal expression in the most unexpected of arenas – the Victorian mental asylum. For, sandwiched between the straw-lined cells of the eighteenth-century asylum and the rubber floors and strip-lighting of its twentieth-century counterpart, the late Victorian asylum was a place of comparative comfort, its interiors increasingly reminiscent of home. Focusing on the period 1880–1914, this chapter shows that, for those running the asylums, domesticity – or 'homeliness' as it was then termed – came to be even more important than did questions of sanitation, security and cure.

In 1847 John Conolly, a doctor at Hanwell Asylum in London, described the ideal accommodation for patients in his care: 'A light cast-iron bedstead, without curtains ... is the best. A little carpet, or a coir matting, a chair or a small bench, are things required in every room; and many patients require the further indulgence of a washing-stand, a box, a little looking-glass, and a small chest of drawers.'[2] Conolly was writing at the very time that the asylum came to be considered the proper place to house the insane. Following an 1845 Act of Parliament, each local authority was responsible for providing and maintaining an asylum.[3] This was in spite of the notorious abuse, overcrowding and corruption observed at existing private and charitable 'madhouses'. Rather than condemn the notion of the asylum, it was argued that such ills would not occur once institutions were publicly owned and managed. Moreover, the Government had introduced a board of inspectors, or 'Lunacy Commissioners', to inspect asylums, regularly and without warning. Aside from these structural changes, by the 1840s a new form of treatment had replaced the beatings, purgings and near-drownings that used to be inflicted upon the insane. This treatment was called 'moral therapy', and was based on the theory that patients fared best when offered a combination of light work and kind and attentive care. For exponents of moral therapy like John Conolly, the asylum would provide a surrogate family, of which the provision of homely accommodation was an integral part.

The range of furnishings set out by Conolly in 1847 was by the standards of the day very generous. But less than fifty years later it had become the minimum an asylum patient could expect. This can be illustrated by four very different English asylums operating at the end of the nineteenth century: Bethlem Hospital; Bootham Park; the Retreat; and Claybury Asylum. Bethlem was England's oldest asylum, established as a charitable foundation in London in 1247; by the 1880s it had around 200 patients, one-fifth of whom paid fees.[4] Bootham Park (formerly York Asylum) was founded in 1777; during the period in question it housed around eighty fee-paying patients in one building and sixty rate-assisted 'paupers' in another.[5] The Retreat, also in York, was established by the city's Quaker community in 1796. By the 1880s it had around 150 patients, two-thirds of them affluent non-Quakers who were charged significantly higher fees than their Quaker counterparts.[6] Financially autonomous institutions like these were known as 'registered asylums'. Claybury Asylum on the other hand was a very different kind of place. Opened by London County Council in 1893, it was typical of the 100 or so asylums built by local authorities after 1845 for the benefit exclusively of 'pauper' patients. Known as 'county asylums', these publicly funded institutions were usually massive: Claybury had 2,000 beds.[7]

6 Ladies' gallery, Bethlem
Hospital, early twentieth
century

7 A sitting room at The
Retreat, late nineteenth
century

8 Ladies' drawing room at
Bootham Park, c. 1910

It was a photograph of an interior at Bethlem Hospital (figure 6) that set in motion the study on which this chapter is based. The photograph, which dates from the beginning of the twentieth century, shows a long carpeted gallery crammed with mahogany furniture, jardinières and flower-vases, pictures, busts and ornaments; in short, a material richness not usually associated with the interior of a mental asylum. Soon afterwards photographs of Bootham Park, the Retreat and Claybury Asylum revealed further surprises. Everything from the tasselled table-cloths, lacquered screen and Persian rugs at the Retreat, through the elegant furniture, lace mats and anti-macassars at Bootham Park, to the genre scenes, drapery and china ornaments at Claybury Asylum, would have sat equally happily in the typical family home of the period [8] (see figures 7, 8, 9).

Photographs can, of course, be deceptive, and as historical documents they must be treated with caution. Indeed, many of these photographs were made for public consumption, to be reproduced in annual reports, prospectuses and even, occasionally, newspapers.[9] There

9 Women's gallery, Claybury Hospital, *c.* 1893

are, however, too few in number to record the entire asylum, and as such they provide only an incomplete picture – one which focuses on the best-dressed interiors and ignores the shabbier back rooms.[10] This would certainly be a problem were it not for a wealth of extant accompanying literature and archival evidence which reveals, in the words of the historian Elaine Showalter, the 'endless thought given to asylum decoration, interior design and decor'.[11]

Much detailed evidence comes in the form of inventories, invoices and management committee minutes. The most comprehensive of the relevant documents is an inventory made at Bootham Park in 1891. It was produced by a firm of York auctioneers for insurance purposes and records the entire contents of the asylum, right down to the last chess-board, magazine and cricket stump.[12] Fee-paying patients' rooms were furnished with mahogany tables, chests of drawers, wash-stands and looking glasses. The floors were carpeted, the curtains bore valances and the beds were finished with white knotted counterpanes. Communal rooms included leather chairs, glazed walnut cabinets, plaster busts and cases of stuffed birds. In fact there was no apparent distinction between the rooms offered to fee-paying patients and and those provided for staff. Invoices from the Retreat reveal a similar picture, with patient accommodation supplied with 'best quality Kidderminster rugs', velvet pile carpets, Liberty & Co. fabrics, and pictures of rabbits, hollyhocks and chrysanthemums.[13]

Most of the furniture purchased for the four asylums came from high-street retailers. Bethlem favoured R. G. Maney, an upholsterer and art furnisher situated near the asylum in south London. The Retreat and Bootham Park gave most of their custom to Hunter & Smallpage and Brown Bros. & Taylor, York's largest furnishing stores. When something really special was required both asylums called in Maple & Co., the leading London furnishing establishment.[14] Claybury's considerable size necessitated the selection of its suppliers by public tender. Predictably, those who succeeded were the big-name wholesalers C. & R. Light, B. Cohen & Sons, Wallace & Co. and C. S. Lucraft, all based in London's East End.[15] Patients might also bring furniture with them, usually for personal reasons and occasionally in lieu of fees.[16]

Since asylums used the same furniture suppliers as the general public, it is no surprise that many of their purchases were the same; but this is not to say that everything in an asylum could be found in the home. Long wooden benches and bentwood chairs appeared in asylums on a scale unimaginable in the ordinary house; invalid beds similarly were commonplace and patients' bedroom doors were fitted with inspection windows. There were also one or two padded cells. However those elements were easily subsumed by the wealth of soft-furnishings and trimmings that characterised interior decoration of the time; and, unlike the late nineteenth-century hospital, asylum sanitation came second to appearance.[17]

The parallels between the asylum and the ordinary family home did not go unnoticed. Speaking generally of asylums, one commentator wrote in 1891: 'There is ... everywhere an upward tendency in furnishing. More objects of interest, and more comfortable, home-like articles are to be met with now than would have been thought necessary, or possible, twenty years ago. Indeed, in the best English asylums the furniture much resembles that of a private house.'[18] In 1887 the governor at Bootham Park described the asylum as a 'prison transformed into a palace'.[19] In the 1890s one visitor to the new Claybury Asylum remarked that he was 'much struck with the magnificence of the accommodation provided', while others jokingly asked when they too could move in![20] Bethlem was likened to 'a first-class hotel', with its 'artistically disposed settees and easy chairs ... and charming floral embellishments on the tables'.[21]

This last comment is especially interesting as it shows that asylum interiors, like hotels, were hybrid spaces: private in the sense that they were open only to a select minority, but public in that they housed large, unrelated and transitory populations. To meet these needs, both asylums and hotels required some small private rooms and some much larger reception rooms, the ratio varying according to the type of institution. The smaller privately-funded asylums tended to offer patients greater privacy: the majority of patients at the Retreat and all the fee-paying patients at Bootham Park enjoyed single bedrooms, while patients at Bethlem appear to have slept around six to a room. By contrast, publicly-funded asylums like Claybury depended on economies of scale and there were sometimes up to sixty patients to a dormitory. Like the dormitory, the asylum dining hall had no equivalent in the family home – furnished with the ubiquitous bentwood chairs, plants, pictures and draperies, it most closely resembled a late Victorian restaurant, another hybrid space.[22] It was perhaps the gallery that presented the asylum authorities with their hardest challenge (see figures 6 and 9). The gallery – a long narrow space which functioned as both corridor and sitting-room – was a standard element of asylum architecture. As such, it was inherently institutional, and much effort was required to break its emphatic linear course.[23] These structural limitations were recognised by a doctor at Claybury Asylum in 1889: 'At the present day [asylums] very much resemble large mansions or hospitals for ordinary cases; or, more correctly, something between mansions and hospitals. The spacious wards – abundant of light and air – remind us of hospitals, while the furniture and home comforts give them more the appearance of mansions.'[24]

Another telling comparison was made in 1914 when the chaplain at Bethlem likened the female wards to a 'ladies' club in Piccadilly' and the male wards to their counterpart, the 'smoking-rooms ... and the billiard rooms of a Pall Mall palace'.[25] Not only does this remark suggest another kind of hybrid environment, but it raises the issue of space and gender. Like all institutions in the nineteenth century, both the architecture and the activities of the asylum were segregated according to sex. The buildings had long been designed with separate wings for men and women, known as the male and the female 'sides'.[26] Furnishings, too, were subject to gender differentiation. The men's gallery at Bethlem housed statues, billiard tables and cases of geological specimens, while the women's galleries tended to have many more soft-furnishings. These kinds of distinctions echoed entirely the home-decorating suggestions made by Lady Barker in *The Bedroom and the Boudoir*: 'boys might be encouraged to so arrange their collections of eggs, butterflies, beetles and miscellaneous rubbish, as to combine some sort of decorative principle with this sort of portable property', while girls would be advised to 'make and collect tasteful little odds and ends of ornamental work'.[27]

Not only were the asylum interiors domestic, but they mirrored changing trends. Indeed it is possible to trace the move from heavy furniture and dark colours, so fashionable in the closing decades of the nineteenth century (figure 7), to the subsequent preference for 'lighter colours, less bulky furniture and less decoration'[28] (figure 8). That the older style persisted at Bethlem into the 1910s (figure 6) is also in keeping with the outside world: as Alastair Service states in *Edwardian Interiors*, 'between 1905 and 1914, the majority of the middle class still furnished their new homes with many of the features deemed fashionable in the 1890s'.[29]

Two important observations have been made. First, there were great similarities between the decoration of the family home, the asylum and other hybrid environments such as hotels. Second, the asylums' furniture tended to be purchased from domestic suppliers and their interiors decorated and redecorated according to changing fashions in interior design. The remainder of this chapter shows that these tendencies were part of a conscious drive towards greater domesticity across the asylum sector – something made abundantly clear by records detailing the time, money and energy put into decorating projects.

The annual report became the principal vehicle used by asylum managers to communicate their aims. Employing almost identical phrases, the management at Bethlem, Bootham Park and the Retreat declared their respective intentions to make their institutions 'more and more homelike and comfortable', 'as pleasant and comfortable as possible', and 'more homelike and comfortable'.[30] All measures undertaken to achieve these aims were carefully recorded in annual reports. In 1881 the head doctor at Bethlem reported that the year's refurbishments meant that 'no ward in any Asylum … is altogether more cheerful and pretty' than those at Bethlem.[31] In 1898 the Retreat proudly announced 'the erection of arches to break the long lines of the galleries, together with other minor alterations, new pictures, etc'.[32] Two years later Bootham Park reported 'a considerable outlay in the purchase of new furniture and carpets'.[33] There are countless further examples. The considerable effort that went into reporting these endless improvements is in itself proof that the asylum managers were serious about homeliness.

If the annual reports bordered on the tedious, then the actual work must have been even more so. Management committees would leave the boardroom periodically to tour the asylum. In May 1877 Bootham Park's committee inspected several wards and 'ordered the papering of certain of the rooms and a new carpet for the 1st Ladies' Corridor'.[34] Managers at the Retreat noted certain 'bedrooms … are extremely plain, and lacking in ordinary comforts … [and] require re-decoration, and furniture. The sitting room needs bookshelves, ornaments and other things to make it more homelike'.[35] At Claybury a salaried steward took on the bulk of the work. Only after he had assembled a range of samples would the management committee consider such questions as whether the long wooden settees should be 'provided with cushions and perforated seats in lieu of plain wooden seats.'[36] Fortunately for the asylum managers, they were not without helpers: government inspectors, lay-visitors, patients, relatives, architects, retailers and medical staff all played a part in either suggesting or carrying out improvements to the asylum interior.

After 1845 a team of inspectors, or 'lunacy commissioners', made frequent visits to each asylum on behalf of the government. At Bethlem in 1889 the inspectors remarked that 'the sitting room in Male Division B is very bare and sparsely furnished, and might easily be made more cheerful and comfortable'. Another year they called for 'the supply of new furniture' and many more 'objects of interest'.[37] Another vocal group were the lay-visitors. With ideas ranging from the grandiose to the prosaic, visitors to Bootham Park proposed everything from a new *port-cochère* to improvements to the male lavatories.[38] Women lay-visitors were especially active and got involved even in the practical aspects of decorating.[39] At Bethlem, for example, 'women totally unconnected with the asylum' visited the institution in the 1880s to paint the woodwork with decorative effects.[40] The Retreat was unusual in having women on its management committee. Predictably they were often appointed to deal with specifically domestic matters. For example, in 1904 it was a female committee member who was given the less than glamorous task of reporting on the 'number of new mattresses required.'[41]

Patient work, or 'occupational therapy' as it is termed today, was a key element of the new 'moral therapy' devised at the Retreat and later adopted across the asylum system. Although the work was strongly gendered – male patients might work on the asylum farm while female patients stayed indoors with their needlework and crocheting – both sexes were enlisted to help with internal improvements. Patients of both sexes got involved in 'artistic painting' projects at Bethlem. These activities were said to leave 'a pleasant impression on the mind[s]' of patients.[42] But whereas patients at these small private asylums were encouraged to get involved for their own benefit, in the huge publicly funded asylums patients were all too often used as just cheap labour.[43]

Indebted relatives, local businesses and affluent managers also contributed to the upgrading of the asylum through numerous material donations. Bethlem Hospital did especially well out of such gifts, as the head doctor commented in 1881: 'We are grateful for the kind presents, not only given as in former years by Governors in the way of engravings and books, but also by patients and their friends; by gifts of this kind we have been able to add cabinets and ornamental furniture to several of the galleries.'[44]

As well as being 'homelike' and 'comfortable', the ideal asylum interior was expected to be 'cheerful' and 'tasteful'. Indeed, rarely were any other adjectives than these used.[45] While the asylum managers were evidently at ease with these notions, they did occasionally defer to design experts. Architects specified the initial decoration of Claybury Asylum and much of the decoration at the Retreat and Bootham Park.[46] Retailers also suggested room-schemes, such as the portfolio of hand-drawn designs for Bootham Park produced by the London furnishers Maple & Co. in 1908.[47]

Much time was invested in studying the furnishings at other asylums. The steward at Claybury visited 'three asylums to inspect the furniture in use thereat and to make any recommendations ... that he may see fit'.[48] In 1896 the Retreat's management committee travelled to Barnwood House, a private asylum in Gloucester, with the sole intention of inspecting the furniture and fittings there. Photographs were taken and notes were made. As a record of another asylum interior, the following observations are invaluable:

> There are Turkey carpets and other rugs on the floors in most of the rooms, also a number of old oak cabinets. There is an abundance of pictures and other ornaments in every department. On the woman's side, there are – as is usual in asylums – more small articles of ornament and knickknacks; but in other respects, little difference ... The decoration of rooms and corridors is very varied. Floors – oak parquetry or linoleum over boards stained, covered with loose oriental rugs. There are no Brussels carpets, but a few Axminster in some of the rooms ... Walls – generally with dado moulding, with lincrusta below. The paper above the lincrusta is generally inexpensive in the dayrooms and bed rooms; but in the corridors, Japanese papers are generally used. This decoration, in some cases, seems to be somewhat overdone.[49]

Nor was it difficult to read-up on the latest interior trends. As well as widely available home-decoration manuals,[50] there were also numerous tips in the psychiatric literature.[51] One such publication, H. C. Burdett's *Hospitals and Asylums of the World*, specified everything from the correct height for a dado-rail to the prettiest shade for a counterpane. The author even described how to create a night-sky effect on the ceiling, reminding his colleagues not to forget to paint a black line around the gold stars.[52]

That such detailed advice should have been given by an asylum doctor is significant. Contrary to what might be imagined, doctors were deeply involved in asylum decoration. They headed project teams, met with architects and suppliers, selected carpets, fabrics and wallpapers, and settled invoices. It was, for example, a member of the medical staff, Dr Jones, who was 'authorised to expend ... a sum not exceeding fifty pounds for the purchase of pictures and ornaments for the wards' of the new Claybury Asylum.[53]

The reason why doctors became so involved in the day-to-day management of the asylum was simple: there was a limit to the medical work they could do. The optimism that had surrounded the mid-century asylum-building boom had very quickly evaporated, and by the 1880s the psychiatric profession was no closer to curing insanity than it had been in 1845. If patients did not make a spontaneous recovery, they were likely to remain in the asylum for life.[54] In such a vacuum, moral therapy and its associated domestic environment were all that was left to make insanity more bearable for its sufferers. In short, homeliness was crucial because for many the asylum really would be their life-long home.

Moral therapy, developed at the Retreat and subsequently adopted across English asylums, laid great emphasis on the environment; although no cure in itself, a homely interior comforted and dignified patients, and thereby assisted their recovery.[55] According to John Conolly there was nothing mysterious about this method of treatment:

> There are few persons ... whose daily habitual pleasure does not arise from the objects around them ... We must not neglect such instincts and capacities if we profess to cure diseased minds. Our practice can only securely rest on the consideration of everything, great or little, capable of affecting the mind beneficially or hurtfully.[56]

As the century wore on and the psychiatric impasse worsened, more and more asylums signed up to the principle that 'patients rise or fall with their surroundings, and the greater [the] tendency to mental deterioration, the greater the need of an inspired environment'.[57] At the Retreat the head doctor claimed that it was 'a well recognised fact that comfortable and homelike surroundings react beneficially upon the most hopeless class of patient'.[58] At Bethlem the lunacy commissioners stressed 'the beneficial influence of pleasant surroundings' on even the most 'excited and violent cases'. They urged the asylum to purchase more 'objects of interest ... so conducive to the recovery of patients'.[59] In 1900 Bootham Park's managers did just that, congratulating themselves on the 'considerable outlay in the purchase of new furniture and carpets ... so conducive to the one great object we have in view, which is the recovery or improvement of our patients'.[60]

Whether these improvements were implemented in order to assist patient cures or simply because there were no cures available, their benefit to the patient was not disputed. At the same time there is evidence to suggest that these improvements were made also for the good of the asylum: to control troublesome patients and to enhance the institution's income and the reputations of those connected with it.

That moral therapy suited the authorities rather than the patient is an idea originally posited by Michel Foucault. Focusing on the Retreat, he argued that patients found the benefits of self-control as preached by sympathetic staff to be as terrifying as the beatings of yesteryear. Patients now lived in fear that any loss of control would bring shame on themselves and disappointment to others: 'madness was controlled, not cured'.[61] For Foucault, moral therapy amounted to 'moral management', and the comfortable domestic environment was not an aid to therapy, but a tool for control. Although Foucault reached this conclusion in the mid-twentieth century, there is some historical evidence to support his interpretation. In 1877 one psychiatrist wrote:

> It is by domestic control, by surroundings of the daily life, by such details or the colouring of the walls, the patterns of floor cloth, the furniture and decoration of the rooms, by the influence of pictures, birds, and draperies ... by moulding and controlling the life of a lunatic, the psychologist hopes to reach, capture and re-educate the truant mind ... We have a great notion of giving patients everywhere an impression of being ... well cared for, and so placing them on their best honour to behave with self-respect and propriety.[62]

In 1896 the lunacy commissioners expressed the same conviction in rather more opaque language: 'A good supply of objects of interest have a marked humanising effect', so reducing 'the turbulence of the rougher patients'. If objects could bring cheer to patients, they could also calm them down.[63]

If the environment encouraged self-control, material comfort was used also as a reward for good behaviour (and austerity to punish bad behaviour). In 1798 a French doctor named Delarive described the process: 'If he [the patient] behaves well, he is preferred to a chamber on the first floor: this is a kind of honourable promotion, which excites his emulation. These rooms, larger and more agreeable than the cells and provided with more furniture, display throughout the picture of neatness.'[64] Erving Goffman, a sociologist writing in the 1960s, argued that such promotionary and demotionary tactics created a malignant hierarchy within asylums: patients whose ravings had become too extreme would be exiled to bare wards, whereas those who had learned to 'play the system' would enjoy preferential accommodation.[65] However Anne Digby's study of the Retreat suggests that moving patients through different comfort zones could be a gentle form of resocialisation.[66] The Retreat, an asylum commonly considered the most enlightened of its day, worked hard to forge trust between patients and staff and any changes in accommodation were applied on a highly individual basis (the ultimate treat was a stay at a luxurious Scarborough villa). Moreover, if the purpose of the asylum was to restore patients to a behavioural state acceptable to the outside world, then such a method of encouraging social behaviour could well be considered an act of kindness. Yet the Retreat was small, privately-funded and generously staffed; and it is unlikely that the huge publicly funded asylums had the resources necessary to ensure the benign application of these promotionary and demotionary tactics. It is here that Goffman's model of an institution ruled by reward and punishment becomes more applicable.[67]

The move towards greater domesticity also had a commercial rationale. As private asylums, the Retreat, Bootham Park and Bethlem had a proportion of fee-paying patients and were commercial entities in so far as they needed to attract sufficient numbers of clients. This was quite a challenge, as the higher a lunatic's social class, the less likely his or her family would be to seek institutional help.[68] And if the private asylum was considered a last resort by the very people on whom its survival depended, it was essential that those who did make it through the door were favourably impressed with what they found. Kind staff, good food and regular entertainment were clearly important; and the interior had a significant role to play in the process.[69]

At the Retreat and Bootham Park the commercial rationale manifested itself in the lavish treatment of rooms reserved for wealthy patients. These patients would pay inflated fees, and the extra revenue thus generated was used to subsidise poorer patients. In 1877 the managers at Bootham Park suggested: 'It might be desirable to keep in view ... the importance of additional light and cheerful private rooms for first class patients who would materially help the Committee to extend the benefits of the Institution to a class of patients whose means are limited.'[70] The fact that the whole institution would eventually benefit was ample justification for spending considerable sums on decorating these reserved areas.[71] It was the redecoration of a suite of rooms reserved for 'first class' ladies, for example, that brought Maple & Co. to Bootham Park in 1908.[72]

The lure of domesticity was also connected to the professional concerns of psychiatrists. The psychiatric profession had developed as an off-shoot of mainstream medicine in the early nineteenth century – and it did so in opposition to the long-held idea that madhouses could be run by any enterprising individual. Psychiatrists argued instead that insanity had a physical origin and that only medical men like themselves were qualified to administer its treatment. However, by the end of the century they had failed to locate those physical origins, and a cure remained elusive. (There was no psychotherapy at that time, and the drugs that were available sedated rather than alleviated insanity.) The secure monopoly that psychiatrists had once enjoyed was now in jeopardy, and one way of buttressing their precarious professional position was to impress the upper classes with the care of its husbands and wives, sons and daughters.[73]

Like all areas of Victorian public life, the asylum was profoundly class-based, and fee-paying patients were desired for their good breeding as much as for their money or influence. Indeed, madness itself was relatable to social class. Whereas the pauper patients at Bootham Park were described as being 'exceptionally noisy and excited', Bethlem's first fee-paying patients, though by their very presence deemed unfit for ordinary society, were thought to exhibit exemplary behaviour. The head doctor, for one, was 'convinced that the admission of such patients has distinctly improved the tone of the rest'.[74] These perceived advantages provided the asylum authorities with yet another reason to entice upper-class patients with accommodation increasingly reminiscent of home.

If the most comfortable rooms in the private asylum were reserved for the wealthier patients, the same class distinctions were replicated across the asylum world at large. The degree of domesticity afforded to patients varied considerably between the different types of institution, and predictably it was the paupers in the publicly funded asylums who came off worst.[75] The managers of public asylums faced a number of obstacles not encountered by their colleagues in the private asylum. First, public accountability meant that it was 'wise to avoid anything in the way of costly embellishment calculated to prejudice the mind of the rate-payer on entering the building'.[76] Second, because pauper patients in the public asylum had no experience of anything other than working-class housing, they were not expected to feel the lack of material comfort as acutely as their wealthier, better-educated, counterparts in the private asylum. For example, in 1847 John Conolly claimed that 'those whose faculties have never been cultivated derive little satisfaction ... and experience little emotion' when introduced to pleasant surroundings.[77] Third, it was considered detrimental to paupers' recovery for them to become accustomed to a degree of comfort unsustainable in the outside world.[78] Add these together and it seems that the interiors of public asylums were never expected to be as homely as those of the private asylums.[79] According to the historian Andrew Scull, most publicly funded asylums were, in any case, so enormous, so short of resources and so lacking in imaginative staff that they could rarely offer 'more than a grotesque caricature of the domestic circle', even had they so wanted.[80]

If the average public asylum presented only a sad parody of domesticity, under the right circumstances a homely interior could be achieved in both the private and the public sector. While the domestic model was followed most easily at small and privately funded asylums like Bethlem, Bootham Park and the Retreat, the successes of the publicly funded Claybury Asylum indicate that a conscious desire to improve patients' accommodation mattered more than anything else. Claybury may have been unusual – indeed London County Council found it 'much too lavish and sumptuous' – but it was no less real than any other publicly funded asylum.[81] As with all institutions, some asylums were commendable, some disgraceful, and many lay somewhere in-between. What is important is that the domestic ideal was a genuine mission with visibly real results.[82]

In conclusion, it is interesting to speculate what the patients themselves thought of the ongoing improvements to their material environment. Did they welcome the efforts to make them more comfortable? Or was their mental anxiety so great that the quality of the interior was entirely irrelevant? Moreover, could patients ever feel truly 'at home' in the knowledge that they were confined to the asylum until told otherwise? Without access to the patients' testimonies, all that can be said for certain is that even the asylum authorities recognised the limits of their work. After dutifully doing the rounds at Bootham Park in the summer of 1906, two committee members dryly observed: 'We are thankful there are such institutions and very thankful that so far we do not require to be kept inside longer than to pay a visit.'[83] Clearly, in spite of everything that might have been done to make the asylum interior more homely, it would never be a place where a 'normal' person would choose to live.

Notes

1 Lady Barker, *The Bed Room and the Boudoir* (London: Macmillan, 1878), p. 92.

2 J. Conolly, *Dr. John Conolly on the Construction and Government of Lunatic Asylums* (London: Churchill, 1847), p. 22.

3 Lunatics Act, 8 & 9 Vic., c. 100.

4 For a full history of Bethlem, see P. Allderidge, *Bethlem Hospital 1247–1997: A Pictorial Record* (Chichester: Phillimore, 1997); J. Andrews, A. Briggs, R. Porter and K. Waddington, *A History of Bethlem Hospital, 1247–1997* (London: Routledge, 1997); E. G. O'Donoghue, *The Story of Bethlehem Hospital from its Foundations in 1247* (London: Fisher Unwin, 1914). The Bethlem Archive is held at the Bethlem Hospital Archive and Museum, Beckenham, Kent.

5 For a full history of Bootham Park Hospital see A. Digby, *From York Asylum to Bootham Park Hospital* (York: Borthwick Papers, 1986). The Bootham Park Archive is held at the Borthwick Institute, University of York.

6 For a full history of the Retreat see A. Digby, *Madness, Morality and Medicine: A Study of the York Retreat 1796–1914* (Cambridge: Cambridge University Press, 1985); S. Tuke, *Description of the Retreat: An Institution near York for Insane Persons of the Society of Friends* (London: Dawsons, 1964 [1813]). The Retreat's Archive is held at the Borthwick Institute, University of York. Some additional archival material is at the Retreat.

7 For a full history of Claybury, see E. H. Pryor, *Claybury – A History of Caring* (London: Forest Health Care Trust, 1993). The Claybury Asylum Archive is split between the London Metropolitan Archive and Ilford Local History Centre.

8 Although no publication has devoted itself entirely to the asylum interior, the decidedly homely quality of the asylum at this period has been acknowledged in works of a larger scope. In *The Cambridge Illustrated History of Medicine* (Cambridge: Cambridge University Press, 1996) Roy Porter described the Retreat as a 'wholly domestic environment' (p. 292). In *Madness, Morality and Medicine*, Anne Digby termed it 'a cosy cluttered cocoon of material abundance' (p. 40). Barry Edginton's article 'The design of moral architecture at the York Retreat', *Journal of Design History*, 16:2 (2003), 103–18, considered these themes in depth. Unfortunately, it came too late to be discussed in this chapter, appearing as it did in the interval between my completion of the text and the book's publication.

9 The photographs of Bootham Park appeared in annual reports and prospectuses, and one photograph in the Bethlem Archive has been stamped with the words DAILY MAIL.

10 'Most institutions possessed a ward or two for show', according to Andrew Scull, *The Most Solitary of Afflictions – Madness and Society in Britain 1700–1900* (New Haven, CT, and London: Yale University Press, 1993), pp. 246–7.

11 E. Showalter, *The Female Malady – Women, Madness and English Culture 1830–1880* (London: Virago, 1987), p. 33.

12 BOO4/1/1, Bootham Park Inventory, 1891. The circumstances under which the inventory was produced mean that it is almost certainly free of bias.

13 H/2/1, Estimate for Complete Furnishing of the Gentlemen's New Lodge, the Retreat, York, submitted by W. S. Rowntree, 1876.

14 BOO4/3/19, Rolled Designs for Bootham Park by Maple & Co., 1908; C/1/1890, Letter to Dr Baker at the Retreat from Maple & Co., 8 July 1890.

15 Identical drapes, bentwood chairs, fire surrounds, wall-clocks, mirrors and light-fittings were photographed in rooms across the asylum. This is a useful reminder that the institution was furnished by contract.

16 In 1998 David Mitchell, estates manager at the Retreat, suggested that this might account for the unusually large number of long-case clocks now in

the building. In *Psychiatry for the Rich: A History of Ticehurst Private Asylum* (London: Routledge, 1992) C. Mackenzie shows how 'some patients brought in their own furniture, such as a sofa or a writing desk ... to establish as domestic and everyday an environment as possible' (p. 43).

17 Questions of sanitation influenced the design of hospitals more than that of asylums. This is evident in the specialist design manuals listed in note 51.

18 H. C. Burdett, *Hospitals and Asylums of the World* (London: Churchill, 1891), vol. 2, p. 41. Burdett also stated: 'The furniture of our English county asylums is often so much like that of an ordinary dwelling-house' (p. 47).

19 BOO1/8/2/1, Bootham Park Visiting Governors' Report Book, 25 April 1887.

20 Claybury Guardian Visitors Book 1893–1921, comments of the St Giles and Bloomsbury Guardians; extract from the trade magazine *The Builder*, quoted in H. Richardson, *English Hospitals 1660–1948* (London: Royal Commission on the Historical Monuments of Britain, 1998), p. 175.

21 Extract from the *London Argus*, 1904, quoted in Andrews *et al.*, *A History of Bethlem Hospital*, p. 543.

22 For this reason dining halls will not be mentioned again; chapels, meeting halls and laundries also had no domestic equivalent and they too have been left out of this discussion.

23 See note 32.

24 R. Greene, 'The hygiene of asylums for the insane', *Public Health*, 2 (1889–90), 270. The choice of the word 'mansion' is interesting because mansions, the very large homes of the very rich, were also organised around public rooms for entertaining and private rooms for guests and family members. See L. Davidoff, *The Best Circles – Society, Etiquette and the Season* (London: Croom Helm, 1973), pp. 86–7: 'The same passion for control through categorisation and segregation of populations and functions as that found in Victorian public institutions coloured the ideal of the gentleman's house ... the ladies' boudoir, the smoking room, billiard room, the guest suites with separate staircases for bachelors and unmarried women'.

25 O'Donoghue, *The Story of Bethlehem Hospital*, p. 350.

26 In the case of Claybury Asylum, even the mortuary had separate sides for male and female corpses.

27 Barker, *The Bed Room and Boudoir*, pp. 13–15. Showalter describes how female patients 'were encouraged to personalise their rooms with rag dolls, bits of shell, porcelain and bright cloth': *The Female Malady*, p. 37.

28 A. Service, *Edwardian Interiors* (London: Barrie & Jenkins, 1982), p. 100.

29 *Ibid.*, p. 106; see also W. H. Fraser, *The Coming of the Mass Market* (London: Macmillan, 1981).

30 Bethlem Hospital Annual Report 1882; BOO1/2/7, Bootham Park Annual Report 1898; A/5/3, Retreat Annual Report 1894.

31 Bethlem Hospital Annual Report 1881.

32 A/5/3, Retreat Annual report 1898; at Bethlem curtains were hung across the galleries.

33 BOO1/2/7, Bootham Park Annual Report 1900.

34 BOO1/1/2/5, Bootham Park Minute Book of Committee of Governors 1877–88.

35 I/2/2, Retreat Miscellaneous Committee Matters 1893–99.

36 LCC/MIN/918, Claybury Asylum Sub-Committee Minute Book 1893–94, 21 August 1893. The asylum was officially opened in May 1893. However, since only a quarter of the building was finished in May, half the furniture was purchased later in the year.

37 Bethlem Hospital Annual Reports 1889 and 1893.

38 BOO1/8/2/1, Bootham Park Visiting Governors' Report Book.

39 BOO1/8/4/3, Bootham Park Lady Visitors' Report Book.

40 Bethlem Hospital Annual Report 1883.

41 A/3/6, Retreat Committee Minute Book 1903–15, 19 January 1904. Interestingly, this kind of involvement conforms to the wider picture of the women's philanthropy movement related in F. Prochaska's *Women And Philanthropy* (Oxford: Oxford University Press, 1980): 'whenever women had a say in the running of an institution they left their domestic touch. Domesticity was the common experience of women charitable workers'. On one level it suited both sexes to adhere to the conventional view of women as expert home-makers. Male managers could appease enthusiastic female volunteers by giving them *something* to do, while at the same time keeping them off the 'real issues'. And though it meant they had to concentrate on the matters of 'domestic management that men found strange and disagreeable' women at least obtained a foot through the institutional door: *Women and Philanthropy*, pp. 140 and 146.

42 Bethlem Hospital Annual Reports 1883 and 1885. Over the next twenty years annual reports would continue to detail the further encroachment of this 'floral panelling'.

43 R. Hunter and I. Macalpine, *Psychiatry for the Poor* (London: Dawson, 1974), p. 129. The authors show that at London County Council's asylum at Colney Hatch male patients painted ceilings and made upholstery, while female patients were given the task of making bedding and clothing for new public asylums.

44 Numerous gifts are recorded in the Bethlem Hospital annual reports. These

included sculptures, prints, Copeland ceramic figures, 'some new settees and a fine case of stuffed seagulls' and a geological collection from the British Museum. Bootham Park benefited from a painting attributed to Zoffany and the Retreat from the sensible presents one might expect of Quakers, such as the bath chair and foot warmer donated by one generous governor. As a newer asylum with fewer notable connections, no gifts were recorded at Claybury Asylum.

45 For example, during a visit to Bethlem in 1880 (reported in Bethlem Hospital Annual Report, 1880: Report of the Commissioners in Lunacy) the commissioners remarked: 'When the time comes for repapering the upper galleries, we trust that paper more cheerful in pattern and colour than the present may be selected.'

46 E/3/11, Retreat Bills and Receipts 1900–01; BOO1/1/2/7, Bootham Park Minute Book of the Committee of Governors 1901–11.

47 BOO4/3/19, Rolled Designs for Bootham Park by Maple & Co., 1908.

48 LCC/MIN/917, Claybury Sub-Committee Minute Book 1891–93. The steward eventually visited Gloucester, Nottingham and Prestwich asylums. A decade later, London County Council's chief asylum engineer was sent on a European tour to observe how foreign asylums were built and furnished. His findings were published in a fully illustrated book.

49 I/2/2, Retreat Miscellaneous Committee Matters 1893–99.

50 As well as Charles Eastlake's famous *Hints on Household Taste*, Macmillan produced the 'Art at Home' series; each book, of which Lady Barker's *The Bed Room and Boudoir* is one, dealt with a different room in the house.

51 These include Conolly's aforementioned *On The Construction and Government of Lunatic Asylums* and Greene's article 'The hygiene of asylums for the insane'; W. H. O. Sankey, 'Do the public asylums of England, as at presently constructed, afford the greatest facility for the care and treatment of the insane?' *Asylums Journal of Mental Science*, 2 (1855–56), 466–79; F. Oppert, *Hospitals, Infirmaries and Dispensaries* (London: Churchill, 1867); M. Granville, *Care and Cure of the Insane – Being the Report of the Lancet Commission on Lunatic Asylums* (London: Lancet, 1877); F. J. Monat, *Hospital Construction and Management* (London: Churchill, 1883); H. C. Burdett, *Hospitals and Asylums of the World* (London: Churchill, 1891); W. C. C. Smith, *Notes on a Visit to Continental and British Asylums Compiled for the Asylum Committee of the London County Council* (London: London County Council Publications, 1901).

52 Burdett, *Hospitals and Asylums of the World*, vol. 2, pp. 41–53.

53 LCC/MIN/918, Claybury Sub-Committee Minute Book 1893–94.

54 See Scull, *The Most Solitary of Afflictions*, and two further works by the same author: 'The domestication of madness', *Medical History*, 27 (1983),

233–48; and 'A convenient place to get rid of inconvenient people', in A. D. King (ed.), *Buildings and Society: Essays on the Social Development of the Built Environment* (London: Routledge, 1980). Scull shows that by the second half of the nineteenth century the asylum population in England had risen to several hundred thousand and new institutions filled as soon as they were opened. Scull relates this rise to a decline in social tolerance rather than a real increase in the number of people showing symptoms of insanity. First, poor families were less able to nurse their relatives than in the pre-industrial period. Second, the asylum-building campaign of the mid-nineteenth century had legitimised, if not encouraged, institutionalisation. The result was ever-larger asylums, over-burdened medical staff and little spare time for psychiatric research. In such a climate, long-term incarceration became common.

55   See Digby, *Madness, Morality and Medicine*, p. 37.

56   Conolly, *On the Construction and Government of Lunatic Asylums*, pp. 9–10.

57   Kent History Centre, MH/Md 2 287, Barming Asylum Commissioners' Visit Book, 26 June 1895.

58   A/5/3, Retreat Annual Report 1893.

59   Bethlem Hospital Annual Report 1883.

60   BOO1/2/7, Bootham Park Annual Report 1900.

61   M. Foucault, *Madness and Civilisation* (London: Routledge, 1991 [1961]), p. 244.

62   Granville, *Care and Cure of the Insane*, vol. 1, pp. 79 and 351–2.

63   Of course some patients were considered too violent to be entrusted with breakable objects. On one ward at the Retreat 'the destructive character of the patients renders it desirable that nothing expensive should be procured, unless very desirable, and not likely to be damaged': I/2/2, Retreat Miscellaneous Committee Mmatters 1893–99.

64   Dr Delarive quoted in Digby, *Madness, Morality and Medicine*, p. 66.

65   E. Goffman, *Asylums: Essays on the Social Situation of Mental Patients and Other Inmates* (New York: Anchor Books, 1961).

66   Digby, *Madness, Morality and Medicine*, pp. 66–72.

67   See Scull, *The Most Solitary of Afflictions*, p. 304.

68   According to statistics offered by Showalter (*The Female Malady*, p. 27), 91 per cent of asylum patients were paupers by 1900. This was because in richer families 'bizarre behaviour would be described as nervousness or eccentricity until the patient became unmanageable, suicidal or violent' (p. 26). For an analysis of rich people's attitudes to asylums, see MacKenzie, *Psychiatry for the Rich*.

69 MacKenzie, *Psychiatry for the Rich*, p. 24: 'Opportunities for privacy and the creation of a domestic environment ... enabled families to be reassured that private patients would continue to enjoy the comforts of a genteel home despite their separation from the family. It was this above all which encouraged families who could afford it to allow their insane relatives to become long term patients in asylums.'

70 BOO1/8/2/1, Bootham Park Visiting Governors' Report Book, 20 November 1877. The Retreat also provided separate accommodation for very rich patients, the Gentlemens' Lodge and the Ladies' Villa, built in 1876 and 1890, respectively. The Retreat's Annual Report for 1882 recorded that an entire suite of rooms had been made over to 'one of the gentlemen patients' so that he might gain 'all the advantages of a private residence, combined with the supervision, and many advantages of the parent institution'.

71 It is interesting to note that when the Gentlemen's Lodge was opened at the Retreat in 1876, a time when furniture was cheaper than ever before, one room alone cost over £30 to furnish: see C. Edwards, *Victorian Furniture: Technology and Design* (Manchester: Manchester University Press, 1993). In 1900 a complete working-class house could be furnished for around £12 and a roll of wallpaper could be purchased for as little as twopence. While this made it easier for asylums to provide a greater numbers of material goods, it also meant that expectation-levels increased.

72 Predictably, photographs of these new rooms were exploited to the full in the asylum's annual reports and prospectuses.

73 See Scull, *The Most Solitary of Afflictions*, pp. 135 and 245. Scull writes that 'without a significant proportion of upper-class patients, the newly emerging psychiatric profession could look forward to no more than a dubious status as a barely legitimate branch of medicine'.

74 While there may be some link between social class and the different behavioural manifestations of madness, patient case notes show as much misbehaviour among 'polite ladies' as among prostitutes dying of syphilis. Even so, the acute class consciousness that pervaded British society during this period meant that asylum doctors believed that the intermingling of patients from different classes would hinder recovery. It was therefore decided to restrict the publicly funded asylum to uneducated paupers and the private asylum to the middle and upper classes. That is why in the 1880s both Bethlem and Bootham Park redirected their charitable income at hard-up but educated members of the middle classes and tried to rid themselves of working-class patients. To appreciate just how natural this seemed at the time, see J. Harris, *Private Lives, Public Spirit: Britain 1870–1914* (London: Penguin, 1994).

75 The ideology of domesticity was not replicated in other nineteenth-century institutions. Although the prison and the workhouse may have undergone

reform, the physical environment remained archetypally institutional and their inmates enjoyed none of the home comforts presented to asylum patients. The preferential treatment of asylum interiors was based on the fact that the mentally ill were increasingly seen as victims rather than as the protagonists of their own downfall. By the end of the period, self-abuse, swearing and other inappropriate behaviour were beginning to be seen as symptoms of insanity rather than its causes: A. W. Beveridge and E. B. Renvoize, 'Mental illness and the late Victorians: a study of patients admitted to three asylums in York, 1880–1884', *Psychological Medicine*, 19 (1989), 19–28. Attitudes towards the mentally ill sometimes bordered on sentimentality: for example, a journalist writing for the *Illustrated London News* in 1860 described Bethlem patients as 'unhappy souls'. In the 1850s Dr Hugh Diamond of Surrey County Asylum put garlands of wild flowers in the hair of his favourite female patients and photographed them as modern-day Ophelias. For a full description of Diamond's work, see S. L. Gilman, *Disease and Representation: Images of Illness from Madness to Aids* (Ithaca, NY: Cornell University Press, 1988), and Showalter, *The Female Malady*.

76 H. Tuke, *The Past and Present Provision for the Insane Poor in Yorkshire* (London: Churchill, 1889), p. 12. A journalist describing the new Claybury Asylum in the June 1893 edition of *The Builder* was careful to assure the public that 'the architectural treatment seems just what it should be', with the interior 'finished in a plain and inexpensive manner'.

77 Conolly, *On the Construction and Government of Lunatic Asylums*, p. 9.

78 As well as wishing to discourage parasitic behaviour, the asylum authorities did not want patients to become too accustomed to a standard of living they would not be able to sustain once discharged. According to Showalter (*The Female Malady*, p. 36): 'In designing [public] asylums, it was … necessary to find a compromise between comfort and luxury, and to avoid the ornamentation that would spoil pauper lunatics and stimulate tastes that could not be gratified in their real lives' Adrian Forty traces similar currents in the treatment of the nineteenth-century hospital interior: 'The modern hospital in France and England', in A. D. King (ed.), *Buildings and Society: Essays on the Social Development of the Built Environment* (London: Routledge, 1980), p. 85.

79 See Granville, *Care and Cure of the Insane*, p. 4: 'It is only natural to expect that the pauper inmates of a mixed establishment will be less carefully provided with comfortable and pleasing surroundings than patients of a higher grade.' It was not only in English asylums that such distinctions occurred. Touring a Dutch asylum in 1901, London County Council's chief asylum engineer observed: 'The interiors of the houses are furnished and decorated to suit the grades of the patients they accommodate; carpeted floors, walls with high-class paper and decorated ceilings are found in the first class houses, while in the third class, sanded floors and painted or distempered

walls are the rule': quoted in Smith, *Notes on a Visit to Continental and British Asylums*, p. 73.

80 Scull, *The Most Solitary of Afflictions*, p. 287. According to Scull, even the lunacy commissioners were complicit, choosing to ignore the lack of material comfort that persisted in many public asylums and instead focusing their attention on private asylums.

81 Scull, *The Most Solitary of Afflictions*, p. 330.

82 The study on which this chapter is based concludes in 1914. It was around this point that psychiatry became increasingly reliant on drug therapy and electrotherapy. It was also during the inter-war period that interior decoration, whether domestic or institutional, was pared down markedly under the influence of modernist design. Taking these facts together, we can begin to understand why asylum interiors became increasingly clinical in feel and why we experience surprise when we first encounter photographs of the kind shown in this chapter.

83 BOO1/8/2/1, Bootham Park Visiting Governors' Report Book, 29 June 1906.

4 ✧ The domestic interior and the construction of self: the New York homes of Elsie de Wolfe

Penny Sparke

So it is, looking backward, that I see my own career in the terms of the houses I have made for myself. They were the cradle in which my desire for beauty was nurtured. They were the laboratory in which its principles were given full and free expression. (Elsie de Wolfe, *After All* [1])

THE MEANING of the domestic interior is not fixed. Rather history has pulled it and pushed it in response to the ideological headlines of the moment. From the mid-nineteenth century until well into the twentieth century, for example, it became the repository, for the most part, of meanings generated by and for women. While men continued to inhabit the domestic arena, and certain rooms in the house were identified as 'masculine' in nature, the belief that the home was nonetheless a predominantly feminine sphere became widely accepted.[2] This belief in the existence of a special relationship between women and the domestic interior resulted not only in their strong presence in that physical space but more fundamentally in their creative efforts to elaborate it and thereby imbue it with meanings. Through the consumption of goods with which to construct a home, through choices regarding its decoration and through direct productive work resulting in ornamentation and display, women increasingly became the key progenitors of the meanings that came to be embedded within the domestic interior. In that process of elaboration women found a means not only of representing the dominant cultural themes of the day – family, class, nation, etc. – but of externalising 'themselves'. As a result, their homes became material manifestations of their personal identities.[3] As economic, social, cultural, technological and political circumstances made women's identities undergo a process of permanent transformation, the domestic interior became an increasingly articulate representation of that process of change.

Women's ability to see their homes as mirrors not only of broad cultural themes but of their individual selves coincided with their growing professionalisation in a number of distinct spheres, especially in areas which were seen as 'natural' extensions of their accepted gendered roles, such as education, nursing and interior decoration. The idea that decorating the domestic interior could be seen as a viable form of paid work for women emerged first in Britain in the last two decades of the nineteenth century as a natural extension of women taking the responsibility for home decoration on an amateur basis and of increasing numbers of women being trained as architects but ending up working on the interiors rather than the exteriors of buildings.[4]

Professionalised interior decorating by women also took off in the USA at the end of the nineteenth century and, by the outbreak of the First World War, the female interior decorating profession was well established, with a number of individuals having set up highly successful decorating businesses.[5] In this period American society was marked by a high degree of mobility and the home took on a key role as a marker of acquired social status. 'In a shifting society', the literary critic Lionel Trilling, has explained, 'great emphasis is put on appearance.'[6] Certainly at this time the aesthetic of the domestic interior came to play an increasingly important role in status formation, and most clients invited a reading of their homes which prioritised their positions in society. Increasingly, also, in those years of growing female emancipation and independence, the notion of 'gender' became uppermost in many women's definitions of 'self'. Through the manipulation of 'taste' values female interior decorators took on the role of representing women's identities through the creation of a visual language for the home. Arguably, however, the identities they created most effectively were their own.

The work of the American interior decorator Elsie de Wolfe is a case in point. Indeed, her creations were so overtly expressions of herself that her clients had to sign up to a de Wolfe identity. While this undoubtedly suited many of her newly arrived clients, who had little confidence in their own tastes and who sought confirmation of their new positions in society through the ownership of an interior decor which had proved its social acceptability, for her more self-confident and creative clients it was less appropriate. The wife of the painter Walter Gay, for example, was unhappy about such an imposition of taste. Commenting on a house that de Wolfe had decorated for herself, she explained: 'I would rather furnish my own place, and express my own personality. This house, exquisite as it is, expresses Elsie de Wolfe.'[7]

Although de Wolfe created a considerable number of interiors in the decade 1905–15, some for the public sphere but mostly for private clients, it was in the interior schemes she created for herself that she developed her language of identity representation most effectively. As it was primarily her own identity she was intent on representing, it was a process which involved a close knowledge of self as well as an acute understanding of the cultural forces which had defined her and which continued to reinforce her own self-image. Her success as a professional decorator undoubtedly stemmed from her ability to focus on those aspects of her own persona with which other women could identify. Indeed the aspects of herself which came to the fore – her enhanced characterisation of her own 'femininity', her social aspirations and her ambivalent sense of her own nationality – proved to be those with which many of the female members of the emergent elite of American society were also preoccupied and which they sought to express through their domestic interiors.

Although de Wolfe quickly became a leading figure in the decorating profession in the first decade of the twentieth century she derived many of her ideas from others. Many of her decorating strategies, for example, were borrowed from the writer Edith Wharton and the architect Ogden Codman who, together, had published the influential book *The Decoration of Houses* in 1897. Unlike Wharton, however, de Wolfe became a prolific practitioner. She turned professional in 1905 in the wake of statements by Candace Wheeler about the possibility of women moving into a career in interior decoration, following the model of Wheeler herself.[8] However she ignored Wheeler's advocation of an extensive training prior to becoming a professional. From the outset she was committed to reaching a wide audience and to taking the private arena of the domestic interior into the public sphere.[9] Indeed she saw the two spheres as being fundamentally interdependent and interchangeable, and she moved freely between them apparently unaware of the barriers that existed for others. She also sought self-expression for others on a significant scale. In her book *The House in Good Taste*, published in 1913 – a compilation of articles which had already appeared in the women's magazines *Good Housekeeping* and *The Delineator*, ghost-written by Ruby Ross Goodnow but with de Wolfe's name attached to them – the decorator was forthright in her view of the importance of the interior as a form of self-expression for women: 'It is the personality of the mistress that the home expresses', she explained. 'Men are forever guests in our homes, however much happiness they may find there.' [10]

The homes de Wolfe created for herself, it can be argued, played a key role in the decorator's construction of herself. She was a highly fashion-conscious woman and perceived the interior as being, following after dress, a layer around the body. Indeed, to a significant extent, for de Wolfe, the domestic interior could be seen, essentially, as a form of identity construction in the manner of dress, created either through disguise or through revelation of what it was covering. Fresh from a career in the theatre, which she abandoned in 1905 to become a decorator, de Wolfe knew all too well the importance of the physical stage set for the drama that is enacted against it.

The interiors de Wolfe created to act as important backcloths for her own life in New York in the years leading up to the First World War were situated in two houses, one of them located on the corner of Irving Place and East 17th Street, where she resided between 1892 and 1910, and the second at 123 East 55th Street, where she lived from 1910 to 1915. While she decorated the interiors of these houses in the capacity of an 'amateur' she also devoted her efforts to professional work from 1905 onwards. In the latter capacity her projects included numerous commissions for private houses across the USA, a woman's club, a school dormitory, an automobile interior, an opera box, theatre sets and a model apartment for an exhibition. [11] The taste values which informed the decoration of her own homes were highly personal ones, informed to a significant degree by her own strong social aspirations, her overt and fine-tuned sense of her own 'femininity' – and of her 'Americanness' which was defined by its juxtaposition with her acquired 'Europeanness'. When she worked for others the same values were frequently in evidence.

The Washington Irving house

Elsie de Wolfe's life as an interior decorator began in 1905 when she was commissioned to design the interior of New York's Colony Club on Madison Avenue, the city's first all-women's club. It was a remarkable commission, coming as it did to someone who was untrained and who had up to that point worked as an amateur. The building was designed by Stanford White, the creator of many of New York's best-known men's clubs.[12] De Wolfe was selected for two reasons. The first was personal. The ex-actress lived with Elizabeth Marbury, a member of an 'old moneyed' New York family and her theatrical agent. Marbury was on the board of the Colony Club and undoubtedly exerted some influence in acquiring this commission for her friend.[13] In addition Stanford White was a neighbour of the two ladies in Gramercy Park and a visitor to the Sunday afternoon gatherings that they hosted for the cultural elite of New York.[14] Like Marbury he also recommended de Wolfe to the board of the Colony Club. His confidence in her ability to undertake the project was rooted in his close knowledge of what she had managed to achieve in her own home.

Marbury had long been a resident of Irving Place, the site of her family home. The couple had first met in 1887, when de Wolfe was still an amateur actress, and their close relationship was to last for the next quarter of a century. They moved into the little Irving Place house in 1892, a year after de Wolfe had become a professional actress and, five years later, in the publication year of Wharton and Codman's book, de Wolfe undertook a major refurbishment of its interior (see figure 10). In essence she transformed it from a dark, gloomy, cluttered, typically Victorian space filled with potted plants and knick-knacks into a brighter, more roomy, set of spaces in which light and air were much more in evidence (figure 11). As she explained later, her plan at that time had been to 'devote all my leisure to making over this tiny old dwelling into a home which would fit into our plan for life'.[15] She clearly used the gaps between her theatre performances to good effect and took the opportunity to experiment with interior decorating strategies which would give the couple a more comfortable and elegant life-style.

The strategies that de Wolfe developed in the Irving Place refurbishment stayed with her for years. Primary among them was a dependence

10 Elsie de Wolfe in the Turkish corner at 122 East 17th Street

on French eighteenth-century decorating style and on antique and reproduction French furniture. In the dining room at Irving Place, for example,
she painted all the woodwork and the furniture white (figure 12). She felt
quite justified in looking to France for inspiration, explaining later: 'Miss
Marbury and I have a perfect right to French things in our drawing-room,
you see, for we are French residents half the year. And besides this
gracious old house welcomed a fine old Louis XIV sofa as serenely as you
please.' [16] From the early 1890s onwards de Wolfe and Marbury went
annually to France, and in 1905 they bought a house in Versailles – the
Villa Trianon – which was to play an important part in their lives – in
de Wolfe's case, until her death in 1950.

The decorator's appropriation of eighteenth-century French taste
provided a means of bypassing the Victorian interior. Her personal dis-
like of what she felt to be the claustrophobia of that idiom was rooted in
her childhood which had been spent in a New York brownstone house.

11 Elsie de Wolfe's dining-room (before decorating) at 122 East 17th Street, 1896

12 Elsie de Wolfe's dining-room (after decorating) at 122 East 17th Street, 1898

Her father had been a doctor of Nova Scotian origin who died penniless, and de Wolfe led an unremarkable middle-class childhood in typically nineteenth-century surroundings. 'I was an ugly child', she was to explain in her autobiography. 'I lived in an ugly age. From the moment I was conscious of ugliness and its relationship to myself and my surroundings, my one preoccupation was to find a way out of it. In my escape I came to the meaning of beauty.' [17]

On one level, therefore, it is possible to see de Wolfe's interest in the interior as social aspiration expressed in aesthetic terms. The gloom could, she felt, be replaced by light and air, qualities she had observed, as a young girl on a visit to England, in eighteenth-century country houses of the aristocracy and in the interior styles and furnishings of the same era, and of the same social group, that she saw in France during her visits with Marbury. From an early date she began to buy French furniture and have it shipped back to the USA. As she became increasingly known as a decorator her knowledge of the French antique furniture trade and her links with key dealers put her in a strong position, and she made as much money from supplying such goods to clients as she did by embellishing clients' interior spaces. The remembered emotional impact of the lightness of those old pieces, compared with their heavy Victorian counterparts, inspired an evocative description of a room she had seen in Europe – 'a room where the windows diffused and undulated the light, where space enveloped one like a silken mantle, where the colors were blended in a gentle camaraderie and where graceful furniture invited repose and comfort, created a kind of peace in me and made me feel at home.' [18] De Wolfe was clearly trying to create something of that sort of ambiance in Irving Place. The result represented a form of personal liberation, a release from both the physical constraints and the melancholia created by the environment in which she had been brought up. The link with Marbury freed her from the limitations of what she had felt to be a suffocating middle-class upbringing and the restrictive taste that had accompanied it. Along with the inclusion of items of French furniture, colour was used strategically to bring light into the house. Her chosen colour scheme – grey–green, rose, dull yellow, white and cream – consisted of eighteenth-century-inspired soft pastels which she was to use in many interiors to come. 'One colour', she explained, 'faded into another so subtly that one did not realise that there was a definite colour scheme.'[19] As was to become a common strategy in many of her later interiors, she took her colours for Irving Place from individual items which were to go into that space, in this instance a Persian rug and a Chinese carpet. The narrow hall was embellished with a green-and-white-striped ribbongrass wallpaper, a feature she was to use again in the foyer of the Colony Club. Many times over in later years the epithet 'spring' was used to describe the tone of the green in question, revealing the regenerative power that decorating held for de Wolfe.[20]

In Irving Place de Wolfe removed a late nineteenth-century 'cosy corner' from the bay window, replacing it with a tiny conservatory, complete with a white marble floor, climbing ivy and a small fountain. This provided a prototype for what was to become a defining feature of her mature decorating language: the indoor garden. It re-emerged in the famous 'trellis' restaurant in the Colony Club and in the many winter gardens that she went on to add to the large houses of members of the 'nouveau riche' across the USA in the first decade of the century. Clients whose interior schemes included winter gardens included Mr and Mrs Ogden Armour in Chicago and Mr and Mrs Ormond Smith on Long Island. She also added one to the New York town house of Mr and Mrs Benjamin Guinness.[21] The idea of 'outdoor–indoor' ambiguity was to reach its zenith in the work of the European modernist architects of the 1930s who took it much further than de Wolfe.[22]

Although the work of this late nineteenth-century amateur interior decorator was both eclectic and historicist in nature it demonstrated, nonetheless, a nascent modern sensibility. From one perspective de Wolfe can be seen to have been working in a transitional mode, rejecting the past in favour of the new, although using models from a deeper past with which to locate that sense of novelty and modernity. Indeed in a number of ways de Wolfe displayed an affinity with what could be seen as a prevailing shift in the USA at that time towards a more rational 'modern' attitude to life, an approach which found an important outlet in another face of contemporary American feminine culture, the 'rational household movement', which took its ideas from scientific management.[23] De Wolfe's often reiterated use of the term 'light and airy' bore witness to the fact that she aligned herself with the idea of modernity to a significant extent and that her vision looked backwards and forwards simultaneously. However stylistically dependent the decorator's work was on eighteenth-century European taste, in the context of turn-of-the-century USA it represented a break with the past and a shift towards a specifically American view of the future. Her commitment to that future was particularly apparent in the practical – non-decorative – faces of her interiors where, in line with the general American confidence in and enthusiasm for technology, de Wolfe incorporated into her interiors all that technology could offer, from electric lighting to steam heating. Even through her evocation of the past, however, de Wolfe's work can be understood as providing a framework for a modern definition of both womanhood and nation, both for herself and for her clients.

The personal tension felt by de Wolfe around the subject of her own nationality – between, that is, her indigenous American and acquired European identities – was a recurrent theme throughout her life and influenced her interiors from an early date. From the 1890s onwards she spent her summers in France, and after the First World War she moved to Paris only to return to the USA when she was forced to do so by the advent of the Second World War. She remained first and foremost an American during her absence, however (in spite of the fact that she married an English peer in 1926), and provided a point of focus for other wealthy Americans travelling in Europe, relying on them as clients and supporters. Paradoxically she needed to embrace French taste in order to be able to define herself as an American while at the same time her only way of defining herself as a modern American was to spend a large proportion of her life in Europe.

If themes arising from her class aspirations and nationality tensions underpinned the interior decor of the Irving Place house, so did those relating to de Wolfe's understanding of her own gender identity. Her transformation of Irving Place represented an opportunity to leave the past behind and to define her new lifestyle as that of an unmarried independent woman living closely alongside another woman in a same-sex relationship.[24] She gave away little about her sexuality in her interiors but they were very revealing constructions of her gendered identity. Her fundamental decision to use the domestic interior, which was understood in this period as a primarily 'feminine' space, as her 'canvas' was in itself a mark of her preoccupation with gender.[25] In her refurbishment of Irving Place de Wolfe has told us that she was setting out to create a home. More than that she wanted to construct an interior space in which she would feel 'at home'.[26] For her, this clearly meant being at one with the cultural trappings of femininity. As an actress she had been better known for her couturier gowns – made by well-known names such as Worth, Paquin and Doucet – than for her performances and she saw the acquisition of 'beauty' as a necessary requirement to keep the 'ugliness' of her childhood at bay. Beauty, for de Wolfe, was synonymous with 'feminine beauty' and she dedicated her life to a pursuit of this ideal using her own face and body as a kind of experimental laboratory. In her later years she underwent extensive cosmetic surgery, and throughout her life she paid great attention to her appearance through careful diet and daily exercise. Her career as an actress had represented one means of moving from the world of reality into one of fantasy where an 'alternative world', provided by costume, make-up and stage sets, facilitated a reconstruction of 'self' in which beauty could be made to play a part even if it was not naturally present. As a decorator de Wolfe came to depend on the domestic interior as a substitute for the stage as a site of identity construction.

The interior decor of the Washington Irving House, as de Wolfe liked to call it, after the writer who was thought to have lived there, was unequivocally feminine. The pastel colours and light decorative touches were offset by a rigorous practicality and a sense of comfort representative of the other face of femininity. The inclusion of many tiny details were witness to the decorator's practical approach. The presence of a little bowl, for example, in Miss Marbury's bedroom, described as being of 'just the proper color' and intended 'to hold pens and clips and odds and ends' was a sign of her commitment to providing a place for everything.[27] She also positioned mirrors, which she used extensively in her interiors to create an illusion of space, to allow her to see the back of her head. The couple's belongings were stored in a highly organised manner in large closets, yet another example of the practical side of the domestic femininity that dominated the interior they inhabited.

A level of domestic comfort was also deemed central to de Wolfe's formula for the successful interior. This was expressed primarily through the soft furnishings that she utilised. Irving Place saw her first use of chintz, a fabric she had seen in English country houses some years earlier. It was used, for example, complete with a bird of paradise print – one of de Wolfe's favourite patterns – as a bedcovering fabric in Miss Marbury's bedroom, and again in the same room as an upholstery fabric on the sofa, on a little side chair and on what de Wolfe herself described as 'an adorable little screen of white enamel, paneled with chintz below and glass above'.[28] The bedroom of each woman boasted a daybed, an item considered by the decorator as an essential component of any woman's bedroom, enabling her to take a necessary daytime nap. Each room also contained a writing table and a variety of lamps positioned conveniently next to the writing and reading areas, which included the bed.

The final manifestation of conventional femininity in de Wolfe's interiors which found its way into Irving Place was a commitment to decorative objects – not the bric-a-brac of the Victorian home but a more selective display of significant items. In her 1897 refurbishment of the house she threw out many of the theatrical momentos which had previously filled her display cases and adorned the mantelpiece in the drawing room, replacing them with paintings and prints which she fixed to the (by then) plain-panelled walls. The hall, for instance, featured a series of fashion plates discovered in France, while a Nattier painting took pride of place over the mantelpiece. (It was to appear again, as did de Wolfe's Breton bed, in the East 55th Street house.) Flowers blossomed in vases on mantelpieces and pattern adorned many of the fabrics. The decorator was restrained in her use of patterned surfaces, however, tending to prefer walls painted in a single colour to wallpaper.

The Washing Irving house played a seminal part in de Wolfe's oeuvre. It was her first attempt at a whole interior and it brought together all the formative influences on her life up to that point, among them the negative memories of her childhood and the positive effects of living in foreign countries and exposure to different cultures. It enabled her to experiment with a new interior language which was at the same time both backward- and forward-looking; it allowed her to align her personal aspirations with her spatial environment; and it provided her with a means of representing 'herself', defined through the cultural filters of class, gender and nationality. More importantly it gave de Wolfe the means of externalising her aesthetic preoccupations and of creating an identity for herself which was in keeping with her new-found freedom and lifestyle. Perhaps most importantly it became her 'home' for a significant period of time, and as such gave her a stable emotional base from which she could move forward with confidence.

123 East 55th Street

If the re-decoration of Irving Place performed an important aspirational role for de Wolfe, that of 123 East 55th Street was the full-blooded realisation of that aspiration. She decorated it while at the height of her success as an interior decorator. By 1910, when she purchased the house, she had already decorated the Colony Club in New York as well as a range of private residences in, among other places, Chicago, San Francisco, New Jersey, Long Island and upstate New York.[29] However, East 55th Street never acquired the same level of personal meaning for the decorator as did Irving Place, and she did not look back at it later in life with the same level of nostalgia. This was partly because East 55th Street, although created for them, was never fully occupied by the two women together, and it remained a 'model' house for others to emulate rather than becoming a real home for de Wolfe. It represented her professional skills at their peak but it did not have the same personal resonance for her as the little Washington Irving house.

In 1901 the architect Ogden Codman, co-author of *The Decoration of Houses* and a frequent visitor at de Wolfe and Marbury's Sunday gatherings when he was in New York visiting from Boston, was commissioned to undertake some work at Irving Place. The historian, Pauline Metcalf, has documented the fact that Marbury and de Wolfe hired Codman to make alterations to the Irving Place drawing room. The brief was to create a 'salon' with the 'mellowed atmosphere of French society'.[30] He achieved it by installing panel mouldings and painting the walls ivory. Mirrors covered the doors and a niche for a statue was built into one end of the room. De Wolfe later claimed authorship of the niche herself, but it is clear that by 1901 she had learned to collaborate closely with architects. This was reinforced four years later through her work with Stanford White on the Colony Club (although White had died before the completion of the project). Indeed, during the first decade of the twentieth century de Wolfe worked with a wide range of Beaux Arts architects, among them Arthur Heun in Chicago and Hoppin and Koen in New York.

De Wolfe's work with Codman on East 55th Street was highly dependent on the project, undertaken by the two, which had immediately preceded it. Earlier in 1910 she had asked him to work with her on what was to become a 'show house' – 131 East 71st Street – in New York. With her new-found wealth the decorator was able to enter into entrepreneurial activity, and the idea of renovating an ordinary New York terraced brownstone, and demonstrating to others what it was possible to achieve, provided her with a perfect opportunity for some publicity. De Wolfe described the East 71st Street house as a 'plain, ugly house like tens of others'.[31] Indeed it undoubtedly closely resembled the house she herself had been brought up in, and the project's appeal was clearly the personal challenge of being able to replace ugliness with beauty, as if by a flick of a fairy wand. The project also served another important purpose: it was a way of demonstrating to that sector of the public which inhabited similar houses all over the USA that they also could transform their interior spaces and bring 'modernity' into their lives. As the decorator herself explained: 'My object in taking this house was twofold: I wanted to prove to my friends that it was possible to take one of the darkest and grimiest of city houses and make it an abode of sunshine and light, and I wanted to furnish a whole house exactly as I pleased – for once!'[32] The implications of those words were, perhaps, that at Irving Place she had not been able to entirely align 'self' with the interior schemes, as Marbury's taste had also had to be accommodated. Seen from one perspective, she was using East 71st Street to show that what she had set out to achieve at Irving Place, for personal reasons, could be emulated by anyone who wished to do so. In other words her work in the private sphere was being exposed in the public arena as an encouragement to others to make interventions within their own private environments. The potential commercial spin-off, of course, was that they might employ an interior decorator, hopefully Miss de Wolfe, to help them undertake that transformation. The project served, therefore, to blur the edges between the public and the private sphere, as well as to reinforce the process of the commodification of the domestic interior, an inevitable result of the professionalisation of interior decoration.

Codman's role in the revitalisation of East 71st Street lay in the significant restructuring that was undertaken on the house.[33] It included taking the entrance from the first floor down to ground level so that a little courtyard with an iron railing and box trees could be added (the only means by which to include the 'outside', which was so important to de Wolfe); replacing the existing stairway with a spiral staircase half way down the house to facilitate the removal of the narrow hallway and allow the rooms at the front to extend fully across the 17-foot breadth of the house; and adding a five-storey servants' quarters to the rear of the house in what had been the backyard.

Most of the decorating strategies employed by de Wolfe at Irving Place were repeated at East 71st Street, though to rather more dramatic effect. Her favourite tactic of applying to the interior scheme as a whole colours deriving from artefacts chosen for the decor was employed again: in the first-floor bedroom, for example, a pair of Chinese jugs, coloured turquoise, mauve, mulberry, black and cream, inspired an intense colour scheme for the interior, which included mauve chintz curtains. A number of items of furniture were specially made for the room. In all her schemes de Wolfe was as happy to have reproduction furniture made for her as she was to use 'genuine' antiques. At other times she had no qualms about painting old pieces of furniture to give them a new lease of life. Her approach revealed her social background: she did not come from a world where fine pieces of furniture were inherited and where it was sacriligious to talk about 'reproduced' pieces. Marbury, who came from an upper-class family, was committed to her inherited pieces, and this could well have caused friction between the two women at Irving Place. At East 71st Street de Wolfe had a free hand and was able to construct new interiors which, rather like the stage sets she had been so familiar with, could create an illusion of the past but which did not themselves belong to that past. Nothing could be more 'modern' than her commitment to sunshine and light, and the freedom with which she blended together disparate pieces of furniture. Describing the drawing room that covered the full width of the first floor she wrote:

> I am growing tired of the plain, white walls and white woodwork, and of the carefully 'matched' furniture of the over-cautious decorator who goes warily. Somehow the feeling of homeyness is lost in such an arrangement. In the drawing room there is furniture of half a dozen styles, but all in harmony. There is a long sofa of gray-painted wood covered with a needlework tapestry in soft gray and rose and creamy tan. There are several chairs of the same wood and tapestry, and still others covered with a dull-rose brocade.[34]

The house at East 71st Street allowed the decorator to exploit her skills to the full and to consolidate an aesthetic which, while still dependent on eighteenth-century French taste, was also very much 'of the moment' in early twentieth-century New York. As in Irving Place, however, practicality also determined many of the decorating decisions. Every possible opportunity to use space effectively was exploited and a storage cupboard was added in every little niche that permitted one. De Wolfe herself coined the slogan 'Suitability, Simplicity and Proportion', and she followed it so ruthlessly that while an elegant loggia with a black-and-white chequerboard marble floor and a highly decorative porcelain stove were considered 'suitable' for the dramatic entrance space, the servants' quarters at the back were much more utilitarian in appearance.[35] The decorator emphasised her commitment to this area of the house, explaining: 'I firmly believe that the whole question of house-hold comfort evolves from the careful planning of the service portion of the house.' [36]

Rapidly following the completion of East 71st Street, which was opened with a grand reception, de Wolfe purchased a very similar house on East 55th Street. This time the intention was to use it as a new home for Marbury and herself. Once again Codman was employed to undertake the necessary architectural work, and exactly the same restructuring programme was implemented. A marble floor was installed; a statue rather than a stove was set into a niche in the entrance hall; and the room arrangement was almost identical to that of the show-house. The multiple mirrors used in the hallway to create a sense of space resulted in the property being christened 'the little house of many mirrors'.[37] Attention to practical detail was in evidence once again, this time through the presence in the hallway of a writing table complete with paper and writing implements which de Wolfe justified with the following words: 'How often I have been in other people's houses when it was necessary to send a message, or to record an address, when the whole household began scurrying around trying to find a pencil and paper!' [38]

De Wolfe's bedroom was on the second floor at the front, with Marbury's immediately above it. They had direct buzzer communication with each other from their bedrooms. She dedicated enormous energy to the interior decoration of this house, conscious that it was to become their home. The distinction between East 55th Street and the show-house became somewhat eroded, however, as the shift from amateur decorating to professional work undertaken in the commercial arena meant that de

Wolfe's private world was becoming indistinguishable from her public sphere.

The drawing room at East 55th Street was a result of what were by then characteristic de Wolfe decorating strategies, tried and tested in a number of projects. Mixed furniture pieces were clustered in groups; rugs covered the floors; the walls were covered with wood panelling; and metal candle sconces (fitted with electric lights) flanked a marble mantelpiece which was topped by a mirror. Light decoration, provided by fabrics, paintings and vases of flowers, contrasted with the plainness of the panelled walls. The interior gave the impression, above all, of having been created over a period of time. This evolved look was something de Wolfe prized and she had commented on how happy she had been with the reading room in the Colony Club because it had the same feel to it. The East 55th Street drawing-room scheme was rooted in a quest for 'homeliness' pointing to the conceptual heart of de Wolfe's decorating philosophy.

The contradictions, tensions and complexities of class, gender and nationality that were Elsie de Wolfe were the essence of her work. She moved from one class to another. She combined an ambivalent sexuality with an exaggerated femininity. She refused to commit herself to life within one country or culture. The only unambivalent thing about her was that she was an interior decorator, though even in that capacity she refused to draw a hard-and-fast line between amateur and professional work and between the public and the private spheres. In the year leading up to the First World War she used interior decoration to represent and constitute 'herself' and, in turn, offered that representation to others. In so doing she helped create a new profession for women, assisted in moving the interior away from the stamp of Victorianism and influenced the tastes of a vast number of women, across a range of social classes, for several decades. In the process she also pushed forward by several stages the domestic interior's potential to represent and constitute personal identity.

Notes

1   E. de Wolfe, *The House in Good Taste* (New York: Harpers & Brothers, 1935), p. 52.

2　For a discussion of the gendering of rooms in the nineteenth-century domestic interior, see J. Kinchin, 'Interiors: nineteenth-century essays on the "masculine" and "feminine" room', in P. Kirkham (ed.), *The Gendered Object* (Manchester: Manchester University Press, 1996).

3　See L. Auslander, 'The gender of consumer practices in nineteenth-century France', in V. de Grazia and E. Furlough (eds), *The Sex of Things: Gender and Consumption in Historical Perspective* (Berkeley: University of California Press, 1996), p. 79, who argues that the domestic interior moved from a representation of class, family and nation to one of women's individual gendered identities.

4　For information relating to professional interior decorators working in Britain in the late nineteenth and early twentieth centuries, see L. Walker, 'Women architects and the arts and crafts alternative', in J. Attfield and P. Kirkham (eds), *A View from the Interior: Feminism, Women and Design* (London: Women's Press, 1989), pp. 90–105. The work of Agnes and Rhoda Garrett is especially interesting in this context. A number of British books, by women, on the subject of the domestic interior appeared in the 1870s, notable among them L. Orrinsmith, *The Drawing Room, its Decoration and Furniture* (London: Macmillan & Co., 1878) and Mrs H. R. Haweis, *The Art of Beauty* (London: Chatto & Windus, 1878).

5　In addition to that of de Wolfe, the businesses (and the names) of Ruby Ross Goodnow (later Wood), Nancy McClelland, Elsie Cobb Wilson and Rose Cumming emerged in these years.

6　L. Trilling, *The Liberal Imagination* (New York: Garden City, 1950), p. 210.

7　W. Rieder, *A Charmed Couple: The Art and Life of Walter and Matilda Gay* (New York: Abrams, 2000), p. 119.

8　In 1897 Scribner of New York published Edith Wharton and Ogden Codman's hugely influential *The Decoration of Houses* (new edn, New York: W. W. Norton, 1978). Two years earlier Candace Wheeler had published a two-part article entitled 'Interior decoration as a profession for women' in *The Outlook*, 6 April 1895, 559–60, and 20 April 1895, 649.

9　De Wolfe undertook a number of projects outside the private sphere of the home, though she continued to work in the domestic idiom in those projects. They included the interior of the Colony Club (1905–7), a dormitory for Barnard College (1907), and the interior of the Vacation Savings Club Headquarters (1913), all in New York.

10　De Wolfe published a series of articles in *The Delineator* (October 1911–May 1912) and *Good Housekeeping* (May 1912–June 1913). They formed the basis of her ghost-written book *The House in Good Taste* (New York: Century, 1913), from p. 5 of which this statement is extracted.

11　Jane S. Smith's biography of Elsie de Wolfe, entitled *Elsie de Wolfe, A Life in the High Style: The Elegant Life and Remarkable Career of Elsie de Wolfe, Lady Mendl* (New York: Atheneum, 1982), gives a brief account of some of these designs. Most remain unresearched in any detail.

12 Stanford White was known for a number of men's clubs in New York, among them the Players' Club (1889), the Century Club (1891) and the Lambs' Club (1904).

13 For Marbury's account of her relationship with de Wolfe, see E. Marbury, *My Crystal Ball* (New York: Boni & Liveright, 1923).

14 Accounts of Marbury and de Wolfe's entertaining and of the Colony Club commission can be found in Smith, *Elsie de Wolfe*, and in A. Lewis, *Ladies and Not-So-Gentle Women: Elizabeth Marbury, Anne Morgan, Elsie de Wolfe, Anne Vanderbilt and Their Times* (New York: Viking, 2000).

15 E. de Wolfe, *After All* (New York: Harper & Brothers, 1935), p. 51.

16 De Wolfe, *The House in Good Taste*, p. 32.

17 De Wolfe, *After All*, p. 3

18 *Ibid.*, p. 48.

19 De Wolfe, *The House in Good Taste*, p. 11

20 E. de Wolfe, 'The story of the Colony Club', in *The Delineator* (New York), November 1911, p. 370.

21 Of the many winter gardens she created in this period, those for Mrs Ogden Armour's house 'Mellody Farm', built in Lake Forest, just outside Chicago, and for Mrs Ormond G. Smith's 'Shoremond', built on Center Island, New York, were two of the more dramatic.

22 Le Corbusier's 'Pavillion de l'esprit nouveau', created for the Paris Exhibition of Decorative Arts in 1925, for example, eliminated the distinction between 'inside' and 'outside', to the extent of leaving a tree on site which penetrated the roof of the pavilion.

23 Scientific management was a form of Taylorism which aimed to rationalise the work process. Applied to the home, it aimed to streamline the housewife's work by reducing the number of her steps and re-organising her tasks. Christine Frederick's publication *Household Engineering* (Chicago, IL: American School of Home Economics, 1913) outlined these ideas most clearly.

24 For a more extended discussion of de Wolfe and Marbury's relationship, see R. A. Schanke and K. Marra (eds), *Passing Performances: Queer Readings of Leading Players in American Theatre History* (Michigan: University of Michigan Press, 2000).

25 For an elaboration of the notion of 'separate spheres', see J. Wolff, 'The culture of separate spheres: the role of culture in nineteenth-century public and

private life', in J. Wolff, *Feminine Sentences: Essays on Women and Culture* (Cambridge: Polity Press, 1990).

26 Smith, *Elsie de Wolfe*, p. 51.

27 De Wolfe, *The House in Good Taste*, p. 41.

28 *Ibid.*, p. 38.

29 Many of the private commissions de Wolfe undertook between 1907 and 1915 resulted from her work on the Colony Club and were for women who were members of the club.

30 P. Metcalf, *Ogden Codman and the Decoration of Houses* (Boston, MA: Boston Atheneum, 1988), 21.

31 De Wolfe, 'Transforming a small city house', in *The Delineator* (New York): February 1912, 132.

32 *Ibid.*

33 Plans of Codman's structural changes to the house can be seen in the Codman Archive, Avery Library, Columbia University, New York.

34 De Wolfe, 'Transforming a small city house', 132.

35 Codman Archive, Columbia University, New York.

36 De Wolfe, *The House in Good Taste*, p. 50.

37 *Ibid.*, p. 42.

38 *Ibid.*, p. 44.

5 ✧ Chintz, swags and bows: the myth of English country-house style, 1930–90

Louise Ward

Ｉ NTERIORS are ephemeral. Although an image captured momentarily in a photograph can give an impression of permanence, interiors are constantly changing through use, and it is therefore unsafe for the historian to treat them as fixed. A room is constructed from more than material things; it is also made by social and cultural conventions and the desire to create an environment that has, or reflects, an identity. A room can act as a projection of personality and/or lifestyle, and can even represent aspects of character: a room is always greater than the sum of its material parts.

Throughout its history, the English country house has existed as both an architectural entity and a cultural symbol. A country house is by no means the same as a house in the country: as an aristocratic family residence which acts as the tangible symbol of a socio-economic and political power structure, it is more than a building type.[1] Composed of references and allusions (both real and mythical), the country house, as a cultural symbol, communicates the life encompassed within and the status portrayed by it. In the twentieth century, when country houses themselves were under threat of destruction, the ideal was the subject of a great deal of 'fanciful, romanticized ... [but] well-articulated veneration'.[2]

The subject of this chapter is the fiction of English country-house living that developed in the inter-war and post-Second World War years, a fictional lifestyle that was the basis of the highly popular English country-house decorating idiom which permeated 1980s' society at large. In order to understand it, it is necessary to acknowledge the wider context from which the country house's identity was drawn.

The moments of fabrication and re-invention of the style occurred in conjunction with the two key phases of country-house preservation. Decline had set in for the country house in the late nineteenth century with the agricultural depression, a situation severely exacerbated by the catastrophic effects of the First World War. However, it was not until the economic and social effects of the inter-war and post-Second World War years had been felt that loss on a large scale began to be seen as inevitable, and a crisis for the future of the country house forecast. The mid-1970s saw a major shift from this first period of crisis to the second, which was brought about by the dual effects of taxation and social change. This shift signalled the threatened country house's transformation from a private home into an integral part, even a symbol, of the national heritage, which was supported by public monies.

Elevated beyond the status of the private home of the privileged, the English country house in the mid- to late twentieth century ceased to depend, as a cultural symbol, on an attachment to a particular property or even to a particular kind of house.[3] Instead – particularly in the 1980s – it became something that everyone could aspire to, or participate in, through the decoration of their homes.

As visual language, however, the country house was highly problematical as it included a number of periods, building forms, decorating styles and living patterns, all of which were put together in a highly eclectic way. This eclecticism, as I show, had specific origins and ingredients, and it involved a specific method.

The post-war country house was epitomised by a house called 'Brideshead'. The fictional creation of Evelyn Waugh in his war-time novel *Brideshead Revisited* (1945), 'Brideshead' and its plight symbolised the erosion of a social order and its inherited values, indeed, the impending destruction of civilisation. Bound together by an ideal of continuity and family inheritance, the house was used not just as a backdrop but as a character, a living entity or a palimpsest, with each generation leaving its mark but never totally removing the evidence of what was there before.

Under threat of extinction, the venerated English country house – as both the embodiment of an idealised way of living and as a symbol of national heritage – found new life in the 1970s, with its appeal reaching a far wider audience. It perhaps comes as no surprise that the archetypal

'Brideshead' should once more have played its part, in the shape of a tele-vision dramatisation of the novel.[4] In the context of an increasingly non-specific nostalgia, this period and the decade that followed wit-nessed the meteoric rise of the appreciation – indeed the fervent worship – of the country-house ideal.[5] It was an identity constructed from what was seen, what was remembered and what was imagined or wished to have been.

In his Preface to the 1959 edition of *Brideshead Revisited*, Waugh wrote:

> It was impossible to foresee, in the spring of 1944, the present cult of the country house. It seemed then that the ancestral seats which were our chief national artistic achievement were doomed to decay and spoliation like the monasteries in the sixteenth century. So I piled it on rather, with passionate sincerity. Brideshead today would be open to trippers, its trea-sures rearranged by expert hands and the fabric better maintained than it was by Lord Marchmain.[6]

The result was, however, that the country house became, more often than not, a museum, no longer an evolving family home. To many, this was an anathema, the antithesis of that for which the country-house ideal of home and history stood. Moving farther and farther away from the real-ity of country-house life and tourism, the symbol of the country house operated almost with a life of its own, with evocative glimpses of how life *might* be lived, or even *had been* lived, within its boundaries.

Veneration of the country house celebrated age and continuity – values represented by the successive generations that occupied inherited family homes. Indeed, one of the founding principles and recurring char-acteristics of such veneration was that the English country house was prized as a home, while the idea that it might also be a demonstration of aristocratic political power was carefully suppressed. Imbued with nostalgia, this embodiment of comfort and sense of place informed visions of how such houses should look. One example, taken from an inspirational (or rather aspirational) American home-decorating book entitled *English Style* (1984), encapsulated the enduring appeal of the English country house:

> There are those for whom the quintessential English interior will always be the grand country house with its enticing clutter, its well-worn

upholstery, and its enviable patina of time. These are the rooms which result from years, if not centuries, of accumulation; layer upon layer of heirlooms; and momentos collected from a family's myriad experiences and travels abroad.[7]

The dressing up of rooms in the English country-house style was intended to evoke this dream, this myth of English life.

In 1989, reassessing the development of the heritage debate since the appearance of his critique *The Heritage Industry* (1987), Robert Hewison offered a useful definition of the nature of a myth:

> If I describe something as a myth, that does not necessarily mean that it is untrue. Simply, that it is true in a special sense, in that it has truth for a great many people, and this general belief gives it temporary validity. It may contain elements that are unhistorical, or ahistorical, but it adds up to a cultural truth. It may indeed contain a great deal of historically accurate and factually testable material, but this is transformed into a touchstone of national, local, and even individual, identity.[8]

In the 1980s, the English country house was one such 'touchstone'. While the country house was being re-invented as a symbol of national heritage, an achievable version of it, a concomitant myth, was created in the form of decorating practices. Effectively, the values encoded in the English country house were transformed into an *image* of it: acting like a veneer that could be applied to the surface of almost any interior, the English country-house style of decorating was presented to consumers as a ready-made status-laden identity. However, although it was drawn in part from actual country houses, this identity did not really *represent* the historical country house. Rather, it was a reinterpretation of something which was itself a fabrication, woven together from numerous sources, including existing elements which were historically accurate, but also some which were unhistorical, some which were ahistorical and many which were not English in origin at all. In fact, the carefully co-ordinated riot of ruffles and swags of brightly patterned chintz, artfully cluttered 'tablescapes' and pictures hung on ribbons with bows which characterise the style bore very little resemblance to anything seen in English houses before the 1980s.

The source of English country-house style as it existed in the 1980s can be traced back to a very specific source – the work of Nancy Lancaster

(1897–1994), the American owner of the English decorating company Colefax & Fowler. Lancaster was born and raised in Virginia, a place which, culturally, socially and politically, was inextricably tied to its English origins. Indeed, it was said of Lancaster: 'Anyone quite so authentically English and authentically American could only be a Virginian.' [9] With the exception of a small number of Europeans and Africans, Virginia had been settled predominantly by the English, with the result that 'the customs, language, and law of the Old Dominion, as Virginia came to be known, were English in origin, and non-English immigrants would be compelled to take on the ways of transplanted Englishmen'. As a consequence, 'the English that Virginia attracted were a special type, and they left an indelible stamp on the social order they created. Like their countrymen at home, they presumed a stratified society that fitted everyone into a hierarchy of vocations'. [10] Although it took some time to develop, by the eighteenth century the lifestyle of southern settlers was based on the structure of an aristocratic rural England. It was the architecture of this time – imported classical styles which were interpreted to suit current needs and tastes – and the quasi-aristocratic manner of country living on plantations and in towns that shaped the appearance of Virginia. It has been said that of all the settlements in British colonial America Virginia was 'the only leisured and class society' [11] – and as such was the closest to England.

The Virginia that Lancaster knew still reflected this quasi-aristocratic lifestyle, albeit one tempered by the effects of the Civil War. Lancaster's was a privileged life, with family connections to prominent social networks in both the USA and England. [12] Unquestionably, Lancaster's upbringing in Virginia, the lifestyle of her family and her social world constituted a powerful and lasting source of ideas about how one should live. Her sentimental attachment to the family home she revered, 'Mirador' in Albermarle County, never waned and is important in understanding Lancaster's approach to decorating houses. As a result of her education in Europe – in the course of which she saw the châteaux of France and became familiar with grand country-house life in England – and her experience of a decaying colonial civilisation in Virginia, Lancaster's notion of 'home' was deeply rooted in the image of grand domestic houses which had mellowed and which showed signs of wear and age.

The ties between Virginia and England were also evident in the hunting-and-shooting lifestyle Lancaster was able to lead in both places. In many ways her ideas about decorating expressed this 'children, horses and dogs' manner of living in which rooms look 'undecorated', understated, but always elegant. The notion of domestic comfort espoused by Lancaster went beyond the physical to include the visual and emotional, coalescing in a general sense of 'well-being', a type of 'English comfort' documented by Jane Austen in so many of her novels.[13] So, even before Lancaster settled in England, she had a nostalgic impression of what the English country house *should* be like.

In decorating, Lancaster was never interested in reproducing exact period style. It was *atmosphere* that she sought most of all, expressed through patina and a sense of history created by the accretions of family generations. Much of the effect Lancaster was to cultivate in her own houses, with her use of faded fabrics and care-worn objects, rests on her non-specific nostalgia for what has been called 'romantic disrepair'.[14] She combined faded colonial grandeur with the informality and sense of history she found in English country houses to create rooms which, while they wore a veil of the past, were underpinned by very American (and modern) notions of comfort and convenience. Much of the confusion as to the supposedly ancient origin of the English country-house look stems from the fact that, drawing on these sources, Lancaster's ideas on decorating and the resulting interiors did not present themselves as either avant-garde or modern. However, while she aspired to create rooms which looked as if they had 'evolved' – as if they had always been there, gradually being improved and mellowed through generations of use – there was a large part of her approach that relied on comforts and conveniences which were not a part of the old English country houses.[15]

Lancaster lived in America and England, but settled permanently in England in the 1920s so that her husband, Ronald Tree, an American educated in England, could pursue his political career. The couple leased one house, 'Cottesbrooke', and subsequently, between 1926 and 1933, Kelmarsh Hall in Northamptonshire. Kelmarsh, with its bright colour, such modern conveniences as central heating and its combination of comfort and elegance which resulted in an atmosphere of understated luxury, witnessed the introduction of Lancaster's ideas to English houses. As John Cornforth has explained, 'not only was Kelmarsh well decorated, but it was immensely comfortable, with a bathroom for every bedroom, a novelty in English country houses at that time; and the bathrooms were treated as rooms'.[16]

Despite her lack of formal training, Lancaster's experience afforded her a reputation for exquisite taste and the confidence to express it. Setting new standards, she was an acknowledged influence on those around her – both decorators and house-owners.[17] At Kelmarsh, she co-ordinated the decoration of the house herself, as she did with all her houses, although she employed the talents of many others to achieve the effect she sought.

'Ditchley' in Oxfordshire, where Lancaster lived from 1933 to 1947, was the house where her talents for decorating really found full expression, in sympathetic collaboration with Tree, who was highly knowledgeable about architecture and art and had a taste for fine furniture and objects (see figure 13). The house, designed by James Gibbs, was Palladian and formal in plan, with austerely architectural decoration. Lancaster introduced an eclectic collection of furniture, furnishings and objects to the house, challenging the dominant period suggested by the architecture in its formal rooms. With the assistance of the French decorator Stéphane Boudin, she combined European, English and many American elements to produce a house which demonstrated to English country-house owners a radically new approach.

Much of the work carried out at 'Ditchley' could be seen as restoration, but it was not a pursuit of *accuracy* as such. It was the kind of restoration that John Fowler, Lancaster's partner at Colefax & Fowler, brought to his work at National Trust properties in the late 1960s, giving life to rooms, through colour, arrangements and furnishings, in a manner underpinned by knowledge of the past but not in thrall to it. The techniques utilised in such decoration transcended the purist's accuracy in that their quest was to provide ambience, or a 'mood', for rooms, to make them support the life that went on within them. Certainly, as a house designed with a view to entertaining on a large scale, Lancaster wished 'Ditchley' to have an atmosphere conducive to a sense of welcome.

'Ditchley' has been described as 'an inspiration to those who inherited or acquired houses in the years before and immediately after the war'.[18] With its bold, bright colours, its blend of informality and

13 *The Hall at Ditchley,* a water-colour by Serabriakoff, *c.* 1948

elegance, and its combination of periods, supported by good architectural 'bones', 'Ditchley' presented a comfortable, less formal alternative to the historic country house or period decoration. Perhaps the originality of Lancaster's approach, and the degree of comfort without opulence that she introduced in England, are most obviously illustrated by noting the experiences of those who occupied such houses and were in a position to compare them to the English country-house living they knew. The comments of Deborah, Duchess of Devonshire, who was well versed in English country-house life, provide an insight to the novelty of the arrangements at 'Ditchley':

> Whatever Nancy touched had that hard-to-pin-down but instantly recognisable gift of style. Her genius (and that is no exaggeration) was in her eye for colour, scale, objects and the dressing up of them; the stuffs the

curtains were made of, their shapes and trimmings, the china, table-cloths ... Even the bathrooms were little works of art. Warm, panelled, carpeted ... A far cry from the cracked lino and icy draughts to which I was accustomed.[19]

Read in conjunction with contemporary descriptions of draughty English houses, exemplified memorably, for example, in the journals of James Lees-Milne and the fiction of Evelyn Waugh,[20] it becomes evident just how inviting and new – at least in England – were Lancaster's ideas about comfortable living. In the light of imitations of Lancaster's interiors, it is important to note, however, that such comfort stems not just from a plethora of soft furnishings but from heat, light, colour and atmosphere, as well as from all the luxuries a well-run house and a supportive staff can offer.[21]

In the 1920s and 1930s, there was a general 'clearing up' of country houses in England through the influence of modern ideas about the use of space and the removal of clutter. Lancaster offered a manner of decorating and arranging which worked very well on both a grand or a reduced scale: in essence, it was not a matter so much of emptying the grand formal rooms, but of making them comfortable as domestic spaces. A contemporary description of her approach can be found in Cecil Beaton's *The Glass of Fashion* (1954):

> Among those who energetically flout all contemporary obstacles or dis-paragements, Mrs Nancy Tree [later Lancaster] has a talent for sprucing up a stately but shabby house and making a grand house less grand. She has an adequate reverence for tradition, observes the rules of style and proportion, and manifests a healthy disregard for the sanctity of 'important' furniture ... Her love of colour, her flower sense, and her feeling for comfort have brought a welcome touch to many an English house sorely in need of such ministrations.[22]

In this way, Lancaster could be seen to be offering an alternative to the real English country house at a time, after the Second World War, when it was in a particularly sorry state, and an alternative to the consciously arranged, *moderne* interiors of decorators like Syrie Maugham or the period style interpretations of such decorators as Sybil Colefax.

Lady Colefax (1875–1951), from whom Lancaster purchased Colefax & Fowler, had set up her business in 1934, taking into partnership a few years later a young decorator, John Fowler (1906–77). Like many others of her station – aristocrats impoverished by the depression – Colefax, a prominent society hostess, traded on her social connections to find clients. Her milieu included the owners of country houses as well as the 'smart' set of people, like Lancaster, who pursued both an urban and a country life. Fowler was not from an aristocratic family, but his entrée to that world was afforded, first, by Colefax and then by Lancaster when she took over the company in the late 1940s. That was a period when interior decoration was not the preoccupation of many owners of country houses: 'The English ... considered it not really the done thing to expend time and thought, let alone money, redecorating your house'.[23] In fact, during the 1950s,

> [clients] were all drawn from a small charmed circle; many were Nancy Lancaster's friends and associates, and almost all were untypical of the owners of grand English houses. Many had influential Anglo-American connections and seem to have had access to money that was not typical of the strapped-for-cash owners of great estates and decaying houses of the day.[24]

Colefax & Fowler worked for a very specific clientele, and Lancaster's social status was clearly pivotal to the success both of the company and of the English country-house look. Although she never practised as a decorator *per se*, her opinion on décor was sought after and her taste admired. She afforded Fowler the opportunity to work in large country houses and to address a circle of clients otherwise not accessible to him.

There are contradictory views of the state of decoration of English country houses after the war. One is that 'before Nancy and John most great English houses were extraordinarily dull'.[25] It is agreed that 'the great houses looked shabby as their owners regarded the subject of redecoration with distaste ... it was not the done thing to discuss one's house or its contents; it existed ... and that was the end of it'.[26]

A second view, espoused by Chester Jones, a decorator with Colefax & Fowler in the 1980s and author of the company's history, presents an altogether different picture of the company as *inheritor* of a tradition of decorating:

> The second influence for this practice [the first being Lancaster] is that of grand English country houses as they were found at the end of the

Second World War: not the formal, controlled interiors of their eighteenth-century conception, but as succeeding generations had adapted them to their own changing requirements. The mood was characterized by comfortable chairs, useful tables piled high with books, lamps to read by, drinks tables groaning with bottles and garden flowers in large vases.[27]

Although there were country houses which may seem to have set a precedent for Fowler's work, there was a marked difference between real cluttered country houses and the carefully orchestrated look created by Colefax & Fowler. The image the company offered to clients through the exemplary interiors and arrangement of Lancaster's houses took a great deal of money to reproduce, but its success depended on far more than money. While it could not be seen as anything other than expensive, the look cultivated by Lancaster, and followed by patrons of Colefax & Fowler, relied on an appreciation of a certain way of living. Those interiors created within a room an aura, or atmosphere, which included, but went far beyond, its fine antiques and pictures. Fundamentally, there had to be an air of casualness and a disregard for the perceived preciousness of things in order for the requisite 'humble elegance' to succeed.

Through country-house sales, and given her considerable funds, it was possible for Lancaster to acquire for herself, and for the clients of the shop, 'real' things: things which had a history, a family history. This added all the more to the effect at which Lancaster aimed. Although her own 'heirlooms' were not very old, she could access the inherited splendour of aristocratic England and imbue her own schemes with a certain *authenticity*. The interior which best signals how Lancaster manifested her comfortable dream of country-house life is one that is tied to the myth of 'authenticity' and the paradox of the English country-house style of decorating in subsequent decades. That interior was the 'Yellow Room', created in 1958–59 through a collaboration between Lancaster and Fowler. Ironically, this model, a paragon of its kind to aspirational pursuers of the effects achieved, was situated neither in a house nor in the country: the 'Yellow Room' was the drawing room-cum-library of Lancaster's *pied-à-terre*, above the premises of Colefax & Fowler in London (figure 14).

The scheme was full of various shades of yellow. The dominant element was the colour of the walls – a high-gloss gorze yellow, created by

14 The 'Yellow Room' decorated by Nancy Lancaster in collaboration with
John Fowler, 1958–59

gradually building up layers of colour and finished with a varnish. The
barrel-vaulted ceiling was painted in three tones of beige to give depth to
the mouldings and to highlight the detail. The curtains were in two
shades of yellow, one set of taffeta and one of shantung (a soft,
undressed, Chinese silk), with cords, tassels and trimmings in yellow and
burnt umber. The sofas and armchairs were covered in a deep citrus
yellow, with marigold cushions, and the few fine chairs were upholstered
with chintz – faded, of course. The room contained many *faux* paint
effects – the marblised cornice, the painted husks and swags in the end

arches and the deep skirting panel. All in all, there was a careful balance in the room between the ease of the squashy, shabby sofas and the grandeur of the scale and the fine objects.

The essence of the look here has been defined as 'a slightly untidy disposition of things that suggests a life lived spontaneously'.[28] Although in later years proponents of the English country-house style were sometimes over-enthusiastic in cramming objects into a room, it could not be said that this interior was cluttered. However, the room did evolve, gradually filling up and being rearranged during its lifespan. It was very carefully structured, with certain objects, such as the pouffe and the squashy chairs, brought in to prevent any of the fine things – the portraits, French chairs and candle stands – looking too perfect. Lancaster thought there should always be things in a room which were 'warm and ugly' to give value to the good things, but also to stop 'important' pieces looking too important.[29] In this overall scheme, there were no pieces pushed forward at the expense of others. In addition, despite the imposing scale of the room, the chairs were arranged to accommodate both a small and a large gathering of people without anyone having to move anything very far. There was always somewhere to put a drink or book, lamps to illuminate areas of the room as required – subtle elements of luxury and comfort. These considerations and, ultimately, the impression that nothing there was so precious that it could not be touched, or even improved by a little use, made these rooms the epitome of humble elegance. The hallmarks of the English country-house look were defined in 1989 by Chester Jones thus: 'Chintz in glorious faded colours, curtains meticulously swagged, fringed and tasselled, the most comfortable upholstery and expertly applied paint finishes, all set in timeless interiors and discreetly lit to show off beautiful antiques and paintings.'[30] If one compares that list to images of the 'Yellow Room', it is not difficult to understand how this single interior, repeatedly cited and even quoted in other interiors, came to stand for all that the English country-house ideal represented.

With its impressive scale and fine decoration, the 'Yellow Room' has been praised throughout its history as one of the most influential interior schemes of the twentieth century. Certainly, to decorators and commentators, and to those who aspired to such a way of life, it represented the epitome of an approach to decorating which blended supreme comfort

with understated elegance. As Lancaster's interiors followed no prescribed
(period) formula, they were in fact very difficult to imitate successfully.
However, looking at her houses, and particularly at the 'Yellow Room', it
is not difficult to see why this wonderfully comfortable impression of
country-house life was adopted by so many country-house owners. Nor
is it difficult to see how this fantasy of comfortable living was taken to be
more than an evocation of how life might be lived – or even had *been*
lived. Essentially, the reality is that an American fabricated an identity for
the English country-house ideal which was later taken to be both a tradition of aristocratic interior decoration and the epitome of Englishness, at
home and abroad.

Through imitation and reinterpretation, led by American decorators
based in and around New York, a rather different version of the country-
house image emerged in the early 1980s. It replaced the understated
appearance of time-worn elegance (still practised by some decorators)
with a more polished version in which characteristic objects and
decorative treatments were accentuated.[31] In 1985, Caroline Seebohm
highlighted the differences between American and English interpretations of the English country-house style. The passage which follows is
succinct in its attributions and its signalling of the classifying markers of
the style:

> With what anticipation does the American visitor set off on his first visit
> to an English country house, with its history, its architectural authority,
> its waywardly charming interiors. As he enters the 'drawing room' …
> with what delight his eye receives the first impressions: light from long,
> high windows with grand valances ('pelmets'), vases of flowers, chintzes
> and innumerable paintings, books, memorabilia … But wait. His glance
> returns to the chintz, so old and worn. To the curtains, taffeta, yes, but
> faded and unlined. He begins to be distracted by the mixture of styles …
> More closely examined, a sofa is covered with what must be dog hairs …
> Books in random piles, unclassified … What can this mean?

Taken aback, Seebohm's imaginary American visitor asks:

> Can this really be the famed original, the prototype from which a deco-
> rating legend sprang? Something seems to have gone wrong – this
> appears to be some impoverished pastiche rather than the real thing. Let
> him return to the other side of the Atlantic, to his own, reassuring house,

filled with brilliant chintzes, swagged valances, unstinting drapery, eighteenth century English furniture, its brass fittings polished to a gleam,
and lavish accessories – knife cases used for bills and invitations,
majolica plates ... Chelsea boxes – all those things that in the United
States have come to represent the 'English country-house look', the most
sought-after look of the 1980s ...[32]

Interestingly, Seebohm presented the country-house look as a tradition of
the English country house; thus, her division of the authentic (English)
from the imitative (American) was not strictly accurate. The English
country house that Seebohm's imaginary visitor would have hoped to
encounter was the result of the ministrations of Colefax & Fowler.

What is offered here is a clear picture of the markers which represent
the identities of the English country-house ideal on either side of the
Atlantic. The understated English look was assumed by a number of
American clients but it was the brighter, more structured and opulent
look of Mario Buatta, based on John Fowler's later work, that formed the
version most widely adopted. His often photographed yellow sitting
room – which he acknowledged to be his John Fowler copycat scheme –
was one of the most influential interiors of the country-house style.
Furthermore, the bulk of interiors decorated in the English country-
house style in locations across the world took this co-ordinated,
controlled, fabric-based American version as their model – aided by the
marketing of Colefax & Fowler products.[33]

As individual components the elements comprising the country-
house style did not have the potential to signify the ideal, although in the
case of chintz this came remarkably close. A brief glance at real English
country houses would indicate, however, that the perception of chintz as
evocative of the English country house was misplaced. The impression
that 'nothing so symbolizes the English country-house interior as
chintz'[34] was created by the dependence of most consumers on soft
furnishings to achieve effects and fill the gaps created by an absence of
antique furniture, pictures and fine decorative objects. The authors of
English Country: Living in England's Private Houses, did, however, go on to
say:

Funnily enough, although chintz is thought to be the *sine qua non* of
every English interior, there is less of it to be seen in the rooms repre-

sented in this book than might be expected. There may be a cushion here, a slip-cover or curtain there, but not much more. It is perhaps true to say that while in the mind an English room is filled with chintz, the reality, as with so many things English, is modified with restraint.[35]

This underlines the fact that, as I have argued, the English country-house style of the 1980s was not based on an accurate historical understanding of how English houses have been decorated. The potential of the signifying objects to be meaningful rested in their relationship to one another. In this way, the various components became the style vocabulary that produced an homogenised image. A paradox, however, lies in the fact that this version of the style, relying for its effect upon soft furnishings, stands as the antithesis of the approach developed by Lancaster. But it was a version that was promoted endlessly through magazine coverage.

The English country-house style was taken up by many consumers because of the aspirational, historical and associational values it suggested. Its unspecific, but powerful, aura served well the re-invention and appropriation of identities. In the 1980s, an insatiable thirst for recreating 'traditional' and 'period' styles reduced the past to a series of visual codes. Nostalgia was created by sampling the history of decoration in a way which imposed an implied, if distorted, lineage. Undisturbed by the lack of historical specificity associated with the English country-house style, the ideal expressed through decorating employed a set of clichéd objects and references to evoke the past. It was the *theatricality* of its effect which was desired and aspired to, whether or not it appeared superficial.

With its 'diverse ingredients that nonetheless combined as happily in a product as deliciously English as a sherry trifle',[36] the English country-house style transcended period definitions. As its initial identity was based not on shared visual characteristics but on associational ones, it presented a greater flexibility, and even a greater potential for meaningful evocations. In addition, its appearance of age and permanence meant that, of all the 'traditional' decorating styles on offer, this instant identity disguised by its very nature the newness, the sense of surface and superficiality, of applied decorating styles. In the home-decor text *Laura Ashley Style* (1987) the English country house was treated as a defined style; it was, however, the *lifestyle* qualities of this enduring decorating tradition, rather than its visual characteristics, that were presented to the consumer:

the style of decoration associated with the country house is still typified by an eclectic profusion, lovingly assembled over the years. But it is no longer a set piece of overwhelming grandeur and aesthetic excellence; rather it is a style which exudes an air of comfort and ease, of faded glory and family memorabilia, and above all of quiet good taste.[37]

This passage *evokes* the country-house style without *defining* any of its material characteristics. However, this was not – initially at least – the way in which Laura Ashley marketed the style.

Representations of interiors used by Laura Ashley to promote its version of the English country-house style give a clear indication of how an aristocratic ideal of the English country house existed alongside popular versions of the style, and how these could be employed to serve the same purpose of presenting for consumption a total (fantasy) lifestyle package. This is also true of their 'how to …' publication *Laura Ashley Style*, which was intended to trigger desire, suggest possibilities and give practical advice. By including in its section on the associated style a history of the English country house,[38] this text also managed to suggest the notion of authenticity and imply the continuation of a tradition.

Taking two examples from the leading British interiors magazines *House & Garden* and *The World of Interiors*, it is possible to see how, in their seductive rhetoric, the division was made between the ideal and the enacted style (see figure 15). While in their representation of the work of decorators the magazines placed the style in the public realm and made it available, there is always the sense that the world it represents could never actually be attained. In the introductory essay to *The House & Garden Book of Classic Rooms* (1989), the reason for this was implied: 'A myriad of influences has gone into making these interiors amongst the best of their kind. The major contribution is, of course, the innate taste of so many gifted amateurs and the contributory flair of professional advisers.'[39] Of course: innate taste and flair – two attributes which are as elusive as the country-house ideal. Seen here is the ability of the country-house ideal (using a constructed image fabricated by Nancy Lancaster) to carry on – in the context of the popularity and wide dissemination of the English country-house style. Similarly, in *The World of Interiors* (1988), editors of the magazine of the same name present the difference between the 'original', which seems to occur as a natural process of living, and the artificiality of the constructed style: 'True clutter

15 Bedroom by Fritz von der Schulenberg featured in *House & Gardens Classic Rooms*

is very different from those artfully arranged tablescapes, piles of expensive books and endless buttons and bows aimed to give an instant lived-in look.'[40]

One of the most notable features of this kind of literature is that it did not seem to trouble either producers or disseminators of the style that the country-house life they offered for emulation may not have been at all real. As the English country-house look was transformed into a decorator style, it was admitted that, 'this is the story of a hoax. Not a whopper, but a misrepresentation, a fantasy of a way of life as seen in its

decorating style.'[41] This was an admission that the decorators were ped-
dling dreams but there was little acknowledgement that the look itself
was not traditional; it was not a 'fantasy of a [real] way of life as seen in
its [really existing] decorating style', but a fantasy of a way of life seen in
an invented decorating style. Although venerated as a historical, English
tradition, this fabricated ideal of Englishness was, at all stages of its conception, practice and re-invention, inherently American. It was indeed, as
claimed in a 1965 article on Colefax & Fowler – though in rather a
different sense than that intended by the unknown author – 'the English
country house as it might have been but never was'.[42]

Notes

This chapter appeared in a similar form in *Things,* Summer 1996.

1 The country house as a non-fortified domestic building type has existed in
England since the sixteenth century. At the heart of a landed estate, this
structure was a statement of power and ownership, and by no means the
same thing as a house in the country. See John Cornforth, *Country Houses in
Britain: Can They Survive?* (London: Country Life, 1974), for a discussion of
what might constitute 'a country house'. For accounts of the place of the
English country house in the twentieth century, see Marcus Binney and
Gervase Jackson-Stops, 'The last hundred years', in Gervase Jackson-Stops
(ed.), *The Treasure Houses of Britain: Five Hundred Years of Private Patronage
and Art Collecting,* catalogue (Washington, DC: National Gallery of Art, and
New Haven, CT: Yale University Press, 1985); and John Gaze, *Figures in a
Landscape. A History of the National Trust* (London: Barrie & Jenkins, 1988).

2 David Cannadine, *The Pleasures of the Past* (London: Fontana, 1990), p. 78.

3 In *Brideshead Revisited* (Harmondsworth: Penguin, 1959 [1945], p. 96),
Evelyn Waugh provides an insight to this phenomenon with a description
of the house 'Brideshead': 'It was an aesthetic education to live within those
walls, to wander from room to room, from the Soanesque library to the
Chinese drawing-room ... from the Pompeian parlour to the great tapestry-
hung hall which stood unchanged, as it had been designed two hundred
and fifty years before ...'. It is an ideal of a house which 'grew silently with
the centuries, catching and keeping the best of each generation' (p. 260), an
ideal expressed (outside fiction) by Vita Sackville-West, in *English Country
Houses* (London: Prion Books Ltd, 1996 [1941]).

4 *Brideshead Revisited* was produced by Granada TV in the late 1970s and
shown for the first time in 1981. It used, albeit with some artistic licence,
Castle Howard in North Yorkshire as the house – which in turn has, as a

result of this alliance, made a great deal of money through tourism. Castle Howard was also used to illustrate Jackson-Stops's Introduction to *The Treasure Houses of Britain* catalogue (1985), once again photographed in a heavy mist to evoke an air of supposed decay and endurance through time.

5 Many writings on the country house in the later twentieth century offer an uncritical, often celebratory, perspective on the formation of public perception of what the English country house should represent. Alternatively, writers criticising the wider phenomenon of nostalgia during the 1980s have a tendency to package the country house as part of the so-called 'heritage industry' and fail to acknowledge its longer history as the tangible evidence of an extant social, economic and political structure. Two early texts which provide insightful commentary are David Lowenthal, *The Past Is a Foreign Country* (Cambridge: Cambridge University Press, 1985), and Patrick Wright, *On Living in an Old Country* (London: Verso, 1985). More recent work offers a new, critical perspective on the place of the country house in English culture and national heritage. See Peter Mandler, *The Fall and Rise of the Stately Home* (London and New Haven, CT: Yale University Press, 1997).

6 *Brideshead Revisited* was first published by Chapman & Hall in 1945.

7 Susan Slesin and Stafford Cliff, *English Style* (New York: Clarkson Potter, 1984), p. 50.

8 Robert Hewison, 'Heritage: an interpretation', in David Uzzell (ed.), *Heritage Interpretation* (London: Belhaven Press, 1989), vol. 1. Hewison's earlier text – *The Heritage Industry: Britain in a Climate of Decline* – was published by Methuen in 1987. In a chapter on *Brideshead Revisited*, Hewison offered a commentary on the country house as an element of the heritage phenomenon and, interestingly, but like so many others, adopts the fictional 'Brideshead' as a model of the English country house.

9 This comment is taken from an article of July 1965 in the Colefax & Fowler Archive on one of Lancaster's houses, additional details on which are unavailable.

10 Wendell Garrett, *American Colonial: Puritan Simplicity to Georgian Grace* (London: Cassell, 1995), pp. 206–7.

11 *Ibid.*, p. 207.

12 For example, one of Lancaster's aunts married into the Astor family, originally from New York but by the late nineteenth century settled in England. The aunt, Nancy Langhorne, became Lady Astor, the first elected woman member of the House of Commons. Her house, 'Cliveden', became one of the last great 'power houses'. It is now a hotel.

13 Discussed in Witold Rybczynski, *Home. A Short History of an Idea* (New York: Penguin Books, 1987), pp. 120–5.

14 Obituary of Nancy Lancaster, *New York Times*, 22 August 1994.

15 The influx of American heiresses into the English aristocracy in the late nineteenth and early twentieth centuries undoubtedly had implications for the appearance of many houses, as well as a great impact on the installation of amenities such as bathrooms.

16 John Cornforth, *The Inspiration of the Past: Country House Taste in the Twentieth Century* (Harmondsworth: Viking–Country Life, 1985), p. 119.

17 The late Duke of Buccleuch, an hereditary owner of an English country house, told Lancaster that 'she had cost his generation a great deal of money'. See Cornforth, *The Inspiration of the Past*, p. 119.

18 John Cornforth, 'Living in her own style', obituary of Nancy Lancaster, *Guardian*, 26 August 1994.

19 From the obituary of Nancy Lancaster, *Daily Telegraph*, 20 August 1994.

20 See Brenda Last's unsuccessful attempts to heat the dining hall at Hetton Abbey in Waugh's *A Handful of Dust* (London: Dell, 1934), and the descriptions of the heating system. In the diaries of James Lees-Milne (who orchestrated the National Trust's country-house scheme and played a pivotal role in country-house preservation) there is an entry in 1942 describing the teasing of a hostess: referring to an upstairs lavatory nicknamed 'The Beardmore', after the Beardmore Glacier as it 'faces due north, the window is permanently propped open ... and the floor is under a drift of snow': Lees-Milne, *Ancestral Voices* (London: Chatto & Windus, 1975), p. 29.

21 Many visitors to Lancaster's houses commented on the central role of the staff in the provision of comforts and a welcoming atmosphere.

22 Cited in Cornforth, *The Inspiration of the Past*, pp. 117–18.

23 Kirsty McCleod, *A Passion for Friendship: Sybil Colefax and Her Circle* (London: Michael Joseph, 1991), p. 141.

24 John Cornforth, quoted in Stephen Calloway, *Twentieth Century Decoration* (London: Weidenfeld & Nicolson, 1994), p. 159.

25 Calloway, *Twentieth Century Decoration*, p. 158.

26 Chester Jones, *Colefax & Fowler: The Best in Decoration* (London: Barrie & Jenkins, 1989), p. 15.

27 *Ibid.*, p. 107.

28 Stephen Calloway and Stephen Jones, *Traditional Style* (London: Pyramid Books, 1990), p. 170.

29 Nancy Richardson, 'The amazing Nancy Lancaster', *House & Garden* (USA), November 1983, p. 226.

30 Jones, *Colefax & Fowler*, p. 2.

31 In November 1986, *House Beautiful in America* ran a feature called 'Style makers today'. Of the seven decorators listed five worked under the aegis of the English country-house style. They were Mario Buatta (very much influenced by John Fowler), Sister Parish (a contemporary of Lancaster), Georgina Fairholme (an English decorator who had moved to the USA and had at one time worked for Colefax & Fowler), Mark Hampton (who had worked extensively in England with David Hicks), and David Easton. Testifying to the popularity of the style – if only with magazine editors – a similar outcome was seen in *House & Garden* (USA) in September 1988. Of the eight listed firms/decorators, five practised the English country-house style. Within the boundaries of the style, their approaches did differ: some were more influenced by the shabbiness of English ideals, while others, particularly Buatta, re-invented the style to suit an American audience and thereby created a distinctly foreign look.

32 Caroline Seebohm, 'To the manner born', *Connoisseur* (July 1985), 77–8.

33 From 1978 Colefax & Fowler worked each year to produce collections, ranges of fabrics and companion papers which, while not exactly mix-and-match, offered a way of literally buying into the style.

34 Caroline Seebohm and Christopher Simon Sykes, *English Country: Living in England's Private Houses* (New York: Clarkson Potter, 1987), p. 117.

35 *Ibid.*

36 Calloway and Jones, *Traditional Style*, inside cover.

37 Iain Gale and Susan Irvine, *Laura Ashley Style* (New York: Harmony Books, 1987), p. 50.

38 There were also the 'rustic', 'romantic'and 'modern' styles, and the general category of 'period' style. The book also included 'The creation of a style' (Laura Ashley's) and a detailed list of the company's shops and stockists.

39 Robert Harling, Leoni Highton, *The House & Garden Book of Classic Rooms* (London: Chatto & Windus, 1989), p. 6.

40 Minn Hogg and Wendy Harrop, *The World of Interiors* (London: Conran Octopus, 1988).

41 Seebohm, 'To the manner born', p. 78.

42 Taken from an article in the Colefax & Fowler Archive: details unknown other than the date of July 1965.

6 ✧ The role of the interior in constructing notions of class and status: a case study of Britannia Royal Naval College, Dartmouth, 1905-39

Quintin Colville

THE ROYAL NAVY in the twentieth century has typically been examined as a professional organisation entrusted with the protection of British interests and sovereignty in peace and war. It can also, however, be approached as an institution within which a range of predominantly masculine identities and lifestyles were assembled, promoted and protected. My research takes this latter perspective on the institution, and its aim has been to explore the role of design and material culture in shaping the various understandings of class and social status arrived at by male naval personnel of all ranks. For the purposes of this chapter, however, the focus has been narrowed to one category of naval personnel and one area of material culture – officer cadets and the interior of the college in which they were trained.

Organised around a comparison between Britannia Royal Naval College, Dartmouth, and the socio-cultural and material characteristics of the English public-school system, this chapter divides into three main sections. The first examines the degree to which the college interior promoted a specifically aristocratic sensibility. The second assesses the conformity of the college to a set of upper-middle-class social characteristics and conventions. The third discusses the significance of the college's material culture in inculcating a particular upper-middle-class identity and mode of sociability.

In recent years it has become generally accepted within historical scholarship that class is one of the most complex and least understood categories of social description. It is beyond the scope of this chapter to attempt any broad redefinition of this much-contested area; and for the purposes of what follows I subscribe to David Cannadine's concise definition of class as 'what culture does to inequality and social structure'.[1] Above all, notions of class are fragile and contingent: people can hold more than one simultaneously, and different ones over the course of a lifetime. Class invariably is related to wealth, or the lack of it, but this is not necessarily its determining quality. Within the navy, during the period in question, notions of class stratification were not the direct expression of a capitalist economy, nor of personal or familial accumulations of property. Instead, they grew out of the interaction of naval personnel with the unequal professional responsibilities, living conditions and socio-cultural amenities deemed appropriate to different ranks by the navy itself.

With this in mind, and without ignoring economic factors, the bulk of the chapter is devoted to the social and cultural aspects of class. From that standpoint, the contribution it seeks to make is to the understanding of the role played by design and material culture in constructing notions of class – and, by extension, in shaping processes of historical change.

Throughout this period, the navy's professional structure was inseparably bound to class divisions. Although a comprehensive survey has not yet been undertaken, the best available evidence indicates that, from the later Victorian era onwards, the great majority of naval officer cadets were the sons of civil servants, doctors, lawyers, the clergy, bankers and businessmen, and belonged within a social fraction termed 'the upper-middle class', or the 'public-school middle class'. In addition, a significant minority of cadets were from upper-class backgrounds.[2] By contrast, the navy's lower ranks came overwhelmingly from the various gradations of the British working class; they were trained separately, and their prospects for promotion to officer status were extremely limited. In the process, and in ways this chapter seeks to explore, the socio-cultural values and attributes of the British middle and upper classes became indistinguishable from the desired qualities, professional and otherwise, of the naval officer. As a result, the navy's officer cadre became, to a large extent, a social and cultural caste.

Now, for the sons of affluent middle- and upper-class families the foundation of this socio-cultural world, and in many ways the passport to these positions of adult respectability, was a public-school education.[3]

It is consequently unsurprising that in the early years of the twentieth century (perhaps the zenith of the public-school system), the Royal Navy began to model its cadet training on the public-school example. Until 1905, cadets had undergone a course of one or more years' duration on board the *Britannia*, an old wooden man-of-war moored in Dartmouth harbour. That year, however, saw the opening of a purpose-built college designed by Sir Aston Webb on a site, chosen by the Admiralty, over-looking the town (see figure 16). Cadets joined at the age of 13 for an expanded four-year course with a revised curriculum, in step with public-school practice, and were taught by a newly recruited staff of ex-public-school masters. The fees charged to parents by the navy (amounting to £150 per annum in 1941), which also paralleled those of the public schools, placed the college beyond the reach of all working-class incomes.[4]

Although upper-class boys almost invariably were sent to public schools, the majority of pupils attending them – and, as already mentioned, most of the cadets at Dartmouth – were from middle-class backgrounds.[5] According to Martin Wiener, among other historians, one of the dominant characteristics of the middle class during this period was its close identification with the traditional aristocracy and its pursuits.[6] That being so, one of the great attractions of the public-school system lay in the degree to which it blurred and narrowed the disparity between middle- and upper-class lifestyles. This was due in part to the shoulder-rubbing proximity to sons of the gentry and the aristocracy that middle-class parents could expect their own sons to experience within those schools; but it was also strongly facilitated by the design and construction of the schools themselves.

Most importantly, they frequently occupied what had previously been, or had been designed to suggest, the country houses of aristocratic families. Aston Webb's design for Dartmouth's Britannia Royal Naval College conformed to that precedent. In its stylistic vocabulary, its use of brick and stone and its roof-scape, the college owed much to a number of large 'English Renaissance' country houses built in the last quarter of the nineteenth century – in particular, Kinmel in Denbighshire, and Bryanston in Dorset, completed, respectively, in 1874 and 1894. The buildings' tripartite massing, the landscaped parkland in which it was set and the sweeping driveways that led visitors to its main entrance also

16 Britannia Royal Naval
College, Dartmouth

17 The great hall of Britannia
Royal Naval College,
Dartmouth

18 The dining hall of
Britannia Royal Naval College,
Dartmouth

placed the college within the long tradition of English neo-classical and Georgian stately homes.

In essence, the building's physical evocation of the public school allowed naval officers to consolidate and internalise a further, and vital, component of middle- and upper-class status. Beyond this, the great majority of naval cadets could never hope to match the college's grandness in their own family domesticity. It therefore seems clear that what it also offered was a supercharged family home. As Jonathan Gathorne-Hardy has put it: 'By going to a public school in a country house you not only absorbed something of the country house way of life, it was almost as though you had been born in one.'[7]

The clear visual analogy with aristocratic life established by the college's exterior was extended in its interior. The proportions of its rooms and the height of its ceilings were far beyond the standards of contemporary middle-class domesticity. Its timber-roofed great hall and its panelled, galleried and vaulted dining hall echoed the residences of Tudor and Elizabethan nobility (see figures 17 and 18). In a variety of ways, the interior also allowed middle-class families to associate themselves with the college and its grandness. For example, in a direct borrowing from public-school practices, the marble fittings of the college chapel were purchased with donations made by naval officers and their families, and the chapel continued for decades afterwards to receive gifts of altar frontals and stained glass. As the college chaplain revealingly commented: 'No doubt most cadets will like to enjoy the sense of proprietorship when they visit their Alma Mater from time to time.'[8]

Beyond this, the interior also satisfied the profound hunger of the middle class for quasi-aristocratic lineage and ancestry. In his 1933 novel *Schools in Turmoil*, St John Pearce described the first day at public school of his protagonist Hedley Templeton, and the moment when he glimpses the carved board listing the school's head boys: 'On it was written a string of names dating back years and years. The first names were practically indecipherable, but the more recent could be plainly made out. "1896 – J. Templeton", read Hedley. His father!'[9] Given the high percentage of cadets who were themselves the sons of naval officers, similar experiences would have awaited many in their first days at Dartmouth's Britannia. For instance, by the 1930s, running the entire length of the building's main corridor were ranks of framed photographs of each term's entry of cadets.[10]

Through material culture, this sense of family lineage was also interwoven with the corporate lineage of the Royal Navy as an institution. To begin with, in a clear reference to the visual vocabulary of aristocratic family portraiture (and one seen also in public schools), the walls of the college's main staircase and of the cadets' dining hall were hung with large oil paintings of naval grandees from the sixteenth century onwards. Elsewhere, depictions of naval scenes and engagements abounded, with a particular emphasis on the Napoleonic and Nelsonian era.[11] Many of these items were gifts from serving and retired officers and their families. And in this way, family and institutional histories and mythologies grew together and reinforced each other. This record of photographs and paintings, together with the college's previously mentioned Tudor and Elizabethan stylistic references, had the effect of mitigating the building's actual (and, within this context, highly undesirable) newness.

By these means, the college became an extremely effective instrument in advancing the socio-cultural aspirations of the middle-class majority of naval officers. As such, it is not surprising to find that from the moment of its completion, the building became the subject of an intense corporate pride. An editorial in a 1905 edition of the college magazine described the transition from training ship to college in terms of the metamorphosis of 'the simple, plain, unpretending grub ... into the brilliant, beautiful butterfly';[12] and the college's twenty-fifth and fiftieth anniversaries prompted further eulogistic outpourings regarding the 'palace ... that nestles in the wooded heights above the ancient town of Dartmouth'.[13]

The class allegiances of naval cadets, and the role of the college interiors in shaping them, were, however, more complex than this. Though genuine, the attachment to aristocratic mores broadcast by the building was only one part of a more nuanced picture. Harold Perkin has noted that from the later decades of the nineteenth century the values of the aristocracy (and also of the Victorian entrepreneurial middle class) began to be challenged by a substantially new social identity. Perkin asserts that this identity, constructed by the professional upper-middle class, was fostered by the growing contemporary demand, both at home and throughout the empire, for administrators, professional men and military leaders.[14] More pertinent still to the purposes of this chapter is Perkin's contention that the key locus for the articulation and propagation of this class-related identity was the public school.

This expanding professional upper-middle class can be defined through its adherence to a fusion of social and cultural characteristics. Although no clear line of demarcation can be drawn between these social and cultural realms, its social priorities can best be described as conformity and corporatism, along with respect for authority and seniority. In cultural terms, notions of duty, service and leadership were emphasised, in combination with specific patterns of etiquette and sociability. Taken together, these components formed the blueprint of what Perkin has characterised as a specifically upper-middle-class reconfiguration of the idea of the gentleman.[15] This re-formed gentlemanliness, frequently referred to as 'character', was what the public-school world aimed to promote. Moreover, by the early twentieth century, the socio-cultural impact of these upper-middle-class values had extended far beyond the boundaries of this social grouping. In the words of Ross McKibbin, and here he is referring to the 1920s and 1930s: 'Not only was the line between the upper and upper middle classes becoming blurred, the upper class was actually losing ground ... In terms of social behaviour the norms were increasingly those established by the upper middle classes.'[16]

With its largely upper-middle-class recruits, its overt aim of producing military leaders for the service of the nation and its close adherence to the public-school model, Dartmouth's Britannia Naval College was at the heart of these developments. At this point, therefore, it is important to qualify the notion that the college interior familiarised cadets with an aristocratic sensibility, and to look instead at the degree to which it advanced the precepts of this newer upper-middle-class identity. The discussion begins by considering the extent to which understandings of status predicated on aristocratic leisured wealth were undermined within the college, then moves to examine the means by which the college set itself in opposition to the world of business and commerce.

To begin with, the emphasis placed by the college on the upper-middle-class notions of duty and service could not have been clearer. Addressing cadets in 1960, but employing phrases that had echoed through the college's buildings for half a century, Admiral Sir Richard

Onslow exhorted them to: 'Put service before self: service to their Queen, their country and their fellow men, without thought of gain or glory or indeed of any reward save the knowledge of a job well done.' [17] More often than not, this notion of service to the nation was conceived in terms of service to the crown, and this ideological conflation was given powerful visual expression in the college's central interior space: the great hall (described as such in the architect's plans, though more usually referred to as the 'quarterdeck'). By the 1930s, a life-size statue of George V stood against its far wall, surmounted by a large royal crest and flanked by portraits of George V and Edward VII. Around its other walls were hung tablets bearing the names of officers who had distinguished themselves in their training and subsequent careers.

Within the navy, this sense of devotion to duty was often expounded with a fervour bordering on the spiritual. Indeed – although the identity of this space as a hall was asserted by the roof timbers and the absence of pews – its design was remarkably similar to that of the college chapel. From this perspective, the grouping of royal images was suggestive of a secular altar or shrine [18] – an impression reinforced by the loosely Gothic, and unmistakably ecclesiastical, slit windows above it. The centrality of this space within the ground plan of the college (designated from the exterior by the vast bell tower) bespoke its symbolic importance to college life. In fact, its visual prominence far exceeded that of the chapel itself, tucked away as it was behind the captain's house at the extremity of the east wing.

Nor were material reminders of this debt of duty to the monarch confined to the great hall. For instance, by the late 1950s the college possessed twenty-one oil paintings and framed photographs of members of the royal family, from Prince Albert Victor to the Duke of Edinburgh, scattered through the building.[19] The college magazine records that when, in 1939, George VI presented the college's captain with a signed photograph the entire college was ordered to march past it in file.[20] Also on prominent display by the 1950s were the naval uniforms of both George V and George VI, as well as two vast hand-steering wheels recovered from the royal yachts *Osborne* and *Alberta*.[21]

Turning to the key upper-middle class, though hardly aristocratic, quality of conformity, the evidence supplied by the college's material culture is equally striking. Here, the messages communicated by the college's interior spaces were also picked up and amplified by cadets' clothing, and it is consequently necessary to examine these two areas side by side. To begin with, in contrast to the idiosyncratically and individually accumulated possessions within an aristocratic home, the navy followed the public-school practice of listing and standardising the items that a cadet could bring into the college.[22] The college's various compendia of orders and regulations bring this situation clearly into focus. For example, in the words of the college's 1934 General Order Book: 'The clothing of cadets must be of the uniform pattern and no other will be allowed. Should a cadet bring clothing which is not uniform it will be returned to his parent or guardian.'[23]

A cadet was forbidden to have more than 5s in his possession while at the college,[24] and was banned from opening accounts with local tradesmen. Parents and guardians were requested not to allow their charges' outfitters to supply clothes or other articles without their authorisation.[25] And any small purchases that cadets did need to make were catered for from the stocks of uniform articles held in the college's own shop.

Besides the standardised objects that cadets brought with them, the college interiors themselves were deeply implicated in this process of homogenisation. For cadets (as for public-school boys), the bulk of their time – when not at lessons, meals or engaged in outdoor sports – was spent within two environments: their dormitory and their common room (the latter known as 'the gunroom'). Though the most domestic of the college's interiors, what is immediately striking about them is the communality of their space (typically 15–40 cadets shared such rooms). Privacy was impossible, and the only concession made to private space was the small lockable drawer, called the 'private till', in each cadet's clothes chest. Even this was subject to examination, and one officer recalled being told, as a cadet that, 'of course you mustn't keep anything in it which is against the rules'.[26] Equally noticeable is the undifferentiated quality of the furnishings. For instance, each dormitory held two rows of identical iron bedsteads, in between which were two more rows of identical wooden clothes chests. Cadets were not permitted to adorn the stark white walls, the windowsills or the tops of the chests with pictures, photographs or personal memorabilia of any kind.

The status of these furnishings as symbols and facilitators of conformity was enhanced by rituals and inspections. To begin with, items of uniform and kit were stored in the chests in accordance with a strict routine. One officer recalled: 'We cadets learned to be tidy, with our uniforms and clothing laid out strictly in regulation fashion, on and in our chests: cap on top in the middle with one sock either side, monkey jacket on the shelf at starboard and trousers to port.'[27] The chests themselves were dressed like ranks on parade. In the words of John Hayes: 'Everybody ... stood by their chests while two cadets at either end of the dormitory gave instructions ... "Up in the middle. Back at the far end. Hayes, yours is crooked," until somebody said "Steady".'[28] Every evening at 9 p.m. the dormitories were inspected. The divisional officer and the cadet captain processed through the rooms scrutinising every detail, while the cadets (arranged in alphabetical order) lay rigidly in their beds.[29] Infractions of the rules invariably resulted in corporal punishment: Cadet de Chair, for example, was beaten for having his toothbrush 'pointing east instead of west'.[30]

In other words, once within the college, the external civilian world of display and consumption was substantially suspended. Statements of individualistic aristocratic expression became harder to make, and the differentiating potentialities of wealth largely ceased to apply. Moreover, ostentatious behaviour – termed 'swanking', 'swaggering', 'side' or 'guff' by cadets – had been negatively classified as vainglorious and fundamentally antisocial.

This process of socio-cultural homogenisation was facilitated by the powerful structures of seniority that flourished within the college – and the public-school world in general. Prior to 1948, when the age of entry was raised to 16, cadets spent 11–12 terms at Dartmouth; and with the passing of each term they became entitled to additional privileges and authority. Each term group was also, to a considerable extent, a self-contained social unit, and had very little contact with groups of older or younger cadets. By these means, an individual's status was further disconnected from personal or familial attributes, and was attached instead to impersonal and automatic staging-posts in the course of training. As John Hayes aptly put it: 'It was like standing on a moving staircase, unable to step up or back, until eventually you got to the top; and each term you went up one in seniority.'[31]

Material culture played a crucial role in realising this system. Most importantly, each new term brought with it a new dormitory and gun-room. Cadets spent the first five terms moving along 'D' block (known as 'junior college'), a large and separate structure completed during the First World War and positioned behind the college's main building. They then relocated to 'senior college', beginning with two terms in a wing of the main building called 'C' block, before processing, over the final four terms, from one end to the other of the college's main façade ('A' block).[32] The communal journals (known as 'line books') kept by cadets of each term group demonstrate their intense awareness of this progression, and the gradually increasing dignity that it conveyed. To quote one of them: 'We came back today feeling very old and superior, as we have got an "A" block gunroom.'[33]

In a multitude of other ways the interior of the college provided an education in this nexus of status and seniority.[34] Certain areas of the college were out of bounds to junior cadets: for example, only twelfth termers were permitted to cross the polished parquet floor of the great hall.[35] Cadets had to pass by the gunrooms of all those senior to them at the double, and older boys displayed a calculated self-confidence when moving through the public spaces of the college. In the words of one new boy: 'We, being greatly terrified, hunched by the side of our notice board like sheep. To add to our discomfiture, the fifth term would charge through our midst, yelling "Gangway" to emphasise their presence.'[36]

The same messages were further inculcated by the clothing cadets wore within these interiors. For instance, junior cadets were not allowed to wear their caps at an angle, and only senior boys could put their hands in their pockets.[37] Describing his final term, Admiral C. C. Anderson noted: '[We] strolled past lesser gunrooms followed by worshipping eyes. A hand, slipped casually into a reefer pocket, drew an almost audible sigh.'[38] Cadets were required to wear knotted lanyards around their necks. As new boys, these were stretched tightly below the collar, but after each term the knot could be lowered an inch, giving a clear visual indication of levels of seniority.[39] And, as before, any and every transgression of these usages counted as 'guff', and would result in a caning. As one officer later put it: 'Guff was Mortal Sin.'[40]

As boys acquired seniority, this system would gradually return to them some of the components of personal consumption and private space that had been stripped away when they first joined the college. In the words of the 1942 General Order Book: 'An additional privilege granted is that cadets of the eleventh, tenth, ninth and eighth terms may bring suitable eatables of their own such as potted meats, jam, honey etc., into the messroom for tea.'[41] Cadet captains (the equivalent of public-school prefects) were permitted to move out of their dormitories into four-berth cabins, complete with desks and cupboards, which they were free to decorate with pictures and photographs of film stars.[42]

Consequently, while drawing on aristocratic formulations of status, and within the quasi-aristocratic shell of the college, the navy had created a system that was entirely opposed to the concomitant aristocratic belief that status could be justified by birth and wealth alone. What the interior of the college provided was, rather, a levelling environment, in which the material and visual props of individuality, personal status and personal taste were systematically removed. Here again, however, the navy was only replicating general public-school practice; and, in terms of class, the consequences of this programme were clear. Writing in 1905, J. Lewis Paton noted that, during his time at public school, a boy 'learns that he is not the most important person in the place ... He loses a few of his angles ... learns to drop rank and wealth and luxury'.[43] The college fees and the interview process ensured that cadets were drawn from the upper middle and upper classes. But, once accepted into the institution, great efforts were made to erode the remaining class distinctions in favour of the upper-middle-class majority.

Within the college, therefore, status was largely determined both by cadets' shared membership of the corporate professional organisation effectively constituted by the navy's officer caste and by the length of time they had spent within it. In that connection it is worth briefly returning to the college's exterior architecture; for, although it did contain many references to the aristocratic country house, it had other and equally immediate associations.

The exterior is best described as Edwardian baroque; and, during the 1890s and the first decade of the twentieth century, this had become *the* architectural vocabulary for government, corporate, collegiate and professional building projects. Important examples with a clear visual kinship to the college include: the Central Criminal Courts of the Old Bailey, by Edward Mountford (begun in 1900); the War Office, Whitehall, by William Young (1899–1906); and the Government Buildings,

Westminster, by John Brydon (1900–8). Moreover, Aston Webb, the college's designer, had not made his name as an architect of aristocratic residences – or indeed of private homes of any kind – but with his designs for precisely this category of corporate and professional building. For instance, among his major commissions during this period were the Royal United Services Institution (1893–95), Birmingham University (1900–9), and the Imperial College of Science (1900–6).

Both the interior and the exterior of the college can be seen as operating together to dismantle the fundamental aristocratic principle of absolute and individual property. The college chaplain, quoted earlier, was correct in believing that cadets would enjoy a sense of 'proprietorship' with regard to their Alma Mater. It is visible, for instance, in the college's annual passing-out ceremony. With a crowd of parents and friends looking on, the leavers would describe a circuit around the parade ground at the front of the college before marching as a body through the main doors, which closed behind them. The spectators would then hear muffled cheers within as the cadets celebrated: a degree of informality impermissible at any other time within Britannia's more public spaces, and one clearly associating the completion of training with a symbolic ownership of the college.[44] However, in this context, ownership (like status) had to be earned, and was at all points contingent on age, rank, membership of the institution and the performance of duty. As Harold Perkin has noted, this corporate and contingent understanding of property was a cornerstone of the professional upper-middle-class social ideal.[45]

The educational priorities of the college were not necessarily either academic or narrowly vocational. Indeed, historians such as Jonathan Gathorne-Hardy have noted how completely it was accepted that public schools were not intended to train for a job, but served to ground boys in upper-middle-class precepts constitutive of 'character'.[46] In adopting and promoting the public-school concept of character, life at the college consequently took the form of a broadly cultural preparation. In the words of an officer-recruitment booklet: 'It is not necessary to specialise in any particular subject ... or, indeed, in any subject at all, in order to get on in the service. It is your character, not the character of your job, that counts.'[47] As a result, the identity of the naval officer became closely associated with a set of predominantly upper-middle-class cultural values.

And it was frequently through material culture that those values were communicated and inculcated.

Moreover, as has already been hinted at, these values were not concerned only with the dismantling of particular aristocratic usages. In rejecting the pursuit of what they might have termed ostentatious and irresponsible property, naval officers were also defining themselves against the world of middle-class business and commerce. The opening remarks of a 1935 officer-recruitment booklet put it plainly:

> To save the reader's valuable time, he should at this stage ask himself one question: 'Do I want my boy to make money?' If the answer is in the affirmative, close the book and take steps ... to destroy it before your son can read it. There is no more money to be made in the service than there is in any other government service.[48]

This, too, was entirely consistent with the upper-middle-class public-school ethic, which claimed for itself a superiority over trade, industry and what was frequently dismissed as 'money grubbing',[49] just as it did over aristocratic leisured wealth. And this should also be seen within a wider process by which the British middle class gradually moved, during this period, from an entrepreneurial towards a salaried professional and managerial social grouping.[50]

The public schools took a variety of steps to protect themselves from the supposedly contaminating influences of commerce. In visual and material terms, perhaps the most important was physical separation from the urban environments with which business was associated. Harrow, for example, was typical in spending fortunes acquiring adjacent landed estates in order, as one historian of that school put it, 'to keep at a distance the rising tide of bricks and mortar'.[51] And it is in this light that we should view the Admiralty's choice of so rural a location for the college.

As well as locating themselves in rural or pseudo-rural settings, public schools also went to great lengths to identify themselves with traditional country pastimes. Britannia was no exception. From the late nineteenth century onwards, its pack of beagles had hunted regularly over the Devon countryside, with cadets acting as whippers-in; and the college field club provided a focus for free time and hobbies. The interior of the college was used to substantiate these associations. Until the

Second World War, antlers and other hunting trophies adorned the walls of the main stairs, and large display cases full of stuffed birds stood in the corridors. Cadets could peruse copies of *Country Life, The Country Lover, The Country Sportsman* and *The Countryman* in the college library.[52]

In this context, it should be remembered that the family homes of most cadets were far more likely to be detached or semi-detached suburban villas than country estates. Equally, many cadets were the sons of businessmen. So what the college provided was a formative – for some, a transformative – environment in which boys could develop the necessary familiarity with the cultural foundations of upper-middle-class life. That they might be placed under some pressure to conform to these norms is revealed by the incredulous words of one master, writing in a 1942 edition of the college magazine: 'One cadet of the first term told us that he was not interested in the country or in any pursuit of the Field Club! We hope that in time he will see the error of his ways. It is hard to imagine a naval officer without country and sporting instincts.'[53]

Beyond this, within the setting of the dining hall, great stress was placed on conformity to upper-middle-class rules of table etiquette. Cadet captains and the ever-watchful officer of the day ensured that boys had clean hands and brushed hair, and that they sat up straight, handled their cutlery 'correctly', conversed and chewed their food decorously, and did not stretch across their neighbours for the water jugs.[54] Training was provided in other upper-middle-class social skills and social situations. For example, dancing lessons were a regular occurrence, with pairs of cadets waltzing, more or less awkwardly, around the great hall. Formal dances were held at the end of most terms, and from the mid-1950s an annual hunt ball was added to the college's social calendar.[55] Within this context, cadets gradually mastered the customs and protocol of upper-middle-class sociability; and commentaries on their socio-cultural progress (under the heading 'Officer-like qualities') were appended to their termly reports.

Alongside conformity of social status, then, the college promoted a cultural homogeneity, and both tended towards the acceptance of upper-middle-class norms. Alongside the particular components of the college interior, this process was facilitated by the college's self-contained and literally boundaried world, from which competing cultural influences could be excluded. In common with public-school practice, there were strict regulations regarding the circumstances under which cadets might venture beyond the college grounds. In the words of the 1935 General Order Book: 'All towns, buildings, houses ... public cinemas, theatres and concerts are always out of bounds for all cadets during term'.[56] The pedagogical quality of the college's material culture was therefore intensified by the fact that cadets were denied access (during term-time) to other physical environments – and their potentially undesirable or culturally disruptive characteristics.

Consequently, the material configuration of the college, and its many borrowings from the public-school example, did much to shape the class affiliations of cadets. Above all, the college interior served to delineate and promote a cluster of specifically upper-middle-class values and characteristics. Through material culture, to a considerable extent, cadets were encouraged to define themselves against an urban middle class of commerce and entrepreneurship. At the same time, the college radically restricted (and in the process stigmatised) individual aristocratic ostentation.

There was a third dimension to this upper-middle-class project. As already mentioned, these intricate notions of gentlemanliness, character and public service were laboriously internalised by cadets through lengthy exposure to the particular material and ideological environment provided by the college (and also by the preparatory school and upper-middle-class home). During this period, such qualities were nonetheless frequently understood and portrayed as the innate and unteachable attributes of the upper-middle and upper classes. The corollary of this belief was the view that the working classes innately *lacked* those same qualities, and it was this rationale that underpinned the upper-middle- and upper-class monopolisation of officer rank. Life within the college must therefore be seen both as conditioning cadets in a particular understanding of working-class identity and as preparing them to accept unquestioningly the reality of an organisation profoundly divided along lines of class.

Notes

1 D. Cannadine, *Class in Britain* (New Haven, CT, and London: Yale University Press, 1998), p. 188.

2 See R. McKibbin, *Classes and Cultures, England 1918–1951* (Oxford: Oxford University Press, 1998), p. 35; D. Cannadine, *The Decline and Fall of the British Aristocracy* (London: Papermac, 1996), pp. 273–5; C. McKee, *Sober Men and True: Sailor Lives in the Royal Navy, 1900–1945* (Cambridge, MA: Harvard University Press, 2002), p. 47.

3 See T. C. Worsley, *Barbarians and Philistines, Democracy and the Public Schools* (London: Robert Hall, Ltd, 1940), p. 20.

4 See A. A. Jackson, *The Middle Classes, 1900–1950* (Nairn: David St John Thomas, 1991), pp. 236–7, footnote 3.

5 See H. Perkin, *The Rise of Professional Society: England since 1880* (London: Routledge, 1990), p. 259.

6 M. J. Wiener, *English Culture and the Decline of the Industrial Spirit, 1850–1980* (Cambridge: Cambridge University Press, 1981).

7 J. Gathorne-Hardy, *The Public School Phenomenon, 597–1977* (London: Penguin Books, 1977), p. 127.

8 Britannia Royal Naval College Archive (hereafter BRNC), Britannia Magazine, summer term, 1907, p. 1285.

9 St John Pearce, *Schools in Turmoil* (London and Melbourne: Ward, Lock & Co., Ltd, 1933), p. 19.

10 BRNC, Catalogue of Artefacts in the College, June 1983, entry E.205.

11 BRNC, Catalogue of Pictures, Models, Silver, etc., March 1969; and Catalogue of Artefacts, June 1983.

12 BRNC, Britannia Magazine, summer term, 1905, editorial.

13 *Ibid.*, summer term, 1930, pp. 3–4.

14 Perkin, *The Rise of Professional Society*, p. 121.

15 *Ibid.*, pp. 121, 368.

16 McKibbin, *Classes and Cultures*, p. 35.

17 BRNC, Speech by Admiral Sir Richard Onslow at Britannia Royal Naval College, 11 April 1960, p. 5.

18 I am grateful to Professor Andrew Lambert for this observation.

19 See BRNC, Catalogue of Pictures, March 1969; Catalogue of Artefacts, June 1983.

20 BRNC, Britannia Magazine, Easter 1939, editorial.

21 See BRNC, Catalogue of Pictures, March 1969; Catalogue of Artefacts, June 1983.

22 J. Wakeford, *The Cloistered Elite; A Sociological Analysis of the English Public Boarding School* (London: Macmillan, 1969), p. 53.

23 BRNC, General Order Book, 1934.

24 *Ibid.*

25 BRNC, General Regulations, 1940, p. 5.

26 Vice-Admiral Sir J. Hayes, *Face the Music: A Sailor's Story* (Edinburgh: Pentland Press, 1991), p. 27.

27 Commander H. G. de Chair, *Let Go Aft: The Indiscretions of a Salt Horse Commander* (Tunbridge Wells: Parapress, 1993), p. 4.

28 Hayes, *Face the Music*, p. 28.

29 *Ibid.*, p. 27.

30 De Chair, *Let Go Aft*, p. 4.

31 Hayes, *Face the Music*, p. 31.

32 Rear Admiral C. C. Anderson, *Seagulls in My Belfry* (Durham: Pentland Press, 1997), p. 8.

33 BRNC, Line Book, Hood Term, 1930–33, regarding 1932.

34 This followed the public-school example; see Wakeford, *The Cloistered Elite*, p. 118.

35 BRNC, Line Book, Grenville House, 1948–53.

36 BRNC, Britannia Magazine, Easter term, 1918, p. 8.

37 This, too, paralleled public-school practice, see Gathorne-Hardy, *The Public School Phenomenon*, p. 117.

38 Anderson, *Seagulls in My Belfry*, p. 19.

39 *Ibid.*, p. 8.

40 *Ibid.*, p. 9.

41 BRNC, General Order Book, 1942.

42 See BRNC, Line Book, Exmouth House, 1947–51.

43 J. L. Paton, *English Public Schools* (1905), quoted in T. L. Humberstone, *The Public School Question* (London: Simpkin Marshall, 1944), p. 10.

44 As witnessed by the author in September 2000.

45 Perkin, *The Rise of Professional Society*, p. 123.

46 See Gathorne-Hardy, *The Public School Phenomenon*, p. 151.

47 Commander E. W. Bush, *How to Become a Naval Officer* (London: Gieves, Ltd, 1935), p. 12.

48 *How to Become a Naval Officer and Life at the Royal Naval College, Dartmouth* (London: Gieves, Ltd, 1935), p. 2.

49 See Perkin, *The Rise of Professional Society*, pp. 119, 121.

50 *Ibid.*, p. 270.

51 E. D. Laborde, *Harrow School: Yesterday and Today* (London: Winchester Publications, 1948), p. 19.

52 BRNC, Britannia Magazine, Christmas term, 1949, p. 23.

53 *Ibid.*, Easter term, 1942, p. 3.

54 *Ibid.*, Christmas term, 1949, p. 14.

55 *Ibid.*, Christmas term, 1956, p. 38.

56 BRNC, General Order Book, 1935; this paralleled public-school practice, got which see Wakeford, *The Cloistered Elite*, p. 71.

7 ✧ Feminine spaces, modern experiences: the design and display strategies of British hairdressing salons in the 1920s and 1930s

Emma Gieben-Gamal

All the young women at the office were having their hair cut short ... my mother and I went to the hairdresser's on Wardour Street ... An hour later, with hats far too large for our diminished heads ... we emerged as new women.[1]

HE BOB, the shingle and the permanent wave remain potent symbols of the inter-war period, signifying social, cultural and political change. Yet the hairdressing salons in which these styles were created have received little attention in any field of academic enquiry. In uncovering the processes by which the hairdressing salon was designed and organised as a space for the consumption of the body and of female beauty, I argue that the hairdressing salon is imbued with a level of signification equally as rich as that attributed to the hairstyles it produced. This chapter looks at the interior design of the hairdressing salon in the 1920s and 1930s, a period in which hairdressing became available for the first time to a large section of society and expanded rapidly as a commercial enterprise.[2] It was also precisely in this period, according to Mica Nava, that a 'modern democratic (and largely feminine) consumer culture ... [became] increasingly normalised and entrenched'.[3] What makes the hairdressing salon an interesting case study is that it affords the opportunity to chart this process of the 'normalisation' of consumption through an analysis of the changing design strategies adopted within the hairdressing salon and the discourses that structured them.

The provision of women's hairdressing services outside of the home dates back at least to the seventeenth century, but the setting up of hairdressing salons exclusively for women appears to have arisen with the growth of department stores in the latter half of the nineteenth century. Following the First World War, the hairdressing trade literature devoted increasing space to the discussion of new independent hairdressing salons for women, in addition to those already located in department stores. An analysis of this literature reveals an increasing recognition on the part of the hairdressing profession that design would play an important part in establishing women's hairdressing as a modern commercial practice. By the 1920s shop-front design, window display, and the layout and decoration of the interior had become a regular – and important – topic of discussion.

After the First World War the design of independent hairdressing salons broadly followed the model of earlier department stores' salons which provided private cubicles for the treatment of women's hair. By the 1920s hairdressing establishments for women universally had adopted the 'cubicle system' as an organising principle in the interior. This was one in which the salon was divided into two spaces: the reception area, which in the early 1920s resembled an upper-middle-class parlour; and the workspace, where clients' hair was attended to, which was organised into a series of private cubicles that were, in contrast to the comfortable reception area, stark in their plain functionality and hygienic atmosphere.

This structuring of space continued throughout the 1920s and 1930s. However, as the 1920s progressed, the reception area became less reminiscent of the parlour, and instead increasingly foregrounded the products on sale. By the end of the 1920s the display of hair and beauty products had become a central feature of the design scheme and display units were positioned as focal points in the room. However, questions about the display of goods had always been a key issue in the hairdressing trade literature. In the early 1920s, the general advice was that goods should be displayed in a subtle manner, and overt displays of merchandise were uncommon. Thus, in 1922, one commentator advised that the display of merchandise 'should be the acme of neatness and simplicity and should be visible without being too conspicuous'.[4] This concern with subtle merchandising displays did not entirely fade with the more commercial style of the 1930s. This is illustrated by the advice given by the proprietor of a salon in 1932: 'I maintain that goods sell themselves if they are displayed properly. Let your customer *discover* them ... Good display is one of the chief things in aiding the discovery of goods. In my own shop I display goods with a suggestion of casualness. I do not crowd them on to the customer with all of them shouting "buy me"'.[5]

What these statements make clear is that from the outset careful attention was paid to the arrangement of goods within the salon, albeit in a style that was restrained rather than conspicuous. Another recurrent point in the literature about displaying goods was that a well-dressed window is one that is not overcrowded, and much advice was proffered on the arrangement of goods according to the aesthetic principles of form and composition.

Interlocking with the development of a more conspicuous display of goods was the development of a distinctly modern style of interior decoration which, by the mid 1930s, expressed a unified interior scheme pulling together the two spaces of the salon into a single visual language.[6] Typically, these salons adopted a smooth, streamlined and 'shiny' aesthetic comparable to the moderne style of luxury ocean liners such as the *Normandie*, or new cinemas like the Odeon at Muswell Hill designed by George Cole.[7] Materials such as washable wallpaper and panels of formica and cellulose lacquer were used to line the walls, inlaid with strips of gleaming metal. Lighting was concealed and back-lit mirrors would provide a wash of light that appeared like magic from hidden sources. Reception areas consisted of streamlined display units and glamorous mannequins, while the cubicles became a lesson in efficiency with their built-in cupboards, hidden hatches for waste disposal and flexible furniture. New materials and technology were used at a practical level to improve the quality of the service and the environment, but they were used also to express the modernity of that service.[8]

The parallels that can be drawn between this emerging modern style in hairdressing salons and the design and decoration of other leisure sites, such as hotels, cinemas and ocean liners, suggest that such interior schemes were part of a wider aesthetic shift. Furthermore, an analysis of the trade literature suggests that the stylistic developments in hairdressing salons were informed by the principles of modern design advocated within the commercial art and architectural literature. But while those principles can be seen as part of the emerging modernist discourse, modernism as a style was not actively promoted.[9] Nonetheless, from the early 1920s, modern principles of design filtered down from the commercial art and architectural journals. Moreover, the references to them and the strength with which they were advocated increased from the mid 1920s and through the 1930s.

Three issues in particular seem to have informed the terms of the debate in the hairdressing trade literature: truth to function, which was applied to the clear expression of the function of space as well as of objects; the use of new materials; and the adoption of forms of decoration appropriate for the modern age. The following statement in the journal *Commercial Art* concerns modern architecture, but it is directly applicable to the principles promoted in the hairdressing trade journals: 'If it possible to isolate two points which seem to stand out more than others when "modernity" in architecture is the topic, these points would surely be on the one hand, clear expression of function, and on the other, decorative qualities which are associated with modern life, rather than the use of worn out motifs.' [10]

Design discourses alone do not, however, fully explain why hairdressing salons looked they way they did, either in the early 1920s or in the 1930s when a more 'modern' stylistic idiom was adopted. Why, for example, was the domestic space of the parlour, or living room, evoked so strongly by the reception areas of salons in the early 1920s? Why, in contrast, were the cubicles so starkly functional and what made this aesthetic of hygiene and efficiency so suitable and sustainable as a structuring principle for design, even in the most stylish modern salons of the 1930s? To answer those questions, it is necessary to move beyond a formal analysis to one in which the hairdressing salon is recognised as a space which is constituted and constructed through a multiplicity of social relations. That is, in order to understand both the signification of the physical fabric of the hairdressing salon and the motivations for the strategies of design that were adopted, it is necessary to look to wider socio-cultural discourses. In particular, it is suggested that those design strategies represented a negotiation of the evolving socio-cultural legitimacy of consumption in the sphere of beauty, and that they interlocked with discourses which structured changing notions both of the body and of the home.

There has been little historical or sociological analysis of the cultural experience of visiting the hairdresser, though histories of consumption pinpoint the 1920s as a significant period for the formulation of new bodily ideals for women.[11] Furthermore, literature about the cosmetics industry suggests that it was in the 1920s that attitudes to make-up began to change and the industry began to gain ground in the public relations battle to make cosmetics respectable and acceptable.[12] At the beginning of the 1920s the majority of editorials in women's magazines were firmly against the use of make-up and lipstick. By the end of that decade, however, the magazines had capitulated and cosmetic advertising in them grew substantially.[13] The following statement in a newspaper article about the opening in 1921 of the new Binns department store hairdressing salons indicates also a shift in ideas about the consumption of beauty: 'Even if it is not every woman's privilege to be beautiful it is her right to make the most of herself.'[14] Although it may be argued that hairstyling was more socially acceptable than 'making-up' one's face, until the appearance of hairdressing salons the process of 'body work' remained hidden within the privacy of the home. Attending to one's hair was a private ritual, but more than that it was deeply personal. Thus while hairstyling may have been more socially acceptable than applying make-up, the act of going to a 'public' commercial establishment may still have been new and daunting.

In this context one might suggest that the visual reference to the domestic space of the parlour in the reception area of the hairdressing salon was a strategy to reassure the new customer and so familiarise her experience. On one level it can be argued that the decoration of the hairdressing reception in the style of an upper-middle-class, or even aristocratic, parlour simply represented an attempt to cater to the domestic tastes of the clientele. However, one problem with this view is that the growth of independent hairdressing salons has been linked to an expanding mass market extending well beyond the confines of the upper-middle-class consumer. One could speculate about attitudes of deference or aspiration among this new clientele, or about the perception that a hairdressing salon decorated in an upper-middle-class style necessarily implies a better service or product. But more than this it is suggested that this strategy of domesticising space was employed in order to imbue the service itself with a sense of solid respectability.

This was not a novel strategy. It had been employed throughout the nineteenth century in the provision of parlours and spaces designated for women's exclusive use, in hotels, trains, department stores and libraries. There the respectable upper-middle-class interior was evoked though the potted plants, the ornaments, furnishings and fittings which were later to be seen in the reception of the hairdressing salon.[15] This same process can be identified in the larger salon receptions which often bore a strong resemblance to department store tea-rooms or to the new suburban tennis clubs which provided a similar model of domesticised space. Significantly, what this style of decoration also reveals is the class-based notion of *domesticity*, in which respectable femininity was equated with a specifically middle-class domestic sphere.[16] As such, the style of decoration in the hairdressing salon did more than reflect the tastes of its clientele: it extended an upper-middle-class aura of respectability to all those who inhabited or passed through the space. Although this expression of a Victorian code of respectability became quickly outmoded, its adoption in the hairdressing salon at the beginning of the 1920s may have reflected the perceived need to establish the service as, above all other things, a respectable one.

As the 1920s passed into the 1930s a trip to the hairdresser had become an established part of the beauty regime of many women, although the chemicals used in treating hair and the growing use of technical equipment could make for a less than comfortable experience.[17] This acceptance and normalisation of the profession was reflected in the demise of the parlour-like reception. And, as the consumption of beauty products more generally gained acceptance through the 1920s and into the 1930s, the display of products became increasingly a defining feature of the reception area. Indeed, the increasing visibility of products in the hairdressing salon can be seen to have reflected the growing visibility of make-up which was shifting from the soft natural look of the 1920s to the more defined and distinctive look of the 1930s with its cupid-bow lips and thin-plucked eyebrows.

It is clear that throughout the 1920s and 1930s the design of hairdressing salons was characterised by variety and individuality of style. Nevertheless, identifiable models of decoration did emerge and become widespread. By the 1930s the conspicuous display of goods characterised the whole sector, but the style of the reception generally fell into two categories: The first was to effect an atmosphere akin to that of the doctor's surgery, in which the display of goods was comparable to that of a chemist's shop. Thus one proprietor stated: 'I was aiming to create a family practice, very much as the doctor does. I have maintained that ladies like a shop with this kind of atmosphere and that they will go to it no matter what part of town.'[18] The second more widespread approach, which was later to develop into a streamlined moderne style, was one in which the display of goods was presented within an environment that emphasised the leisured nature of the service through comfortable seating, the provision of magazines and even a telephone. The aim, as the following remarks made by hairdressers suggest, was to create a sociable environment where women might arrange to meet. 'My clients will make appointments to meet their friends in the shop. "Meet me at my hairdressers." How satisfactory it is to hear this from your customer when she is using the telephone!'[19] Another hairdresser commented: 'It is the best compliment possible to one's shop … [to be seen as] a *suitable* rendezvous … [and] it is a nice place for friends to wait in'.[20]

If the decoration of the reception area changed at that time to reflect the increasing commercialisation of beauty, the cubicles continued to be modelled along the lines of those of the early 1920s' salons. 'Functional', 'efficient' and 'hygienic' were the words that continued to structure the debate. But why was this aesthetic adopted in the first place? Given the ominous appearance of much of the electrical equipment used in the hairdressing salon – such as the permanent waving machine that looked like a metal jellyfish on a stand – and the still novel experience of using electrical equipment, especially on the body, one might have expected the decor of the cubicles to be designed to compensate for the crudeness and alarming appearance of the technology. Little attempt, it seems, was made to do this. Again, this may be seen as reflecting a concern with respectability – which was of particular relevance to a space in which the intimate activity of attending to another person's hair was carried out. Thus, while a sociable, comfortable and ornamented reception spoke of a genteel respectability, once in the privacy of the cubicle, where a male hairdresser might tend to a female customer, the atmosphere had to be one of strict professionalism from which any sexual overtones were purged. One indication of this was the use of frosted-glass partitions, as can be seen in the Eugene salon cubicle, or curtained partitions which provided a level of privacy while maintaining sufficient visibility to preclude any suggestion of impropriety (see figure 19).

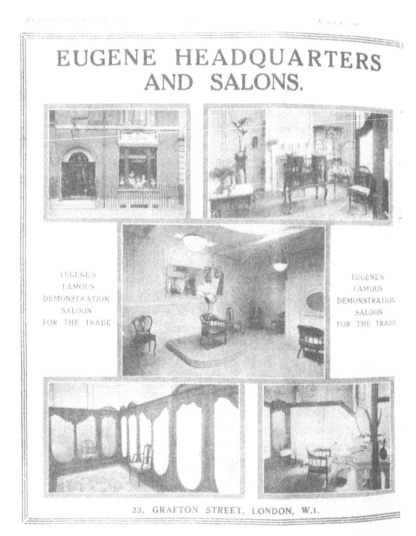

19 *Hairdressers' Weekly Journal* advertisement for Eugene headquarters and salons

In the journals a number of articles held up the hospital or doctor's surgery as a suitable exemplar for the cubicle area, or consulting area, of the salon. But, more than that, they were dominated by discussions of hygiene, efficiency and utility. The strategy was intended not only to improve the service, but to reassure the customer of its professionalism. Thus, in the advertisement for the Viabella salon, the customer is tempted to relax in the reception room as if it were her sitting room, but her confidence in the service is invited on the basis of the clean and efficient atmosphere of the cubicle [21] (figure 20).

The belief that the hygienic appearance of the salon would secure the customer's confidence structured every level of advice promulgated on the design and decoration of the salon. It structured a discussion of materials in which it was advised that 'the prime reason for using marble in the salon is the assistance it gives to cleanliness'.[22] It informed a debate about colour schemes in which white was recognised for its suggestion of cleanliness, but soft blues, greys and pinks were recommended because they looked clean, were easier to keep clean and were restful to the eye.[23] And it informed the shift towards more simple furniture, furnishings and finishes: 'The modern tendency is towards plain panelled surfaces, and an elimination of ornament. The effect is to ... provide less harbourage for dust and dirt.' [24]

This zealous promotion of cleanliness and hygiene may have stemmed in part from the need to distance contemporary hairdressing salons from some of the older West End establishments known for strong and unpleasant odours caused by London's poor Victorian drainage system.[25] But what also becomes clear from an analysis of the hairdressing trade literature of the period is that the debate about hygiene was rooted in – and reflected – a wider social concern. Thus, an article in the *Hairdressers' Weekly Journal* from 1921 stated: 'For the hairdresser ... there is a factor compelling him to treat his patrons to the luxury of perfectly hygienic surroundings whether he wishes it or not':[26]

amongst other things fifty years of compulsory learning ... has made us a people more particular about personal cleanliness than we were before ... [and] is causing a general levelling up in the popular views and ideas of cleanliness everywhere ... The hairdresser needs to keep up to date with developments ... which express these ideas and sets a standard that cannot be ignored by the humbler business.[27]

VIABELLA

Culture de Beauté

102 Baker Street
London   W.1

Telephone – Mayfair 3835

Above is the private consulting room where you can talk as freely as if you were in your own comfortable sitting room. On the right is the treatment salon, where an atmosphere of cleanliness and efficiency invites your confidence.

Treatments which include Radio Active Mud Treatment, Electrolysis, removal of Blemishes, Facial Treatment for every skin condition and Flesh Reducing are carried out by fully qualified masseuses under the most hygienic conditions in the latest scientific manner. At 102 Baker Street you are visiting trained skin specialists. Write with full confidence or call to-day for particulars of the Viabella treatments in which you are interested. Below will be found two useful adjuncts to your dressing table.

BUTTERMILK LOTION

An antiseptic cleansing fluid which instantly revives the skin, rendering it beautifully white, clear and smooth. In generous size bottles **5 6 & 10 6**

FOUNDATION CREAM

A delightful greaseless cream to be used before powdering, imparting a wonderfully youthful appearance to the complexion. In attractive jars **3/6 & 5 6**

20 *Vogue* advertisement for Viabella's 'Culture de Beaute'

This concern with hygiene and the war against germs can be dated back to the nineteenth century when both the home and body were targets for reform.[28] By the 1920s the discourse of hygiene, in relation both to the environment and to the body, had translated itself into one of maintenance and scientific management. Throughout the 1920s advertisements for hair and beauty products built on a tradition of justification premissed on the health-improving virtues of the product, but repackaged this message in the rhetoric of scientific management and rational methods of production. An advert for the INECTO salons in London thus claimed: 'At last the English woman has recognised the vital importance of the scientific care of her hair to such an extent that its beauty has become as proverbial as the charm of her traditional complexion.'[29] Another advert in the same magazine proclaimed 'Hair beauty – By rational methods'.[30]

In her book *Good Hair Days. A History of British Hairstyling*, Caroline Cox acknowledges the impact on hairstyling of discourses of scientific management, hygiene and efficiency, alongside those of beauty and glamour. She suggests that the adoption of the bob in the 1920s was bound up with female emancipation and fashion, but that it also reflected the modern woman's busy lifestyle, which necessitated easy-to-care-for styles, and changing attitudes to hair cleansing.[31] References to 'cleanliness' and 'efficiency' permeated the language of advertising and promotional campaigns throughout the beauty industry; they were even used qualitatively to describe women themselves. In his influential 1931 book *The Art and Craft of Hairdressing*, Gilbert Foan noted: 'There is no doubt that our women have never looked so chic, clean and neat, both in head-dress and clothes, than at this period.'[32] The frequent qualitative as well as descriptive use of 'cleanliness' and 'hygiene' would seem to further contextualise and explain the sanitary and functional aesthetic adopted in the salon cubicle.

The ramifications of this discourse, however, reached beyond the confines of the beauty industry. In many ways it was the home that represented the epicentre of this discourse: the role of women in the home, the physical space of the home and the running or 'management' of the home were all affected. The impact of scientific management on the home is a relatively well-charted field;[33] and while there is no space here to elaborate on that dimension, four points which provide an important backdrop and parallel to developments taking place in the hairdressing salon should be mentioned.

First, the movement towards a rationalisation of housework and the household into a science of management was intended to professionalise the housewife.[34] Second, the movement focused its attention on questions of design – in particular kitchen design – which in its most extreme form resulted in what Penny Sparke has called 'the de-aestheticisation of the kitchen', as it was redesigned on Taylorist principles – in the pursuit of hygiene and efficiency.[35] Third, these discourses of cleanliness and efficiency were taken up and exploited by the electrical, gas and associated industries in promoting their life-enhancing, labour-saving and time-efficient products. And, fourth, such was the impact of the discourse that 'hygiene and efficiency' became a yardstick by which to measure a woman's competence as a wife and/or mother and, by extension, the status of her family.[36] In this wider context, therefore, it seems hardly surprising that articles on design in the hairdressing journals should emphasise the need to express the hygienic quality of the service in the decor of the cubicle. One final point to draw in this parallel between the hairdresser and the modern housewife in her new (often suburban) home is that the functional, efficient and hygienic appearance of the new cubicles did more than 'streamline' the service – it was intended also to signify the professionalising of hairdressing, just as the newly modelled kitchen signified the professionalising of housework.

I have argued thus far that notions of utility, hygiene and efficiency were pivotal to the design of the hairdressing salon of the inter-war-years, reflecting wider social discourses that structured women's consumption, their domestic role and the physical organisation of spaces within the home. I conclude by calling attention to a further powerful idea that also can be seen at work in the design of the hairdressing salon. It is the notion that hygiene and cleanliness were themselves perceived as *luxuries*. For many of the new and expanding lower-middle class of the inter-war period, the new suburban home, with its supply of electricity, its modern kitchen and bathroom, represented a level of comfort and, by extension, luxury previously unattainable.[37] In many respects, however, the notion that cleanliness and hygiene were luxuries persisted. The new standards of hygiene were difficult to meet and maintain without the aid of expensive electrical products or full-time servants, something that, according to

Gwynne Howell writing in *Ideal Home*, the promoters of the utility and appliance industries recognised when they complained: 'There has been a tendency in the past on the part of the average housewife to regard electricity and its uses – apart from lighting – as a luxury.'[38] In another *Ideal Home* article, J. F. Saunders expressed the same lament: 'Many people are under the impression that, apart from its use as an illuminant, electricity in the home is a luxury.'[39]

One consequence of the perception that products which facilitated the achievement of hygienic surroundings were luxuries was that a hygienic space became an expression of luxury itself, since it signified the use of luxury objects in its creation. This conflation of luxury and hygiene was recognised by the author of a *Hairdressers' Weekly Journal* article about design in which he stated that the hairdresser should treat his customer to the 'luxury of perfectly hygienic surroundings'.[40] Although a seemingly casual remark, this, together with tone of many more articles in the hairdressing journals, expressed a subtle but significant conceptual shift in the connotation of 'hygiene' through which it became a signifier of luxury. During the early 1920s this notion was still expressed in rather crude terms. Conspicuous luxury was most clearly expressed in the reception area, while the cubicles remained functional and efficient, but not especially comfortable or luxurious. Indeed, one might say that the early cubicles reflected a de-aestheticisation similar to that identified by Penny Sparke in the early scientifically planned kitchens.[41]

As a more commercial style of design developed in the 1930s, this notion of the luxury of hygiene was expressed in an increasingly sophisticated way, being articulated through the re-aestheticisation of the cubicle area. This was exhibited most clearly in the hairdressing salons that adopted the modern and commercial style of design that can most closely be described as a form of the moderne. The most flamboyant examples of this new style were to be found in the newly refurbished salons of large department stores like Harrods and D. H. Evans in London. But smaller department stores, like Medhurst's in Bromley, south London (featured in the Haskins advertisement), also adopted this style to great effect (see figure 21). Within these salons the increasing rationalisation of the service was represented in the design and decoration of the cubicles. Built-in cupboards, fittings that were designed to be packed flat against a wall when not in use, hatches for waste disposal and cupboards

★ skilled planning

and designing by

159 ST. JOHN ST., CLERKENWELL, LONDON, E.C.1
Phone : Clerkenwell 6700

★ Medhursts' Hairdressing Saloon, Bromley, is an example of Haskins' planning
and designing. The walls are cellulosed green, decorated with horizontal bands
of stainless steel. Each cubicle is decorated in different colours, with brilliant
cut mirrors and lighting immediately overhead and each side of chair. The
Beauty Parlour and Chiropody cubicles are in ivory, and scarlet lake. The floor
is of cream grained rubber squares, and an air washer is included, which supplies
fresh and perfumed air. May we call upon you and proffer our suggestions?

21 Advertisement in *The Hairdresser & Beauty Trade* for Haskins's Shop Fronts &
Fitting, featuring the Medhursts' hairdressing salon, 1935

accessible from both corridors and cubicles created a clutter-free, efficient environment. All these features improved the efficiency of the service and the level of hygiene. But the use of modern materials, such as linoleum on floors and washable coverings or formica panelling on walls, together with the abundant use of glass, also created a luxurious effect in which everything was highly polished and gleaming.

Unlike the salons of the 1920s, in which the style of decoration in the cubicles was in stark contrast to that of the reception area, those of the 1930s adopted a new stylistic scheme in which the two spaces were designed as part of a unified interior aesthetic. More opulent materials, such as carpeted floors, expensive wood veneers like walnut, birch or mahogany, and areas of glass and smooth lustrous panelling, broken up with brilliant metal inlays, were being used in the reception. The display of goods continued to play a central part in the design scheme, but the products on offer were in glittering display units set into the wall, or in sleek display cabinets with hidden lighting. One significant effect of the new design schemes was that the sense of luxury was no longer limited to the reception area, just as hygiene was not specific to the cubicle. The predominance of smooth, satiny materials and glittering glass and metal throughout the reception and the cubicles communicated a sense of both luxury and hygiene. Throughout the salon the customer was confronted with highly polished and sparkling clean surfaces. It can also be argued, as Juliet Kinchin does in her article on the gendering of space in nineteenth-century domestic interiors, that there was an association of smooth surfaces, femininity and 'social polish'.[42]

This strategy of developing an aesthetic of cleanliness and hygiene was not, however, unique to the hairdressing salon. The application of streamlining to the design of such domestic appliances as the vacuum cleaner, refrigerator and electric iron gave them a sleek and efficient look. With their mechanical parts encased within their smooth, gleaming shells, their re-styling spoke of high technology and luxury. They were symbols of cleanliness as well as aides to hygiene. Ellen Lupton and Jane Abbott Miller have argued that the streamlined style of design symbolised the new ideals of bodily hygiene,[43] though, as Adrian Forty has pointed out, hygiene was linked also to beauty: 'The idea that cleanliness might be beautiful took hold with such force that every new product that purveyed an appearance of hygiene was felt by consumers to be fulfilling a genuine need: far from being hard to adapt to, cleanliness was an aesthetic that satisfied many desires.'[44] One such desire was for the luxury, as well as the beauty, of hygiene, and while objects were increasingly designed to express this notion, it was in the hairdressing salon that its most sophisticated expression was to be found.

Hairdressing salons continued to evolve and change to reflect developments both within and outside of the industry. Already by the late 1930s, articles were creeping into the hairdressing journals about the new American 'open system' which swept away the cubicles and restructured the space into an open-plan work area.[45] However, this chapter has set out to show that the design of the hairdressing salon was of particular significance in the *inter-war* period, during which it not only symbolised the transformation of hairdressing into a modern commercial practice, but reflected and negotiated a wider shift in the normalisation of consumption. Strategies expressive of this normalisation which were employed in the hairdressing salon have been linked to socio-cultural discourses that structured women's lives in the home and as consumers. Images of domesticity have been shown to have played an important part in the developing design of the salon, initially as a means to impart respectability and later locking into the discourse of health, hygiene and efficiency. Within these processes the design of the hairdressing salon may also be seen to reflect the notion of rational consumption which formed part of the discourse of scientific management.

In this context women were urged to think about and organise their consumption habits in more rational ways.[46] Mica Nava has suggested that ideas about rational consumption and the housewife as a manager became 'a means of regulating and controlling disorderly (female) shoppers'.[47] One might infer from this that control over female shoppers was imposed by men. However, women were themselves active in the development of this discourse, which suggests that they were complicit in instituting these strategies of control and were not just its passive victims. Women were at the centre of organisations which promulgated theories of scientific management in the home and framed consumption within a discourse of rationality. They were vocal advocates of domestic science, propagating their theories in flourishing women's magazines such as *Ideal Home, Good Housekeeping* and *The Ladies' Home Companion*, and through new organisations such as the Good Housekeeping Institute.

They formed pressure groups like the Women's Labour League, an off-shoot of the Labour Party which sought to improve conditions for the working-class housewife. And they were at the centre of the promotion of the electrical industry, in 1924 establishing the Electrical Association for Women, which sought to educate women about the advantages of using electrical appliances in the home. Throughout this literature, the terms of debate were framed within the drive for rationalisation, efficiency and hygienic surroundings. Furthermore, women hairdressers actively shaped the debate about appropriate styles of design for their salons, in which utility, cleanliness and efficiency were key considerations.

This is not to suggest that consumption was transformed into an entirely rational activity. The design of the hairdressing salon locked into notions of glamour and aspiration as well as those of hygiene, efficiency and utility. In fact what these discourses and the design of the hairdressing salon do suggest is that the simple classification 'rational' or 'irrational' is inadequate to convey the complex system of desires, wants and needs which characterised consumption in this period.[48] Furthermore, this dichotomous way of thinking, which has tended to structure and constrain the terms of the debate in relation to female spaces, is challenged by an analysis of the hairdressing salon which demands that the space is understood as relational and multi-layered – one in which public and private, rational and irrational overlap.

In conclusion, the decoration and design of hairdressing salons in the inter-war period embodied the passing of an old world of Victorian values of respectable femininity and the negotiation of a new world in which new modes of consumption, new leisure pursuits and the discourses of new technology and scientific management shaped women's lives, homes and bodies. The bob and the permanent wave have been posited as symbols of women's entry into modernity,[49] but it was in the hairdressing salon that the visual transformation of women into *new women* took place, and it is arguably the space within the hairdressing salon which best expresses some of the complexities of this transition.

Notes

1 Quoted N. Williams, *Powder and Paint: A History of the English Woman's Toilet* (London: Longmans, Green & Company, 1957), pp. 162–3.

2 S. Zdatny, 'Fashion and class struggle: the case of the coiffure', *Social History*, 18:1 (January 1993), 53–72; also see G. Foan, *The Art & Craft of Hairdressing* (London: New Era Publishing, 1931), pp. 1–6.

3 M. Nava, 'Modernity tamed? Women shoppers and the rationalisation of consumption in the interwar period', *Australian Journal of Communication*, 22:2 (1995), 3.

4 R. Merton, 'Beauty parlour management: an American view point', *Hairdressers' Weekly Journal*, 41:2110 (30 September 1922), 1893.

5 Lady Vincent Caillard, 'How I built Pascal et Cie', *The Hairdresser and Beauty Trade*, 1:1 (2 September 1932), 14–15 (italics added).

6 This stylistic unification of the reception area and the cubicles did not extend to the more modest salons. However, a more considered approach to the decoration of these salons can be identified, in which fixtures and fittings were bought as co-ordinated sets or were carefully matched in terms of style.

7 Like cinemas, hairdressing salons which adopted this moderne style did so to varying degrees, some adopting a more restrained style like that exhibited in the Muswell Hill Odeon cinema, while others, typically the department store salons, adopted a more luxurious and flamboyant style.

8 In 1929, Edmund Maxim, a prolific writer on design in the hairdressing trade journals, referred to the use of new materials in conjunction with modernist designs in 'Panelling materials for the modern hairdresser', *Hairdressers' Weekly Journal*, 48:2449 (30 March 1929), 119–120; and in 1935 he stated that 'these days [are characterised by the] lavish use of gleaming glass and bright metals for decorative purposes': E. Maxim, 'More modern materials for interior decoration', *Hairdressers' Weekly Journal*, 54:2771 (1 June 1935), 2593.

9 Elsewhere I have argued that an analysis of the hairdressing trade literature and the design of salons in this period can provide us with a key insight into the ways in which modernist discourses of design were interpreted and applied to an area which remained outside the strictures of modernist design *per se*: E. Gieben-Gamal, 'Gendered spaces: the design and display strategies of British hair salons in the 1920s and 1930s', unpublished MA dissertation, Royal College of Art, London, 1999.

10 Quoted B. Hillier, 'Diluted deco: the British affair with the modernistic', in B. Hillier and S. Escritt (eds), *Art Deco Style* (London: Phaidon Press, 1997), p. 181.

11 M. Featherstone, 'The body in consumer culture', in M. Featherstone, M. Hepworth and B. S. Turner (eds), *The Body, Social Process and Cultural Theory* (London: Sage, 1991), p. 180.

12 For a social and cultural account of the cosmetics industry in the nineteenth and twentieth centuries, see K. Peiss, 'Making up, making over. Cosmetics, consumer culture and women's identity', in V. de Grazia and E. Furlough (eds), *The Sex of Things. Gender and Consumer Culture in Historical Perspective* (Berkeley: University of California Press, 1996).

13 Featherstone, 'The body in consumer culture', p. 180; see also the discussion of the growing cooperation between advertisers and women's magazines in all areas of consumption in Cynthia White's *Women's Magazines 1693–1968* (London: Michael Joseph, 1970), pp. 113–15.

14 University of Glasgow archives, Records of the House of Fraser, newspaper (unidentified) cutting, 1921, HF2/15/5.

15 For an interesting account of the development of women's reading rooms in US nineteenth-century public libraries which explores the domesticisation of public space as a strategy for maintaining respectability, see Abigail A. Van Slyck, 'The lady and the library loafer. Gender and public space in Victorian America', *Wintethur Portfolio*, 31:4 (1996), 222–41.

16 For a discussion of the class implications of representations of women and the city, see J. Ryan, 'Women, modernity and the city', *Theory, Culture & Society*, 11 (1994), 35–63.

17 In 'Making up, making over', p. 311, K. Peiss has argued that women's expenditure on beauty treatments and cosmetics rose dramatically in the inter-war period, and that by the 1930s, make-up had become integral to self expression and the belief that identity was a purchasable style. Mass Observation surveys carried out in the late 1930s also suggest that women had, for some time, regarded hair care as an important part of their beauty regime, and that it was one of the last areas of expenditure to be surrendered in times of financial strain: University of Sussex, Mass Observation Archive, M-O A Directive, April 1939 – Personal Appearance, M-O A File Report, July 1939 – Personal Appearance Part 1 and M-O A File Report A10, December 1938 – Reactions to Advertising.

18 W. Dietrich, 'It's the master that makes the business', *Hairdresser & Beauty Trade*, 1:7 (25 November 1932), 10–11.

19 R. G. Langworthy, 'Ten points that make a prosperous business', *Hairdresser & Beauty Trade*, 1:8 (December 1932), 9.

20 *Ibid.* (italics added).

21 Although the advert is for a beauty salon rather than a hairdressing salon, it nonetheless epitomises the ideas promoted in the hairdressing trade literature.

22 A. W. J., 'Marble in the saloon', *Hairdressers' Weekly Journal*, 40:2061 (22 October 1921), 2017.

23 Merton, 'Beauty parlour management', 1893.

24 E. Maxim 'Panelling materials for the modern hairdresser. Compositions, compressed wall-board, three-ply, laminated woods and walnut veneers. Interesting developments foreshadowed by new metal processes', *Hairdressers' Weekly Journal*, 48:2449 (30 March 1929), 1120.

25 C. Cox, *Good Hair Days: A History of British Hairstyling* (London: Quartet Books, 1999), p. 76.

26 A. W. J., 'Hygienic fitting-up of the salon', *Hairdressers' Weekly Journal*, 41:2090 (13 May 1922), 942.

27 *Ibid.*, 941.

28 See E. Lupton and J. A. Miller, *The Bathroom, the Kitchen and the Aesthetics of Waste: A Process of Elimination* (Cambridge, MA: Princetown Architectural Press, 1992), p. 19.

29 Advert for INECTO hairdressing salons, *The Queen*, 157:4086 (15 April 1925), xviii.

30 *Ibid.*, advertisement for Dorothy Stuart.

31 Cox, *Good Hair Days*, pp. 38, 55.

32 Gilbert A. Foan, *The Art and Craft of Hairdressing: A Standard and Complete Guide to the Technique of Modern Hairdressing, Manicure, Massage and Beauty Culture*, ed. N. E. B. Wolters, 4th edn (London: New Era Publishing, 1958), p. 141.

33 See, e.g., Adrian Forty, *Objects of Desire: Design and Society since 1750* (London: Thames & Hudson, 1995); and Lupton and Miller, *The Bathroom, the Kitchen and the Aesthetics of Waste*. Literature on suburban housing in the inter-war period also discusses the question of scientific management in the home: see, e.g., Helena Barrett and John Phillips, *Suburban Style: The British Home 1840 – 1960* (London: Macdonald & Co., 1987) and *Little Palaces. The Suburban House in North London, 1919–1939*, Exhibition catalogue (Middlesex Polytechnic, 1987).

34 Among the key proponents of scientific management was Christine Frederick, whose book *Scientific Management in the Home* was first published in the USA in 1915 and then in Britain in 1920. During the nineteenth century, Catherine Beecher had been a prominent proponent of 'domestic economy' and household reform in the USA, publishing a *Treatise on Domestic Economy* (Boston, MA: Marsh, Capen, Lyon & Webb, 1841), and *The American Woman's Home* (New York: J. B. Ford & Co., 1869). Beecher's books provide an important backdrop to the development of scientific management and pre-empted many of the principles of modern kitchen design.

35 P. Sparke, *As Long as It's Pink: The Sexual Politics of Taste* (London: Pandora, 1995), p. 85.

36 Ruth Schwartz Cowan also remarked on this, writing: 'cleaning the bathroom sink was not just cleaning, but an exercise for the maternal instincts, protecting the family from disease': R. S. Cowan, 'Two washes in the morning and a bridge party at night: the American housewife between the wars', *Women's Studies*, 3:2 (1976), 151.

37 Before moving to the newly built suburbs, the lower-middle-class woman would have been used to a scullery; a plumbed in bathroom was also a novel experience for most.

38 Mary Gwynne Howell, 'Good housekeeping – electricity and the housewife', *Ideal Home*, 6:4 (April 1925), 310.

39 J. F. Saunders, 'Newer aids of electrical power', *Ideal Home*, 11:2 (February 1930), 106.

40 A. W. J., 'Hygienic fitting-up of the salon', *Hairdressers' Weekly Journal*, 41:2090 (13 May 1922).

41 See Sparke, *As Long as It's Pink*, p. 85.

42 J. Kinchin, 'Interiors: nineteenth-century essays on the "masculine" and the "feminine" room', in P. Kirkham (ed.), *The Gendered Object* (Manchester: Manchester University Press, 1996), p. 21.

43 See Lupton and Miller, *The Bathroom, the Kitchen and the Aesthetics of Waste*.

44 Forty, *Objects of Desire*, p. 180.

45 It was not until the 1950s that the open-plan system fully replaced the cubicle system.

46 In an article entitled 'The business aspect of household economy', Mary Gwynne Howell states: 'Haphazardness has given way to scientific household management, which calls for powers of organisation and execution such as are found in any other business': *Ideal Home*, 6:5 (May 1925), 416.

47 Mica Nava goes on to state that the market and consumption can never be fully contained and that the anarchic nature of desire can never be fully managed: 'Modernity tamed?', 15.

48 The literature on retailing in the inter-war period is fairly sparse, but theoretical models for understanding consumption, in particular female consumption, are dominated by a view of women as passive victims of their own irrationality, or of manipulation by advertising: see, e.g., Stuart Ewen, *Captains of Consciousness: Advertising and the Social Roots of the Consumer Culture* (New York: McGraw Hill, 1976); and Rosalind Williams, *Dream Worlds: Mass Consumption in Late 19th Century France* (Berkeley: University of California Press, 1982). However, in *The World of Goods: Towards an Anthropology of Consumption*, 2nd edn (London: Routledge, 1996), p. vii, Mary

Douglas and Baron Isherwood suggest that the traditional dichotomy of 'rational' and 'irrational' consumption is a gross simplification which denies the complexity of consumer behaviour. Mica Nava, in 'Modernity tamed?', 6–7, also suggests that consumer behaviour needs to be understood both as a rational and irrational activity.

49 A. Light, *Forever England. Femininity, Literature and Conservatism Between the Wars* (London: Routledge, 1991), p. 10; see also B. Hillier, *The Style of the Century*, 2nd edn (London: Herbert Press, 1998), p. 94.

8 ✧ Pragmatism and pluralism: the interior decoration of the *Queen Mary*

Fiona Walmsley

MUCH OF THE LITERATURE on luxury liners, their histories and their interiors is style-oriented, focusing on the liners as visual icons of modernity.[1] This account of the *Queen Mary*, in contrast, seeks to unpack the process that resulted in its design, looking in particular at the conflicting views of its designers and of the Cunard representatives responsible for its commission. In addition I describe the way in which ideas about the market influenced the appearance of its interiors.

Cunard commissioned the *Queen Mary* in 1930. Several factors led to its decision to do so. Firstly, a change in America's immigration policy had brought about diminished earnings for the shipping companies from the steerage market, as approximately one-third of their business was derived from Europeans travelling westwards.[2] This change in immigration policy forced the steamship companies to redefine their markets, requiring that they find a new type of client. By 1930, 80 per cent of the travellers were American. These were not the pre-war 'rich' but a new type of traveller – Americans with European ancestry or with knowledge and experience of Europe gained during the First World War. Secondly, the Wall Street crash of 1929 brought a fall in shipping-line freight and passenger revenues. Thirdly, other European countries launched liners to attract the new American customers then travelling eastwards.[3] These European liners directly threatened Britain's pre-eminent position in the marketplace for the transatlantic crossing.

Cunard's management decided to change its operational policy and to reduce its weekly three-ship express service to a two-ship service. The

two-ship service, however, could be implemented only by commissioning ships of great size and power that would be financially viable.[4] These
'super-liners' were to travel backwards and forwards from Southampton
via Cherbourg to New York. Commentators often refer to the inter-war
period as the golden era of transatlantic travel, as the European super-
liners competed with each other for passengers. The emphasis was on the
speed at which the liners, competing for the 'Blue Riband', crossed the
Atlantic and the conspicuous display of their interior furnishings,
particularly those aimed at the first-class traveller.

   The architectural press of the 1930s chose to all-but ignore the *Queen
Mary*. Instead it concentrated on the *Orion*, the *Orcades* and the
Normandie, despite Winston Churchill's description of the *Queen Mary* as
both the pride of Britain and the symbol of Britain's recovery from the
Depression.[5] As far as the architectural press was concerned, there was
nothing to be proud of in the *Queen Mary*. For those journalists the ship's
interiors represented a missed opportunity: here, they believed, had been
a chance to promote modernism, one that really *could* have stood for
Britain's recovery from the Depression. Because the idea of the ocean
liner was so symbolic to followers of the modern movement, as had been
clearly expressed by Le Corbusier in *Towards a New Architecture*, the conservative interior decoration of the *Queen Mary* could not have been more
disappointing.[6] An article in *The Architect & Building News* described the
general effect as 'mild, but expensive, vulgarity', and concluded: 'The
architecture of Queen Mary is, on the whole, a testimony of indifferent
taste and feeble imagination; that it will give almost universal satisfaction
to those who travel in it is perhaps a matter for congratulation, but
hardly a happy augury for British art.'[7] Throughout the period leading up
to *Queen Mary*'s launch, the architectural press had expressed concern
that the ship's interiors would follow a historical theme, 'a Jacobearia, a
Georgia or a Tudoria?'[8] It pointed out that Cunard was in competition
with foreign ship-owners with the freedom to interpret contemporary
taste in their ships' interiors.[9] Associated design professionals had
concerns that the 'New Cunarder' would follow nineteenth-century traditions, remarking that 'Decorations, enrichments, mouldings, have been
added in excess to tempt the patronage of the traveller'. The Design and
Industries' Association article 'Shipshape design' argued that now was the
time to drop the 'period pilot' and give architects and interior decorators

an opportunity to show that English ships could be an expression of the age, manifesting as much 'genius' in their interior decoration as in their exterior design.[10] The architectural press used the Orient Line's *Orion* as the model with which to compare the *Queen Mary*.[11] They praised the former for its overall scheme of design, implemented under the supervision of the New Zealand architect Brian O'Rorke who had designed all of the furniture and the light fittings. Here, at last, they claimed, was a ship's interior decoration that had no historical references and which followed the aesthetic standards of the modern movement.[12]

This was the first example of a commissioned architect having sole responsibility for the integrated design of a liner's passenger accommodation. While architectural journalists looked to the *Orion* for their comparison, other commentators looked to the French *Normandie*.[13] That liner was part of the French strategy of fostering the prestige luxury trades with the help of subsidies from the government of France. It gave French craftsmen an opportunity to undertake commissions for one of the country's national symbols.[14]

Cunard tendered for all aspects of the building of the *Queen Mary*, and, as Colin Anderson has shown, the company worked within the British tradition of using furnishing companies to provide the shipbuilder with decorative schemes.[15] John Brown & Company carried out the exterior construction.[16] Together the furnishing companies and John Brown provided both the engineered aspects of the internal environment of the ship and the more domestic settings. Cunard took responsibility for the decoration of the public rooms, and both the architects and the contracted firms of decorators worked under Cunard's supervision and to Cunard's designs. John Brown & Company was responsible for the tendering and contracting of the decorating firms that worked on the passenger accommodation, but not on the special staterooms. The two main characters involved in the ship's interior decoration were not, as might have been expected, the New York architect B. W. Morris (of Morris & O'Connor) and A. J. Davis, of the English architects Mewes & Davis, both of whom had already worked for Cunard, but rather Sir Percy Bates, Cunard's company chairman, and Ernest Leach, the eventual head of furnishings at Cunard.[17] (Morris had been the architect–interior designer responsible for the Cunard Building at 25 Broadway, New York, and Davis had had previous experience of both naval and architectural projects for Cunard, including the interior of the *Aquitania*, built in 1914.[18])

Cunard set out the requirements for the *Queen Mary* in a document entitled 'Q.S.T.S. No 534 General Particulars'.[19] The number of passengers in each class and the necessary crew numbers associated dictated the overall design of the ship. Cunard was aware that an increase in the allocation of space in the public and private areas was an important consideration for attracting passengers and this was used to differentiate between the three classes of passenger – i.e. cabin, or first class; tourist, or second class; and third class.[20] Several of Cunard's departments had responsibilities with regard to the ship's internal decoration. The naval architect's office, in conjunction with the furnishing and passenger department, supervised the implementation of the interiors at John Brown & Company under the direction of the shipbuilding committee.[21]

Individually numbered and area-specific designs and drawings were sent from the naval architect's office in Liverpool to John Brown in Clydebank. Sir Percy Bates had ultimate responsibility for the interior decoration of the ship and thus had the final approval for the architectural projects undertaken by Morris, which were interpreted by Davis in the form of drawings. He took an active interest in the inspection of the sample cabins which had been constructed at John Brown's yard; he had the final veto on the commissioned artists' work; and he wrote outlining the Cunard board's relationship with Frank Pick from the Council of Art and Industry.[22]

As superintendent of the furnishing department Leach, too, played a major role in establishing a design philosophy at Cunard.[23] He was responsible for setting out the initial proposals for the use of an outside advisor and, if one were to be appointed, for the definition of that role; he also suggested artists and architects for the project.[24] Furthermore, Leach reminded Sir Percy Bates that the directors had had the final say over several of the successful liners, recently completed. It was Leach who presented to the Shipbuilding Committee the preliminary drawings and models of the decorative schemes for the public spaces.[25]

In response to the committee's general criticism of the overly detailed ornamentation in all the designs, Leach observed that this was perhaps an impression arising from the small scale of the drawings and models, and that it would not be so marked in the actual work. He also strongly advised Sir Percy Bates against using Morris's early designs for the smoke room, the American Bar, and the card and drawing rooms, all of which had been worked in a traditional manner.[26] Leach visited the Exhibition of British Art and Industry at Burlington House as Cunard's representative, and wrote a report to accompany the annotated exhibition catalogue for the shipbuilding committee.[27] Additionally, Leach assisted Morris in the selection of works of art for the liner, and in that capacity he wrote the rejection letter to Duncan Grant, explaining why the directors had rejected his painting *The Flower Gatherers.*[28] Finally, in a memo to the chairman, he wrote what appears to have been the design philosophy for both the Cunard Line and the *Queen Mary.*[29] The memo also outlined the need for the interior decoration to be both modern and conservative. However, Cunard interpreted 'modern' to mean the inclusion of up-to-date conveniences for the cabin-class traveller, among them individually controlled ventilation systems, private bathrooms and/or toilets attached, electrical heating and accessible telephones and call bells.[30]

The construction of the ship was not without problems, the most dramatic of which was the lay-off of the workforce at John Brown's Clydebank yard five months away from the original launch date. Cunard's depreciation policy failed them. The workforce remained out for twenty-seven months. Throughout the lay-off Sir Percy Bates was busy negotiating governmental intervention and financial subsidy, negotiations that eventually led to the takeover of the White Star Line.[31] Neville Chamberlain, the chancellor of the exchequer, used the merger to strengthen Britain's position on the North Atlantic.[32] Work resumed in early April 1934, with emphasis placed on the recasting of the passenger accommodation, which commenced the following June. B. W. Morris, a personal friend of Sir Percy Bates, had been appointed in 1931, not as consultant architect but in the more diluted role of personal advisor to Sir Percy.[33] It is thought that Sir Percy wanted an American on the design team to give an insight on the likes and dislikes of the large number of Americans expected to travel on the ship.[34] He was pleased with the appointment but was very aware that having an American in the role of personal advisor was a delicate matter and he asked specifically that no publicity be given to the appointment in New York.[35] Morris travelled to England at the beginning of the project and conferred with other arts-related professionals. These included Kenneth Clarke, director of the National Gallery; Grey Wornum, an architect associated with the Royal Institute of British Architects; Frank Pick, head of the British Council of Art and Industry; and Dudley Tooth of Cunard's shipbuilding committee.[36] Much of the collaboration was over the commissioning of artists. Clarke is said to have recommended McKnight Kauffer; Wornum recommended James Woodford, Morris Lambert, George Ramon, Bainbridge Copnall, Jan Juta and Norman Forest; while Tooth recommended Duncan Grant, Rex Whistler, Paul Nash, Edward Wadsworth and Stanley Spencer.[37] Several of the artists suggested were actually commissioned. Leach assisted Morris in the selection of the works of art, but the final veto on all the commissioned work was with Sir Percy Bates.

Following Morris's visit to England, Cunard's directors commissioned him to undertake architectural projects in relation to the ship. He had already made some criticism of the original plans.[38] Davis in turn was commissioned to prepare scale and full-size drawings of Morris's decorative schemes. Davis's role was to interpret Morris's drawings for the various Cunard departments involved in the interior decoration of the ship.[39] The drawings had to be approved by the naval architect's office, the furnishing department, the shipbuilding committee and, finally, by Sir Percy Bates, before they could be sent to John Brown & Company, who then supervised the work of the sub-contractors.

Morris and Leach looked to contemporary manufacturers for the design sources for the furnishings of the ship.[40] They obtained samples from reputable companies such as Heals & Sons in London.[41] Some designs were altered slightly to make them more 'suitable and comfortable'. The designs were then forwarded to the decorating firms, via John Brown,[42] all of which worked concurrently in their respective areas during the 'fit' of the ship. They included Waring & Gillow (see figure 22); Hampton & Sons; Trollope & Sons; Bath Cabinet Makers; White Allom; Maple & Company; and Martyn & Company in connection with the cabin-class public rooms and communal spaces. Fifty-four cabins were designated as 'special staterooms' (see figure 23), responsibility for the design of which going to several of those companies.[43]

Waring & Gillow, Maple & Company and Trollope & Sons also worked extensively in the tourist-class accommodation in conjunction with local firms, such as Wylie and Lochhead. Additionally Maple &

Company was contracted extensively for the third-class public areas in conjunction with McIntosh & Company. Interested parties wrote to Cunard putting forward both suggestions for the style of the interiors and the artist or architect they felt should be commissioned. The suggestions ranged from adopting the naval atmosphere of seventeenth- and eighteenth-century sailing ships, furnishing one of the saloons and dedicating it to Thomas Gainsborough, RA, to the adoption of modern movement decoration instead of period styles.[44] J. H. Early, a shareholder, brought to the attention of the Cunard board the Design and Industries' Association article 'Shipshape design', and it was passed, in turn, to Morris in New York.

On a political level governmental offices and national bodies wrote to Cunard to promote British manufacturers who were engaged in both industrial and rural production. Frank Pick, acting for the Council of Art and Industry (CAI), tried to engage Cunard in a working relationship with the CAI. He envisaged the CAI's role as advisory, ensuring that the ship would become a 'travelling exhibition of British art and design'.[45] Cunard viewed its relationship with both Pick and the CAI as informal. Although Pick had been involved initially in the selection of dining equipment, china, earthenware, glass and cutlery, he had serious concerns about the equipment, the furniture and the overall decoration of the dining room. Pick and Cunard differed considerably in their approaches to the overall design. Pick hoped to design the dining room equipment in conjunction with the furniture and fittings, but Cunard felt no need to make decisions until after the equipment had been designed.[46] Pick made various suggestions, ranging from a complete re-designing of some areas to pictorial treatment of others, and he felt that this harmonising process should be carried out in the 'modern manner'.[47] Cunard politely ignored most of his suggestions, and when it began to place orders for the equipment elsewhere Pick was in the embarrassing position of having had a few only of his own and the Council's suggestions taken up.[48] In concluding his affairs with Cunard Pick wrote: 'We do not seem to have been effective towards establishing a modern standard of design in the ship unhappily.'[49] Pick had discovered that there was overall a lack of coordination – not just of the dining-room but of the whole process of creating the interior decoration. Cunard had prior experience of public criticism for its lack of coordination in ship interiors, the issue having already been raised by external as well as internal commentators. Pick wrote to Cunard asking who had the responsibility for the detailed coordination of the dining room. In its letter of response Cunard set out the procedure it was following to implement Morris's designs. The letter reveals that the arrangements were working well until Davis had been taken ill six months earlier.[50] This was a critical time for Cunard. The interior 'fit' was underway. Davis's illness left a gap in the supervision of the designs being implemented. Cunard was aware of the gap and considered bringing in a 'temporary assistant', such as Oliver Hill, to supervise the situation.[51] Mewes and Davis suggested that J. C. Whipp, a colleague of Davis, take over the supervisory role.[52] Meanwhile Morris, at the request of Cunard, travelled to and fro between Britain and New York in the attempt to oversee the situation.

Two months after Pick had aired his concerns about the lack of coordination for the dining room Morris expressed his own, mainly in connection with the lack of implementation of his designs. The list of items for which his suggestions had not been accepted was growing

22 The Forward Cocktail Lounge of the *Queen Mary*

23 A special stateroom of the *Queen Mary*

24 The Verandah Grill of the *Queen Mary*

longer, as was the case with Pick's.[53] Morris realised that Cunard lacked
the ability to coordinate the design either of the ship overall or of its
specific areas. To overcome this lack of coordination, he suggested to
Cunard that all the public rooms and the cabin-class staterooms
should have a consultant to ensure that the materials for furnishings and
upholstery related to the finish of the respective rooms. He recommended, for business reasons, that 'cultivated feminine thought should
have expression', and proposed a list of ladies, many of whom already
had contracts with Cunard as decorative artists, to work in conjunction
with the firms which had tendered for each specific area.[54] Many of Morris's suggestions were not accepted by Cunard, though there is evidence
that Cunard followed his recommendation of Anna and Doris Zinkeisen
(see figure 24).[55] Nevertheless Morris continued to emphasise the importance of requesting the artists' advice and opinions on each area. He
wrote to Cunard throughout the year of the 'fit' expressing his distress
and concern over the deviations from his original proposals. He reiterated the need for experts to be involved in the selection of the furnishings
and fittings for both public and private areas.[56] His correspondence with
Cunard reveals that Morris became disillusioned with the overall design
of the ship: his ideas were ignored and, with Davis ill and because of his
own physical distance from the work itself, he lacked direct control of the
situation.

John Brown & Company also had difficulty with Cunard's decision-
making by committee.[57] The construction company had recommended a
small committee with a few directors, to include Morris, Leach and the
naval architect Paterson, but Cunard reduced the committee members to
four. S. J. Pigott, a senior member of staff at John Brown, had visited the
Normandie, and then wrote privately to Morris. He expressed his surprise
at finding out, from Paterson, that Morris was responsible for the coordination of the 'various decoration' of the *Queen Mary*.[58] Morris's
response is reiterated in a second letter from Pigott:

> I confirm receipt this morning of your night letter telegram, reading as
> follows: – Coordination weak account lack of single authority witness
> Committee Brocklebank Morris Davis Whipp Leach stop Brocklebank
> informally suggests return November too late best results but immediate
> sailing impractical account business here stop Have no further commit-
> ment for services letter follows confidential. B. W. Morris.[59]

Morris's disappointment is clear in his final sentence. In a letter of response to Duncan Grant he confirms that from June 1935, the time when Whipp had begun to take a more active role, he had little to do with the shipbuilding committee and its decision-making process.[60] Whipp was much more conservative in his approach. He undermined Morris's decisions in relation to the choice of artists and he conveyed to Cunard's board of directors his opinion that most of the suggestions put forward by the various artists were not in harmony with the board's intentions.[61] His report dismissed much of the art work that had already been commissioned and expressed his wish to have artists redirect their efforts. He also felt that artists had been given 'unlimited liberty to interfere in the decorative treatment of the rooms', a view very much against Morris's recommendations.[62] Duncan Grant originally had been commissioned to design the panels and other features for the first-class lounge, including the carpets and curtains, and he had given advice on the textiles.[63] Regarding the recommendation of Vanessa Bell, Whipp, in his typically conservative manner, wrote: 'The suggestion that Mrs Vanessa Bell should design the carpets and curtains and direct the general colour scheme for this room gives me serious concern.' [64] The ship's interiors expressed Cunard's contradictory approach to interior decoration. The directors wanted the interiors to be both modern and traditional,[65] and the combination of grand hotel and English country house allowed them to realise their philosophy.[66]

The idea of the English country house was evoked for the American market in the literature's treatment of cabin-class accommodation. By emphasising the ships's interior Cunard hoped to keep passengers's attention away from the external climatic factors, particularly the swells of the Atlantic. Cunard realised that the ship did not posses the innovative lines of her main rival the *Normandie*,[67] and in order to compensate for this the American campaign placed great emphasis on British sailing traditions:

> In all that touches the building and the navigation of ships, the British tradition is inexorable … a code of principles founded in the hard-learned lore of the race, made clear and definite through 96 years of Cunard White Star Line. But the British tradition will distinguish the 'Queen Mary' in another sense. The way in which you are served tea, the intuition of the stewardess in suggesting milady's breakfast, the thought-

fulness of the gardener in bringing her a corsage for evening ... all this is part of it. These men and women share the same heritage. Service is to them a life-long career, carried on through successive generations ...[68]

The *Queen Mary* was the first liner to rename first-class accommodation 'cabin class', a change of name that enabled Cunard to sell more berths. Other liners, including the *Normandie*, followed suit, and they became known as 'cabin ships'.[69] There had previously been a cabin class on liners, the class, that is, between first and second on a four-class ship, as the *Queen Mary* had been in the original design.[70] The change meant, in effect, that Cunard could charge a cabin-class rate of $262 – $8 less than the first-class rate. This was an effective way for Cunard to undercut its competitors. The 'cabin-class' designation represented the luxurious accommodation in the larger, faster ships of all the transatlantic lines.[71]

Cunard advertised to the widest possible market as the social divisions within the liners changed. No longer did the thousands of steerage passengers provide the profits for the shipping lines while supplementing the prestige passengers in first class. The pluralism of the decor in each class related directly to the types of passenger to whom Cunard anticipated catering: 'cabin', the most prestigious and luxurious, catered for the celebrity market; 'tourist' catered for business and commercial travellers; and 'third' catered for 'ordinary' people, a new class of traveller, of which teachers and students were typical.[72]

An important consideration was the amount of space for both public and passenger accommodation allocated to each class, which were divided vertically. Cabin-class public and passenger accommodation was allocated mid-ship, with tourist-class accommodation at the stern and third in the bow. The reasons for this vertical division were two fold: first, the effects of the ship pitching were least noticeable in the mid ship area and most pronounced in the bow; and, second, it helped guard against interaction across social classes. Additionally wooden barriers between the different classes physically reinforced the vertical social divisions. They also ensured complete segregation during the embarkation and disembarkation of the passengers as well as throughout the voyage.

The *Queen Mary* was designed with twelve decks which ran from the uppermost sports' deck to the hold, via the sun, promenade and main decks, and decks A–G. The highest continuous deck was designated A;

decks B, C and D also ran the full length of the ship. In cabin class the principal public rooms were on the promenade deck, while its passenger accommodation was on A and B decks outboard. In tourist class the smoking room was on the promenade deck and the lounge on the main deck. Third-class passengers were provided with a garden lounge on the main deck, a smoking room on A deck and a lounge on B deck. All dining rooms were on C deck. The kitchens were situated between the cabin-class and the tourist-class dining rooms. Cunard was able to expand the passenger capacity of the different classes. Crew would be moved from their cabins when the number of bookings necessitated extra passenger accommodation.[73] The crew's accommodation was behind tourist-class 'aft' and in front of third-class 'for'ard.

The shipping companies promoted the luxurious features of all areas of the liner. To fill the passenger accommodation Cunard provided several choices for travellers so that all 'types' would be catered for. Each class had its own decor, each area having been designed to appeal to the type of consumer Cunard placed within it. The accommodation was divided into public and private spaces, the public rooms being the areas for the passengers to mingle and be 'seen' in. Cabin class had conspicuous public rooms – these areas which Cunard's publicity department depicted as designed specifically to allow passengers to escape from their land-based life and enjoy the distractions of life aboard ship.

The transatlantic crossing took approximately five days, during which time the passengers were encapsulated, both physically and socially, in a contained vertical world. This division was reinforced by the use of lifts, stair-wells and wooden barriers which ensured that passengers mixed only in those social circles familiar to them on land. Cunard's conservative approach to the design process reinforced the notion that aesthetic decisions had been led by the perceived tastes of the market. The cabin-class interiors combined the styles of the modern grand hotel and the traditional English country house The tourist-class interiors were, in the main, traditional, while allowing for the odd intrusion of modern elements. In contrast, the third-class interiors were very utilitarian in their design and finish.

The pluralism of the interior decoration reflected Cunard's intention that passengers in every class should enjoy the different aspects of the ship's interior. It worked on two levels. First, all consumers paid for what they wanted in terms of comfort, space and service. Second, within each class, Cunard offered a variety of interiors to suit a range of customer requirements. This was particularly evident in the decoration of the cabin class, decreasingly so in the other two classes.

New technology was used as a selling point for all three classes. For example, cabin-class accommodation included a passenger-controlled ventilation system, telephones in every cabin, en-suite bathrooms supplied with hot-and-cold fresh water, sea-water facilities for plunge or shower baths and the use of electrical equipment – reading and dressing lamps, clocks, sockets for curling irons and supplementary heaters; additionally, the individual cabins had a greater floor area than the other two classes, with no need for upper berths. In tourist class as well as a general improvement in the decor, private toilets were introduced to raise the standard. Cunard considered the provision of good beds, hot-and-cold running water, good lighting, fresh air and practicable wardrobe space attractive to the 'best' kind of third-class passenger.[74] Leach's design philosophy, followed by Cunard, was in keeping with company policy – 'A foundation of conservatism in finance with the readiness to exploit the best of twentieth century ideas in administration, but firm resistance to the merely fashionable and ephemeral, attendant with frequent change . . .'.[75]

From conception to completion the *Queen Mary* was a commercial undertaking to ensure that Cunard stayed in the competitive North Atlantic market. The interiors reflected a combination of modern grand hotel and traditional English country house to attract American travellers, and the liner came to symbolise the regeneration of Great Britain. Cunard kept firm control of all pre-launch publicity material, so the press had no knowledge of what the liner contained until journalists were invited to the 'Organised Press Parties'.[76] All the sub-contractors and architects involved had signed contracts at the tender stage, and in doing so signed over to Cunard the rights to their specifications, models and drawings; Cunard even reserved the right to allow any reproductions of the sub-contracters' work for their own publicity material.[77] Similarly, the artists commissioned signed over copyright of their work to the company for illustrative reproduction and advertising purposes.[78] In his speech at the launch, George V referred to the *Queen Mary* as 'the stateliest ship now in being',[79] a phrase that Cunard lifted and used in its publicity material.[80]

The contemporary media lauded and promoted the ship, and little real criticism was forthcoming. The architectural press was the least warm in its response. Rather than criticise the ship, however, it chose to all-but ignore its launch. Cunard employed the traditional British shipbuilding method for the commission and creation of the interior decoration of the ship. Its ambivalence during the design process with regard to the role and the suggestions of its in-house architect Morris, and those of associated design professionals, was apparent. Cunard chose to have an 'informal' relationship with those whose opinions it sought, reflecting its lack of commitment to design. The lack of overall supervision was exacerbated by Davis's illness during the 'fit'. Decisions were taken by committee, a process found difficult by all those who were trying to implement ideas. The process allowed the individual managers to impose their own opinions on the style and format of the interior decoration. The ship was criticised for its Odeon–American-English suburban interiors. Yet from a financial perspective Cunard ran the ship successfully;[81] and one factor contributing to that success was the prestige the *Queen Mary* gained by winning the Blue Riband from its rival the *Normandie*.[82]

The *Queen Mary* was a juxtaposition of ship and hotel. Cunard's emphasis was on speed and technology, however, rather than on ideas of leisure, comfort and traditional service, all of which were linked with the metaphor of the hotel. Cunard use the term 'modern' in relation to the ship's technology, and it supplied all three classes with modern materials and modern conveniences, in the form of sanitation. Leach's policy document set out the dangers of the modern movement, i.e. 'the feeling of cubism'.[83] In reality, however, the notion of a 'rational' interior did not fit with Cunard's philosophy of interior decoration. Any potential cohesiveness of the interiors appears to have been lost in the pragmatic application of the design process, as Morris's schemes were transferred from drawingboard to reality, and the result was a set of interiors characterised by a high level of stylistic pluralism, though realised with a high level of pragmatism.

Notes

1   J. Steele, *The Queen Mary* (London: Phaidon, 1995); W. Miller, *The Great Luxury Liners 1927–1954: A Photographic Record* (New York: Dover Publications, 1991).

2   J. Maxtone-Graham, *The Only Way to Cross* (New York: Macmillan, 1972), p. 152.

3   H. Johnson, *The Cunard Story* (London: Whittet Books, 1987), p. 97.

4   F. E. Hyde, *Cunard and the North Atlantic 1840–1973* (London: Macmillan, 1975), p. 203.

5   The Right Hon. Winston Churchill, PC, 'Queen of the seas', *The Strand Magazine* (May 1936), 42–53.

6   Le Corbusier, *Towards A New Architecture*, trans. Frederick Etchells (London: Architectural Press, 1923), pp. 96–7.

7   Anon., 'R.M.S. "Queen Mary"', *The Architect & Building News*, 29 May 1936, 240–5.

8   Anon., Notes and Topics: 'The new Cunarder', *Architect's Journal* (December 1933), 732.

9   *Ibid.*, 813.

10 Traveller, 'Shipshape design', *DIA Quarterly* (May 1931), 9–12.

11 W. Tatton Brown, 'Architecture afloat the "Orion" sets a new course', *Architectural Review* (October 1935), 130–9.

12 J. E. Blake, 'Fifth in line', *Design*, 65 (1954), 9–11.

13 Glasgow University Business Archive (hereafter GUBA), Letter by J. S. Pigott, 1 August 1935.

14 M. Battersby, *The Decorative Thirties* (London: Studio Vista, 1969), p. 25.

15 C. Anderson, 'Ship interiors: when the breakthrough came', *Architectural Review*, 844 (June 1967), 449–52.

16 Hyde, *Cunard and the North Atlantic*, p. 204.

17 Anon., Notes and Topics: 'Queen Mary', *Architect's Journal* (April 1936), 649.

18 A. Forsyth, 'Floating palaces: British liners of the 1930s', *The Thirties' Society Journal*, 4 (1984), 10–15.

19 GUBA, Quadruple Screw Turbine Ship/Steamer No. 534, General Particulars.

20 *Ibid.*

21 N. Potter and J. Frost, *The Queen Mary, Her Inception and History* (London: George G. Harrap & Co., 1961), p. 47.

22 GUBA, Letter by Sir Percy Bates, 18 November 1931 and 10 November 1934.

23 Liverpool University Archives (hereafter LUA), Memo by E. Leach, completion date 28 November 1930.

24 *Ibid.*

25 LUA, Extracts from Minutes of the Shipbuilding Committee held on 8 and 9 December 1930.

26 LUA, Memo by E. Leach, 19 February 1932.

27 LUA, Memo by E. Leach, 12 January 1935.

28 LUA, Letter by E. Leach, 21 September 1935.

29 LUA, Memo by E. Leach, 18 December 1930.

30 GUBA, Quadruple Screw Turbine Ship/Steamer No. 534, General Particulars.

31 Hyde, *Cunard and the North Atlantic,* pp. 214–15.

32 Johnson, *The Cunard Story,* p. 105.

33 LUA, Extracts from Minutes of Meeting of Executive Committee held on 11 March 1931, 163.

34 N. Potter and J. Frost, *The Queen Mary,* p. 47.

35 LUA, Letter by Sir Percy Bates, 26 March 1931.

36 Anon., '"Queen Mary", a floating gallery of art', *Art Digest,* 1 May 1936, p. 20.

37 See the Southampton City Art Gallery catalogue, by A. Forsyth, to accompany the exhibition 'Art on the Liners: A Celebration of Elegance at Sea', May–June 1986; see also LUA, S.S. 'Queen Mary', names of artists under consideration and possible allocation of work (undated).

38 LUA, Re.: Steamship, No. 534, by B. W. Morris, 10 June 1931.

39 LUA, Memo by E. Leach and G. Paterson, 29 September 1931.

40 LUA, Memo by E. Leach, 12 January 1935.

41 GUBA, Letter by John Brown & Company, 16 July 1935.

42 LUA, Notes by B. W. Morris of meeting at Clydebank, 6 June 1935.

43 GUBA, Letter by John Brown & Company, 2 July 1935.

44 LUA, D42/C3/381 Suggestions as to the general style of decoration (undated); LUA, Letter by J. H. Early, 4 June 1931.

45 LUA, D42/C3/377, Letter by F. Pick, 24 May 1934.

46 LUA, Letters between Sir T. Brocklebank and F. Pick (various dates).

47 LUA, Letter by F. Pick, 31 December 1934.

48 LUA, Letter by Sir T. Brocklebank, 4 November 1935.

49 LUA, Letter by F. Pick, 24 December 1935; LUA, Extract from letter sent by Sir Ashley Sparks to Sir Percy Bates, 26 March 1931; GUBA, Letter by S. J. Pigott, 1 August 1935.

50 LUA, Letter by Sir T Brocklebank, 22 March 1935.

51 LUA, Letter by H. J. Flewitt, 22 January 1935.

52 LUA, Letter by Mewes and Davies, 25 January 1935.

53 LUA, Letter by B. W. Morris, 19 July 1935.

54 LUA, Memo by B. W. Morris, 14 June 1935; LUA, Letter and lists by B. W. Morris, 27 June 1935.

55 LUA, Letter by Sir Percy Bates, 2 August 1935.

56 LUA, Memo by B. W. Morris, 1 June 1935.

57 GUBA, Report for the Clydebank Committee, 30 January 1935.

58 GUBA, Letter by S. J. Pigott, 1 August 1935.

59 GUBA, Letter by S. J. Pigott, 22 August 1935.

60 LUA, Letter by B. W. Morris, 24 February 1936.

61 LUA, Letter by J. C. Whipp, 9 September 1935.

62 *Ibid.*

63 LUA, Copy of accounts relating to Duncan Grant's designs, 30 May 1936.

64 LUA, Letter by J. C. Whipp, 9 September 1935.

65 Anon., 'Passenger accommodation', *The Shipbuilder & Marine Engine Builder* (June 1936), 122–61.

66 B. Dennison. '534 and all that: Shades of the Waldorf', *Architect's Journal* (January 1934), 149–56; *New York Times*, 31 May 1936; Merseyside Maritime Museum Archive (hereafter MMMA) Publicity Leaflet 'The Stateliest Ship Now In Being' (undated).

67 *The New York Times.* 31 May 1936.

68 Advertisement, *New Yorker*, 30 May 1936.

69 Maxtone-Graham, *The Only Way to Cross*, p. 320.

70 LUA, D42/C3/292. Letter by H. J. Flewitt, 11 March 1931.

71 Hyde, *Cunard and the North Atlantic*, Chapter 8.

72 Conversations between the author and E. Swindle Hurst, archivist for Thomas Cook, in London, and Ted Scull in New York, autumn 1990.

73 LUA, Memo by G. Paterson, Q.S.T.S., no 534, 10 April 1934.

74 LUA, D42/C3/405, Report on Inspection of Sample Cabins, 20 November 1934.

75 LUA, Memo by E. Leach to chairman, 18 December 1930.

76 LUA, Letter by E. Leach, 20 November 1931.

77 LUA, Decorative Contract and General Specifications (1931).

78 LUA, Letter by Duncan Grant, 11 June 1935.

79 R. O. Maguglin, *The Queen Mary: The Official Pictorial History* (Long Beach: Sequoia Communications, 1985), frontispiece.

80 MMMA, publicity leaflet (undated).

81 W. H. Miller, Jr, *The Fabulous Interiors of the Great Ocean Liners in Historic Photographs* (New York: Dover Publications, 1985), p. 91.

82 Maguglin, *The Queen Mary*, p. 36.

83 LUA, Memo by E. Leach to chairman, 18 December 1930.

9 ✧ 'Constructing contemporary': common-sense approaches to 'going modern' in the 1950s

Scott Oram

The working man is a great realist and he has great common sense. He is not governed by theories but by facts and common sense. (Ferdynand Zweig, *The British Worker*, 1952 [1])

THIS CHAPTER considers how the working- and lower-middle-class residents of a provincial city in Britain encountered, experienced and made sense of the idea of 'going contemporary' in the home in the 1950s. The word 'contemporary' carries two meanings in modern parlance. In its most common usage it denotes 'of the same age' or 'belonging to the same time or period';[2] but in design historical discourse it refers also to a British furnishing style of the 1950s.[3] This chapter is a contribution to the study of *the contemporary* in the second sense. It is not simply a study of a series of reactions to the style; nor is it another bid to 'test the effectiveness of the [design establishment's] drive to re-educate public taste in the working-class sector';[4] it is an attempt to look at the common-sense considerations and reasoning procedures of a provincial city's working-class residents in setting up homes in the 1950s.

Although a 'model' of contemporary style was clearly available in the Council of Industrial Design's efforts to promote the production of 'objects' characterised by 'sound construction, modest proportions, simple lines, careful choice of timber and fabrics, attention to finish and detailing and generally a decent, well-bred elegance',[5] there is no reason to assume that these ideals were automatically transferred piecemeal to the British public at large. The whole notion of the transference of cultural ideals via designed objects is complex; for, as Roland Barthes suggested, 'the unity of the "text" lies not in its origin but in its destination'.[6] Furthermore, Penny Sparke has argued that in the 1950s the general public was 'much more interested in the symbolic content of the new furniture and its relevance to the new post-war lifestyle and values' than it was with the ideals promoted by the Council of Industrial Design.[7]

In considering how this particular group of people in a provincial city in the 1950s made sense of 'contemporary' within the complex web of motivations inherent to their lived experience, this chapter focuses primarily on information derived from an oral history exercise. It draws on a series of in-depth interviews [8] with working- and lower-middle-class couples who married and, in most cases, set up home in Lincoln during the 1950s. It draws also on other source material, primary and secondary, that both supports and, sometimes, works independently of the oral testimony.[9] It is acknowledged that 'working class' and 'lower-middle class' are difficult categories with which to describe people individually; however, they represent groups that, considered collectively, could be 'socially mobile',[10] on the one hand, while retaining varying degrees of 'cautiousness and pragmatism', on the other.[11] As Richard Hoggart was eager to point out in 1957, the attitudes he was attributing to the 'working classes' were 'sufficiently shared' by 'other groups':

> In particular, many of the attitudes I describe as 'working-class' might also be attributed to what are often called the 'lower middle-classes'. I cannot see how this kind of overlapping is to be avoided ...[12]

As far as the *taste* values of the working classes were concerned, however, Richard Hoggart was uncompromising:

> Some other classes have changed the outward expressions of their taste a great deal during the last fifty years, but on the whole working-class people have been little affected. They make nothing of Scandinavian simplicities ... Of all present-day middle-class styles the one nearest to their own ethos is that commonly represented in drawing-room dramas about upper suburban life – flowery chintz and bits of shiny brass.[13]

The main concern of this case study is with taste. Moving away from Hoggart's proposal and, in turn, from the Veblenian notion that taste automatically trickles downwards through society, I look instead to the common-sense values that have been attributed to the working and lower-middle classes.[14] This is not a study simply of reactions to a style but rather an investigation into how people made sense of their domestic interiors within the complex interaction of 'social, economic and anthropological factors that [were] outside their immediate control'.[15] To interpret the given information effectively I have relied on a twofold method that borrows from the disciplines of social anthropology and ethnomethodology: the latter[16] because it sheds light on the common-sense considerations and reasoning procedures of the individual; and the former because it provides a broader structure through which issues relating to the whole cultural system can be explored. The consumption decisions of the residents of Lincoln cannot possibly be isolated from the complexities of change that were happening worldwide during the period in question. As Penny Sparke has written,

> more than ever before the effects of the press, the radio, television and the cinema entered the lives of practically every individual in the industrialised world, providing new sources of information, creating new expectations and suggesting new values.[17]

It would seem necessary to consider, at this point, how far the combined national media contributed to consumers' perception of 'contemporary'. This chapter proposes that the national media reflected a 'look' of the 'ideal' domestic interior – one that, at least to some degree, the Council of Industrial Design had been instrumental in creating – a look that was 'clean, bright and new', and made up of a number of different components, including furniture, decor and consumer durables.[18] It would, however, be naïve to suggest that this 'look' was intrinsically British, as the UK's media did not particularly discriminate in the type of goods it portrayed or where they were from: British, American, Scandinavian and Italian goods combined together to form images through which the media could promote *lifestyles*.[19] Nor was this a static 'look'. It was, as Jean Baudrillard has suggested when referring to 'the model', an ideal that was always just out reach 'Because the model is, in essence, only an idea it can continually flee as we advance'.[20]

In an earlier piece of work, entitled ' "Common-sense contemporary" ',[21] I discussed the ways in which constraints relating to ideology, economics and the availability of 'the contemporary' affected complete 'ownership' of the concept. This chapter, however, concentrates on the links between consumption and the constructed domestic environment, investigating how aesthetic notions of 'lightness and brightness', and the 'true pattern' of modernisation in the household, worked as markers of ongoing modernity, especially if purchasing the complete ready-made environment was not possible.[22] The chapter also looks at the impact of 'doing-it-yourself' (DIY) – in particular, how people's skills, time and ideas about what could and could not be attempted were constraining factors in constructing the complete 'built-in' environment.

'Lightness and brightness'

I certainly wanted something very different to what I was used to at my parents home, which was all very traditional; carved – not exactly carved, but the twisted legs on tables and the heavy moquette type upholstery materials. I wasn't very keen on these; I just wanted something that was a little more up-to-date ...[23]

'Going contemporary', or 'going modern', seems to have been something of an abstract concept for householders in Lincoln during the 1950s. Rejection of the 'traditional', the 'ornamental' and the 'heavy' was evident, but other than desiring something that was 'a little more up-to-date', Mrs Malone is perhaps typical in failing to express, in her comment (quoted above), any concrete ideas about what 'up-to-date' actually meant.[24] The notion, then, is problematical insofar as it defies positive definition. Yet if we consider its characteristics in terms of opposites, clarification of what constituted 'contemporary' or 'modern' becomes a little clearer.

Styles that traditionally had been associated with the domestic interior were, as Mrs Malone suggested, out of vogue, but that is not the complete story. Clearly anything considered old fashioned, and anything associated with the – constantly referred to (if historically inaccurate) – Victorian age, was likely to be rejected. Mrs Toyne reflected:

I was thinking about the generation thing, that they weren't young parents – they were from the Victorian age almost, you know, with brown paint, and we sort of reacted against that, I think.[25]

There were many references to 'brown paint', which was used almost as a synonym for the ambient darkness and heaviness associated with many working- and lower-middle-class domestic interiors in the 1950s. It is perhaps not surprising, therefore, that a number of the interviewees stressed that they desired opposite aesthetic values for their new homes. Because of their symbolic importance to the household, certain items of furniture tended to be dominant in their role as signifiers either of the old or of the new lifestyle; fireside chairs, dining-room tables and chairs, sideboards and bedroom suites are examples, and they provided constant points of reference for the interviewees. Indeed, if a hierarchy of household objects were to be constructed, those same items would undoubtedly be near the apex. Lightness and brightness were not restricted to furniture alone, however: 'going modern' required that the complete domestic environment be an expression of lightness and brightness, as the discussion below indicates:

> *Mrs Malone:* In the kitchen ... the woodwork was painted white but we did the wallpaper to make it lighter and brighter than the dingy cream.
> *Scott Oram:* So brightness was important?
> *Mrs Malone:* Brightness, oh yes, lightness and brightness, certainly. The windows weren't very big. So, yes – it just needed pepping up really.
> *Scott Oram:* Was that a reaction to a situation that you had lived in before that was particularly dark?
> *Mrs Malone:* I think fashions generally were that your skirting boards – and of course in most places you had picture rails – were usually dark wood or stained. I think it was fashion, and fashion was moving on now to perhaps lightening things.[26]

The acceptance of the situation here was almost unquestioned: the shift towards modernity was almost as inevitable as the fact that fashion was 'moving on'.[27] Modernist calls for 'the rejection of historical style and enhancement of purity'[28] may have had something to do with the general public's reaction, but it is unlikely that people were following the philosophy directly. In most cases, as Paul Greenhalgh has suggested, theirs would have been an 'oblique response' to a 'well heeled' rhetoric.[29] For the residents of Lincoln, then, the concern seems to have been less with *why* they wanted to 'go modern' and more with *how* they were going to do it.

Regardless of the majority of the interviewees' power to purchase major furniture items, couples made it clear that they had been able to make a considered and measured contribution towards the construction of their own 'contemporary' environment. The lightness and brightness, just referred to as markers of 'the modern', were available to house-holders through means other than furniture. Wallpaper, paint and curtaining material played their part in creating the required aesthetic for the interior. By doing it themselves, by creating their own environment, in their own way and at their own speed, couples at least had the chance to negotiate 'the modern' on their own terms.

'Doing it yourself' made a great deal of sense to working- and lower-middle-class householders of the 1950s for a number of reasons. Firstly, it presented them with a financially viable way of modernising their properties; secondly, it gave them an opportunity of applying aesthetic and intellectual judgement in a creative way; and, thirdly, the DIY move-ment openly encouraged the utilisation of both latent and conspicuous skills. Of course, individuals' abilities had always been required to con-tribute to the general upkeep of the household, but never before had they been channelled towards a stylistic goal in such a collective manner. For the majority of householders, however, inroads into the practice of DIY were dictated by economic necessity rather than any ambition to test their own versatility. Hiring in professionals to do the work on their newly acquired properties was simply out of the question.[30] Mr. Vose reflected: 'I couldn't afford to get people in to do it. The only jobs we had people in to do on a professional basis were the plumbing jobs, which I, at that time, thought I couldn't tackle.'[31] Not that professionals were easy to track down even when they *were* wanted. An article in the *Lincolnshire Echo* in 1955 stated:

> When the time comes houseproud folks will find that professional home decorators, or beautifiers as they are termed in some parts of the country, are hard to find and when found are prone to be all but per-manently busy.[32]

There was a widespread realisation that people's skills, newly found or otherwise, could perhaps match those of some professionals. 'The intelligent and practical amateur can always score over the tradesmen', David Johnson wrote in *Do It Yourself*. 'He can choose his own time and thus suffer the minimum of inconvenience. He can take as long as he likes to do the job – he has no 5s–0d an hour bill for Labour mounting up.'[33]

This criticism was just one in a series of sorties in a long-running battle with tradesmen who had insisted that the DIY industry was both taking business away from them and undermining the professional status that they and other tradesmen had earned. As F. J. Camm, the editor of *Practical Householder*, had stated in 1956, apart from the money saved through not hiring tradesmen, in many cases, householders may have felt that by 'doing-it-themselves' they could do 'a better job' than some 'professionals'. Mrs Cant, for instance, had employed a 'decorator' to do some wallpapering:

> I'd got a little cleaning job, and I saw this wallpaper in the shop … so I saved my money, and I was going to have my front room done nice … And I bought this lovely wallpaper and got this decorator guy down the road to do it – instead of doing it myself – and he put it on upside down.[34]

Reflecting on her experience Mrs Cant remarked that had she undertaken the work herself she would have done 'a much better job'. That, however, was not simply a matter of taking up the tools herself; the situation was far more complex.[35] Mrs Cant implied in her interview that she had offered the job to the decorator because he was a friend of the family. He may have been a tradesman in his own right – she did not say – though the fact that he put the wallpaper on 'upside down' would suggest otherwise.[36] After saving up for the wallpaper and believing that her front room would, at last, be nicely decorated, Mrs Cant had every right to be both disappointed and annoyed with the final result. She avoided confrontation, however; her disappointment was overridden by her belief that friendship, and perhaps the continuity of extended 'family' ties, were more important than falling out over this minor material upset.[37]

The practice of appropriating and loaning close friends and relatives to do work on the home was almost as common as the tradition of 'borrowing and lending' *per se*, and in some working- and lower-middle-class communities, it was all but obligatory behaviour.[38] If a job should arise that required a particular skill, and if a member of the community was well known as 'expert' in that field, he or she would often volunteer a service or wait to be asked to carry it out. Families and friends, therefore, would often 'trade off' their skills for 'favours owed' in a time-honoured way, as the following interview with Mr and Mrs Rushton seems to confirm:[39]

> *Mr. Rushton:* When it comes to doing-it-yourself, I was very fortunate in that I've got a friend, Gordon, who is a carpenter and joiner, so any do-it-yourself that needed doing I used to holler for Gordon and he used to come and do it.
>
> *Scott Oram:* That's interesting. Did you pay him for this or did you 'trade off' with something else?
>
> *Mrs. Rushton:* Oh no, he wouldn't have accepted payment.
>
> *Mr. Rushton:* But we had a car and he didn't, and so, you know, this was the sort of thing that happened. And then, when he eventually got a car, if anything went wrong with his car I used to go over and work on it for him, to sort of pay him off . . .[40]

Transitional measures involved in the move forward from using tradesmen to DIY, then, were quite complex. As I have suggested, if labour was intrinsically tied into some form of communal bartering system then the idea of branching out on one's own may have been stunted. And not all, as the Rushton's case would seem to confirm, were dissatisfied with bargaining for what they wanted. Where the working and lower-middle classes are concerned, therefore, I have difficulty with Camm's claim that DIY rose like a phoenix from the ashes of poor professional conduct.[41] But if poor professional conduct alone was not sufficient to motivate the rise in DIY activity, how can one explain the measured contributions that householders were beginning to make towards the construction of their own home interiors?

There would seem to be three possible avenues one may take in giving an answer, and they cross and integrate at various points. Firstly, post-war migration to housing estates and the 'new towns', near and far, had been instrumental in the breaking up of many communities. Another motivating factor, however, may have been the monotony of daily work in the office or factory which, for many, involved little responsibility or skill. 'There are satisfactions in tangible achievement in the mastery of knack,' F. J. Camm had insisted in 1956: 'away from the discipline of factory employment, it is a pleasant change to be one's own boss on a project and to set one's own pace and quality standards'.[42] Bereft of opportunity to express their individuality in working hours, Richard Horn has suggested, many men felt that they *'needed* such work'.[43] Thirdly, an increase in the time available to pursue 'leisure' activities is often cited as accounting for the growth of DIY, but just what DIY counted as leisure and what counted as necessity remains a controversial issue. Nonetheless, given that householders had more time on their hands to pursue such activities, DIY allowed people opportunities both to educate themselves and to use skills that perhaps would have otherwise remained latent. C. J. Bartlett referred to the 'Do-it-Yourself' or 'Teach Yourself' book series as having 'offered splendid opportunities for people to broaden their skills and knowledge'.[44]

Many of the skills required for the activities that now came under the label 'DIY' – wallpapering, for instance – had, of course, to be acquired; but to those who already had related skills in other areas found the new occupations reasonably easy to adjust to. Mr Macnamara explained how his wife was particularly good at wallpapering: 'We were a dual partnership in a way, but Ed is a nib at papering – she is a nib at anything – but she has got a flair for papering especially. I'm amazed how she does it. When it's finished – it just fits perfectly.'[45]

As confidence in their own skills grew, householders were encouraged, and felt increasingly able, to experiment with their own ideas without the assistance of professional help. Many couples believed, in fact, that through DIY they got their homes somewhere near to how they really wanted them and were equally under the impression that had they employed someone to come in and do the job for them they may not have got what they wanted.

'The true pattern'

I followed the true pattern, basically. There was only a little glass lean-to at the back for a kitchenette, as it were, so I had to build on a kitchen at the back. There was a coal house built in to the dining room area of the house, with an outside door, so I covered that over with the kitchen extension and then knocked the inner wall down ... put sliding doors in the dining room area ... The staircase I boxed in. All the lovely panelled doors I panelled over in hardboard, of course, like everybody did ...[46]

When the Voses moved into a 1930s' house that appeared to have been 'built the day before',[47] apart from the fact that 'it was wrecked'[48] and that 'nothing had been changed, not even the wallpaper',[49] the modernising procedure they embarked upon, according to Mr Vose, followed the 'true pattern'.[50] This was not simply a matter of carrying out repairs, decorating and installing modern conveniences, however, but a systematic course of action that embraced preconceived notions of constructional and aesthetic alteration. Nor was Mr Vose's unprompted list a mere rendering of solo enterprise. On the contrary, it was an account of a well-rehearsed, common and generally accepted procedure.

Although such undertakings were common practice, exactly why they wanted, for instance, to knock two rooms into one, box in the banisters and cover up panelled doors remained hazy to most of the interviewees (see figures 25–27). 'It was the fashion that people did that', Mrs Burgess remarked, 'everyone was doing it. Well, someone does it don't they? And it sort of gets handed down.'[51] There is no hint here that any philosophical ideals were being followed; the mere fact that 'everyone was doing it' was enough to make the practice standard and therefore generally acceptable.[52]

A broader reason for modernising, one which involved removing the 'dark brown' from the interior in favour of elements of 'lightness and brightness', has already been discussed; and in that quarter there was no lack of encouragement from the media. DIY magazines, for example, presented doctrinaire anti-Victorian–pro-modern interior campaigns with great relish: 'Transforming an ugly Victorian house into a charming contemporary and comfortable home' was a task requiring 'originality and skill', Roger Smithells remarked in Do it yourself.[53] Tony Wilkins, then assistant editor of Do it yourself, explained how the magazine would tell readers 'to cover over their staircase banisters and panelled doors and give them the "modern" look. Everything had to be smooth and flush and probably painted white.'[54]

By the late 1950s, magazines like Do it yourself were enjoying a boom period. 'In the space of three years', the editor David Johnson proudly boasted, 'it is no mean achievement to have reached a readership of something like 3,750,000 monthly.'[55] There is no evidence to suggest, however, that the influence of DIY magazines was of paramount importance: 'handyman' books, local newspapers, national exhibitions and TV programmes all sang from the same songsheet, though some of the householders interviews failed to cite even these as sources of inspiration. For instance, when I enquired whether the idea to panel his doors came from friends or from magazines, Mr Hopkins replied: 'I think it was more likely to be possibly seeing what they were building at the time, because they were putting up – if I remember rightly – I think they were putting up doors, and they may only have been hardboard covered …'.[56]

The use of hardboard to cover up banisters, fireplaces and doors was widespread (see figure 27). Articles and advertisements promoting the panelling of doors selected their copy and their targets carefully. J. R. Burt's 'New doors for old' feature in *Do it yourself*, for instance, gave this encouragement to the reader:

> Give your doors that new look with hardboard panels. Flush doors give the whole house a sleek well-groomed appearance. The out of date panelled doors tends to provide a series of dust-collecting ledges that are a nuisance to the busy housewife.[57]

Likewise, K. Halliday claimed that 'some of the drudgery can be taken

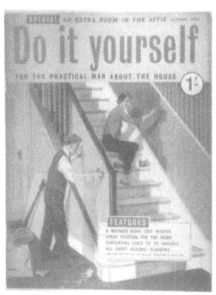

25 'Covering up'   26 'Knocking through'

out of housework by panelling stairways in hardboard or some similar material'.[58] In pursuit of modernity, some householders followed the 'covering up' procedure without question. Mrs Burgess said that although the doors in their property were 'lovely panelled ones',[59] all of them were eventually 'covered up'.[60] 'To modernise them', Mr Burgess intervened, 'I bought sheets of hardboard and nailed them on each side and then cut it, you know, around the door – I must have used six-inch nails to put them on.'[61]

Mr Hopkins's reasons for panelling were based on practical considerations, but with a slant towards the aesthetic:

> Well, they were poor quality doors, and we did think it gave them the appearance of being more solid and [they] weren't so old fashioned. You know, I think that was the main thing that we thought – they looked old fashioned, and we thought [panelling] would make it look a bit more modern.[62]

The procedure of knocking through two rooms to form one (figure 26) was subjected to the same commonsensical scrutiny. I asked the

27 'Modernising your doors'

Toynes whether they had knocked through from the dining room to the lounge. 'No', Mr Toyne replied, 'just the kitchen. We couldn't go dining room–lounge because the staircase was in-between – it was a centre, it was a kitchen wall to the pantry'.[63] The thought of having an open-plan or through lounge had occurred to Mr Toyne, but the structure of the house made the exercise impossible to carry out.

Apart from minor structural alterations carried out in order to modernise their properties, the interviewed couples contributed to the ambience of the interior by carrying out a number of small but significant jobs. Painting and wallpapering were quite a common practice, allowing whole areas of the interior to be given a modern look in reasonably short time. Most of the women interviewed contributed to the design of the interior by making their own curtains, rugs, quilts, and so on, some going to great lengths to wait for the sales when contemporary materials would be affordable.[64]

Other minor contributions to the furnishings were made using new materials. Formica, for instance, allowed for table tops and work-surfaces to be changed 'to suit the decor'.[65] Attempts were also made to construct pieces of furniture, coffee tables being prime examples. Mrs Burgess recalled:

> We had some coffee tables made with those plastic legs where you tiled the top – you know, like they had little brass feet and you just screwed them in ... You used to make them – two rows of tiles and then put some beading around the edges ...[66]

Working- and lower-middle-class couples were able to enter into the contemporary spirit by constructing the ambience of their environment, by decorating and by carrying out the 'true pattern' of modernisation. Where the completion of the look of the domestic interior as a whole was concerned, however, householders were still reliant on purchasing the furniture items that signified contemporary and all that it encompassed. If a complete – purchased – environment was out of the question for the majority of the working and lower-middle classes, so too was a completely 'constructed' environment. DIY may have offered a way of accessing the contemporary but, due to both the limitations and the expectations of its participants, it could never provide the whole answer.

'Contemporary' as a complete style did not filter down to the residents of Lincoln. They were aware of its existence from the beginning, however, and desired it. The language of 'going modern' or 'contemporary' dominated the concerns of the majority when they were setting up home, but this was not to do with an adherence to theoretical notions about *why* they should be doing it. The rejection of the Victorian interior was motivation enough for most couples to take up the quest for 'the modern'. *How* they were going to do it was the area of most concern, and 'lightness and brightness' offered welcome alternatives to the 'brown paint' of the 'Victorian' house's interior, and it was sought through whatever means were available.

DIY may not have provided all the answers to those who sought the contemporary or modern. It did not enable them to say 'we have arrived', but it certainly allowed the householder to display sufficient markers through the 'true pattern' of modernisation to suggest that they were, indeed, on their way. The latent and manifest skills of the householders, again in keeping with working-class traditions, were utilised to good effect. Even here, however, there were some things that would not be tackled – furniture's symbolic content was too embedded in their culture to allow anyone, but the expert, to make it.

If a single finding emerges from this study it is that the tastes of this particular sample of working- and lower-middle-class people from a provincial city in the 1950s cannot be gauged by using the discriminating values of the design establishment of the day as a yardstick. What I have called 'common sense' was exercised time and again by the householders in considering what should be included in their homes and how they would go about the task.

Notes

1 F. Zweig, *The British Worker* (Harmondsworth: Penguin, 1952), p. 224.

2 J. M. Hawkins (ed.), *The Oxford Reference Dictionary* (London: Guild Publishing, 1987), p. 185.

3 C. Boyce, *Dictionary of Furniture* (Oxford: Roundtable Press, 1985), p. 70.

4 C. Morley, 'Homemakers and design advice in the postwar period', in T. Putnam and C. Newton (eds), *Household Choices* (London: Future Publications, 1990), p. 89.

5 P. Reilly, 'Look before you buy', in F. Lake (ed.), *Daily Mail Ideal Home Book* (London: Daily Mail Publications, 1955), p. 62.

6 R. Barthes, *Mythologies* (London: Cape, 1972), p. 114.

7 P. Sparke, *An Introduction to Design and Culture in the Twentieth Century* (London: Unwin Hyman, 1986), p. 117.

8 Unless otherwise indicated, all oral testimony is taken from interviews carried out by the author between September and November 1993; see Appendices 1–9 of S. Oram, ' "Common-sense contemporary": the ideals and realities of the popular domestic interior in the 1950s', MA dissertation, Royal College of Art, 1994.

9 As all of the interviewees defined themselves as being from the 'working or lower-middle classes', and as it is with their self-perception, among other things, that this study is concerned, I use these terms throughout the this study. All ten of the householder couples lived in Lincoln at the time the interviews took place, though only six of the couples resided in Lincoln during the 1950s. The remaining four couples were based in other provincial towns and cities, or else were 'mobile' because of their employment. Although they had initially rented their accommodation most of the couples interviewed purchased a house early on in married life, and thus the term 'householder' is used in preference to 'tenant'. It is recognised that this study fails to represent adequately a large section of the community that resided in council accommodation at the time. Given that part of this study touches on aspects of modernisation, however, it was felt that, because council properties were often subject to regulations that prohibited tenants from carrying out structural alterations, evidence from potential interviewees as to the interior design of *those* dwellings would constitute the grounding for a further study.

10 R. Hoggart, *The Uses of Literature* (Harmondsworth: Penguin, 1957), p. 13.

11 Qualities that Krishan Kuman aligns with the 'working classes' in his definitional entry on the working class in A. Bullock, O. Stallybrass and S. Trombley (eds), *Modern Thought* (London: Fontana, 1988), p. 909.

12 Hoggart, *The Uses of Literature*, p. 19.

13 *Ibid.*, p. 149.

14 See T. Veblen, *The Theory of the Leisure Class* (New York: Macmillan, 1899).

15 Sparke, *Introduction to Design and Culture in the Twentieth Century*, p. 111.

16 'Ethnomethodology' refers to the sociological study of 'everyday activities, however trivial' and concentrates on 'the methods used by individuals to report their common sense practical actions to others in acceptable rational terms'; see entry by M. Barrett in Bullock *et al.* (eds), *Modern Thought*, p. 287.

17 Sparke, *Introduction to Design and Culture in the Twentieth Century*, p. 143.

18 H. Hopkins, *The New Look* (London: Secker & Warburg, 1963), p. 271.

19 Although a great deal of the media's concern was to sell 'lifestyles' through advertising, not all images would have been compiled for commercial reasons. The 'look' would also have been made up of, for example, background settings for magazine articles and stage sets for TV dramas, etc.

20 J. Baudrillard, 'The system of objects', in J. Thackera (ed.), *Design After Modernism: Beyond the Object* (London: Thames & Hudson, 1988), p. 182.

21 Oram, '"Common-sense contemporary"'.

22 *Ibid.*, Malone interview, Appendix 9, p. 3; Vose interview, Appendix 2, p. 6.

23 *Ibid.*, Malone interview, Appendix 9, p. 6.

24 For comments on 'traditional', the 'ornamental' and the 'heavy', see *ibid.*, Malone interview, Appendix 9, p. 6, and Rushton interview, Appendix 8, pp. 5–6.

25 *Ibid.*, Toyne interview, Appendix 3, p. 12.

26 *Ibid.*, Malone interview, Appendix 9, p. 3.

27 *Ibid.*

28 P. Greenhalgh, 'Introduction', in Greenhalgh (ed.), *Modernism in Design* (London: Reaktion, 1990), p. 4.

29 *Ibid.*

30 See Oram, '"Common-sense contemporary"', Vose interview, Appendix 2, p. 8, Cant and Burgess interview, Appendix 1, p. 9, and Rushton interview, Appendix 8, p. 8.

31 *Ibid.*, Vose interview, Appendix 2, p. 8.

32 Anon., 'Do-it-yourself spring clean', *Lincolnshire Echo*, 14 January 1955, p. 4.

33 D. G. Johnson, 'Tradesman versus amateur', *Do It Yourself* (December 1958), 1171.

34 Oram, '"Common-sense contemporary"', Cant and Burgess interview, Appendix 1, p. 9.

35 *Ibid.*

36 *Ibid.*

37 *Ibid.*

38 Young and Willmott, for instance, stated that neighbours in Greenleigh 'borrow and lend little things to each other, and when this accommodation is refused, it is a sign that acquaintance has turned into enmity': M. Young and P. Willmott, *Family and Kinship in East London* (Harmondsworth: Penguin, 1957), p. 149.

39 Oram, '"Common-sense contemporary"', Rushton interview, Appendix 8, p. 8.

40 *Ibid.*

41 F. J. Camm, 'Welcome to new readers', *Practical Householder* (October 1956), 841.

42 *Ibid.*

43 R. Horn, *Fifties' Style: Then and Now* (London: Columbus Books, 1985), p. 28.

44 C. J. Bartlett, *A History of Postwar Britain 1945–74* (London: Longman, 1977), p. 153.

45 Oram, '"Common-sense contemporary"', Macnamara interview, Appendix 6, p. 5.

46 *Ibid.*, Vose interview, Appendix 2, p. 6.

47 *Ibid.*

48 *Ibid.*

49 *Ibid.*

50 *Ibid.*

51 *Ibid.*, Cant and Burgess interview, Appendix 1, p. 5.

52 *Ibid.*

53 R. Smithells, *Do It Yourself* (March 1957), 60.

54 Tony Wilkins in a letter to the author, quoted in Oram, '"Common-sense contemporary"', Appendix 10, p. 1.

55 D. G. Johnson, 'Fourth year term', *Do It Yourself* (March 1960), 237.

56 Oram, '"Common-sense contemporary"', Hopkins interview, Appendix 5, p. 5.

57 J. R. Burt, 'New doors for old', *Do It Yourself* (April 1957), 153.

58 K. Halliday, 'Why not try glass panels?' *Do It Yourself* (May 1959), 467.

59 Oram, '"Common-sense contemporary"', Cant and Burgess interview, Appendix 1, p. 5.

60 *Ibid.*

61 *Ibid.*

62 *Ibid.*, Hopkins interview, Appendix 5, p. 5.

63 *Ibid.*, Toyne interview, Appendix 3, p. 6.

64 *Ibid.*, Vose interview, Appendix 2, pp. 4–5.

65 *Ibid.*, Rushton interview, Appendix 8, p. 11.

66 *Ibid.*, Cant and Burgess interview, Appendix 1, p. 12.

10 ✧ After modernism: the contemporary office environment

Jeremy Myerson

FOR NEARLY 100 years, from around 1890 to 1990, the office was an archetype of modernism, a place of rational production and administration, its design almost entirely determined by considerations of management efficiency and its importance to contemporary culture marginalised by a fixation with mechanistic process. Over the past decade, however, the corporate office interior has entered a new post-industrial phase of development which reflects a new plurality of cultural perspectives in workplace design and could be described as post-modern in character.

This chapter explores the reasons for this shift from modern to post-modern, relating stylistic and planning changes in the contemporary office interior to four areas of tension and conflict in workplace design: the needs of the organisation versus the needs of the individual; the demand for space for work versus that for space for public and social interaction; the fixed office versus the flexible office; and the importance of architecture versus the role of design. The chapter looks in particular at schemes that have reflected the re-introduction, over the last ten years, of historical reference and cultural quotation to workplace design, including medieval town planning and garden-city metaphors.

Back in 1990, however, office design appeared almost hermetically sealed from the post-modern discourse in design. Dr Francis Duffy, architect and founder of the workplace designers DEGW, described the office as 'the dominant economic and environmental experience for the vast majority of workers in the developed, and even the developing world today. The landscape of the late 20th century is the office.'[1] Duffy warned: 'Future historians had better hurry up. So far scholars have treated one of the most remarkable changes in 20th century life with almost complete neglect.'² Despite his promptings, the office remained on the fringes of popular cultural analysis. Commentators were largely silent on the implications of a massive transfer of the work experience from the factory to the office.

The design of the furniture and products which comprised the material environment of the office also appears to have been neglected if one compares the literature's coverage of workplace design with the more searching analysis given to objects for a domestic environment. This had little to do with the *volume* of coverage: in 1990 a segment of the publishing industry was entirely dedicated to producing texts, magazines, guides, brochures, catalogues and books about office design. But little in this literature or the thinking it reflected was cultural in nature. It did nothing to challenge effectively the powerful link between the office aesthetic and the modern movement – a link encapsulated in Mies Van Der Rohe's description of the office as 'a machine for working in'.

The office and the factory, rational places of a total production process in which systems could be applied, were the first places to demonstrate the key ideas of modernism in the early twentieth century. In their planning, organisation, furnishings and equipment, they adopted design characteristics which suited the dominant economic model. This was Fordism (after Henry Ford), which depended on well-run offices and factories to deliver mass production and mass marketing to a mass audience within highly planned, centralised and regulated economies.

As the twentieth century progressed, so there was a progressive separation of factory from office conditions, just as a century earlier there had been a progressive separation of the home from the workplace with the onset of industrialisation – a phenomenon described by historians as 'the separation of the spheres'. Design historian Adrian Forty explains in his book *Objects of Desire* how corporations, in an era of relatively full employment during the 1950s and 1960s, competed with factories for staff, not by paying higher wages but by offering more respectable and pleasant surroundings. Despite attempts by some designers, and their clients, to make the workplace more like the world outside in its aesthetic response to individual human needs, however, the office adhered largely to a mechanistic model, and its furniture and interiors accordingly followed a system-based approach.

Adrian Forty ascribes the dominance of this mechanistic model to management's need to control the work process:

> The inescapable reality was that efficiency was the ultimate aim of the office. Though the means of attaining it may have changed, efficiency has been the main consideration behind the selection of every design for every article of office furniture and equipment during the twentieth century. However hard designers tried to blur the distinction between home and office, management aims remained at the root of all design for the office.[3]

The twentieth-century office incorporated none of the democratic–cultural dialogue surrounding such artefacts as, say, domestic furniture. Indeed, while the crisis of design after modernism and the reaction to 'black-box' design were making themselves felt throughout the home, the street and the city, the office was curiously insulated from such change. Behind their concrete-glass-and-steel façades, office buildings continued to be filled with rectangular reception sofas in black leather, sharp-edged steel filing cabinets and miles of look-alike systems furniture in shades of grey and beige. Even today most people would be hard-pressed to differentiate a facsimile machine from a photocopier from a laser printer at more than five paces, such is the modern technical aesthetic's stranglehold on the office.

Le Corbusier was not slow to recognise the symbolic value of office furniture to the cause of the modern movement. In *Towards A New Architecture*, he wrote: 'Our modern life has created its own objects; its own costume, its own fountain pen, its eversharp pencil, its typewriter, its telephone, its admirable office furniture.'[4] But, as the twentieth century drew to a close, his influence and that of his peers in developing a fixation with a year-zero modernist style among the office-based American corporations was increasingly ridiculed by commentators, most notably Tom Wolfe in *From Bauhaus to Our House*.

Wolfe dubbed Le Corbusier 'Mr Purism'. 'He showed everyone how to become a famous architect without building buildings. He built a Radiant City in his skull.'[5] Architect and fellow-modernist pioneer Ludwig Mies van der Rohe also came in for the Wolfe treatment: 'White

God No. 2. He put half of America inside German worker-housing cubes.' [6] Wolfe expressed his disbelief at the way corporate America, at the peak of its unparalleled economic power, bowed down before White God No. 1, Walter Gropius, and other European refugees, who had brought the Bauhaus to big business:

> ... a box, of glass, steel, concrete, and tiny beige bricks ... In short, the reigning architectural style in this, the very Babylon of capitalism, became worker housing. Worker housing, as developed by a handful of architects, inside the compounds, amid the rubble of Europe in the early 1920s, was now pitched high and wide ...[7]

Lance Knobel's lucid historical analysis *Office Furniture* made the point less rhetorically: 'One of the decisive ironies of our century is the transformation of the modern movement, from a radically-based approach to design, largely inspired by the needs of the working class in turmoil following the First World War, into the perfect encapsulation of corporate style.' [8] Knobel charts how the post-war development of steel-framed structures in architecture led to office buildings on expensive city-centre sites with large, clear, lettable floor spaces unhindered by columns or obstructions. So ideology and commerce became twinned. Mies van der Rohe as early as 1919 had envisaged a towering glass office block on a triangular site; once the technology was available, he realised his aims, in 1958, with the Seagram Building, New York. That building, and the tower of Union Carbide nearby on Park Avenue, designed a year later by Skidmore Owings and Merrill, set the pattern for office design for the next twenty years.

Office interiors became machine-like in the modular assembly of their component parts. Desks were carefully laid out in rectilinear patterns, the clerical staff inside large bull pens within the deep space and the more senior personnel given, progressively, window access, perimeter offices, larger desks, domicile-like furniture (usually in wood), artworks and private dining rooms, as they moved up through he corporate hierarchy. Billy Wilder's classic 1960 film *The Apartment* immortalised the process as Jack Lemmon ingratiated himself with senior managers in a bid to escape the office–factory floor and so gain a key to the executive washroom.

While new technology has, over the past decade, created new forms of Taylorist office environments, such as dealing rooms and call centres, it has also sown the seeds of liberating change. This point is well understood by Dr Francis Duffy, who has observed: 'Increasingly widely diffused information technology, which is killing the old-fashioned clerical office factories, is equally putting paid to Fordism.' [9]

Duffy was among the first commentators to suggest how new technology might transform the modern office from factory-like paperpushing, number-crunching, production house – often employing large numbers of low-paid workers for regular hours – to post-modern interactive hothouse of creative and strategic thinking, employing smaller numbers of better-paid, more highly qualified people working irregular hours. During the 1990s, as the mass production and mass marketing principles underpinning Fordism broke down, so the location, and even the very nature, of office work itself became ripe for reassessment.

Office designers trained to work within a strict discipline – functionality dedicated to furthering traditional notions of management efficiency and an accompanying imagery rooted in the machine – now began to glimpse a new creative scenario as the traditional 'modern' notions of the office started to break down. But what would the new, post-modern, landscape of the workplace look like? And what would be the cultural agenda for furniture and equipment designers within this changing environment? A mosaic of diverse impressions and pieces of evidence immediately piles up before any researcher contemplating the future of the office. Historical development suggested that progress would not be uniform: some offices would stick stubbornly to manual typewriters, bare floors, trailing wires and the glare of exposed fluorescent tubes, while others would embrace the latest cable-less technologies, design thinking and management theories about team-working.

The study reported in this chapter indicated that the subject would be most clearly discussed as a series of conflicts in office design so that all the contradictions, tensions and anomalies could be brought into view. The four conflicts selected as means of exploring the characteristics of the office after modernism are now considered.

Organisational v. individual needs

This is the oldest and most profound conflict in office design – between the corporate needs of the organisation in terms of output, productivity and efficiency and the needs of the individual worker in terms of morale, privacy, comfort and health. For most of the twentieth century, since the first offices were developed, it was an uneven struggle. Adrian Forty explains in *Objects of Design and Society* [10] how first the division of labour and then scientific management eroded the status of the office clerk. Furniture design played a key role in this. The standard nineteenth-century office desk – ornamental, designed to store papers and indicative of a master in charge of his own domain – was gradually replaced by a modern design dedicated only to shifting papers as swiftly as possible.

By 1911, the year of 'efficiency fever' in America, [11] the ideas of Frederick Taylor had decisively given organisations the whip-hand over its individual workers, and they did not stop whipping for the next eighty years. Even the 1980s, supposedly the decade of consumer choice and individual liberty, saw some of the worst manifestations of organisational control in the outbreaks of such workplace diseases as sick building syndrome and tenosynovitis among office employees. At least, by then, staff were allowed to talk. In the early days of Taylorist scientific management, conversation in the office was forbidden on the grounds that it interrupted concentration.

Frederick Taylor's ideas were held up in American business schools such as Harvard and Wharton, says the writer and consultant James Woudhuysen, as 'the means to crush trade union syndicalism and so overtake the mighty engine of British industry once and for all'. [12] But Taylor's thinking was important in terms of more than just the political economy: as the ultimate time-and-motion man he had a profound effect on the design of the workplace. Woudhuysen argues that Taylor's influence on the office aesthetic has been as profound as that of the Bauhaus. Certainly Taylor cast an analytical eye over the material environment. In 1912 he wrote:

> The analysis of a piece of work into its elements always reveals the fact that many of the conditions surrounding and accompanying the work

are defective. Knowledge so obtained leads frequently to constructive work of a high order, to the standardisation of tools and conditions, to the invention of superior methods and machines.[13]

As late as 1984 Woudhuysen, writing in *Design* magazine,[14] could claim that offices were still being organised in Taylor's image. That was one of the many paradoxes of the 1980s: in a political and economic era supposedly dedicated to liberating the individual from the shackles of state bureaucracy and converting the economies of the USA and Britain to those of services-led societies, the corporate organisations squeezed their junior staff all the harder.

Environmental psychologist David Tong, of the British consultancy Building Use Studies, described how this was done against the background of the property and services boom. He termed the 1980s the 'decade of corporate efficiency' and outlined a scenario in which the workplace was streamlined ruthlessly to meet business objectives: high-speed lifts and regulated environments with computer-controlled lighting and centralised air-conditioning took away individual control and allowed management to set the agenda. People seated within the deep space of large city-centre blocks no longer knew if it was day or night, or what the temperature was outside – things that even Frederick Taylor had not denied the office clerk seventy years earlier.

At the end of the 1980s, as sick building syndrome hit the headlines together with such other work-related illnesses as repetitive strain injury and tenosynovitis, the pendulum began to swing against the organisation for the first time. This movement was aided by the publication of new and mandatory European Community health and safety directives concerning working with visual display units and a demographic picture which suggested a shortage of skilled young office staff during the 1990s.[15]

Amid the conflicting needs of organisations and individuals, office interiors began to be rethought. Architects and designers sought to soften the mechanised formulas of the 1980s in favour of the individual. In the search for new inspiration and ideas, they adopted a broader set of cultural and historical references. In the medieval city plan, they found models of socially cohesive and economically sustainable communities that, with the right client, could be replicated on the floorplate of the corporate workplace. The modernist compound was breached.[16]

Work space v. public space

Taylorism viewed every inch of office space as work space, a sweatshop crammed full of desks dedicated to getting every spare ounce of effort out of every staff member. During the twentieth century, most office managers the world over had the same idea. The American writer Judith Merkle [17] has documented how scientific management influenced Japan, Germany and the rapidly industrialising USSR under Lenin (who was critical of Taylorism) and Stalin (who was not).

Office developers also faithfully adhered to the work-space concept with deep uninterrupted floorplates and low floor–ceiling heights to enable the maximum number of workstations to be incorporated in a building. Functionalist principles made this possible. But in the late 1980s something strange started to happen to the allocation of space in office buildings. The 'modern' insistence on efficient use of space began to be eroded.

Again, the catalyst for change was a demographic picture predicting long-term shortages of skilled white-collar staff, the so-called 'knowledge workers'. These employment trends coincided with a show of white-collar trades union strength, especially in the Scandinavian and German economies, and new management studies suggesting that smart companies seeking to raise productivity should reassess where the really productive work in the office was being done. This was no longer at the desk, apparently, but rather in informal gatherings around the coffee machine or on the squash court, so encouraging the cross-disciplinary focus and interdepartmental communication promoted by management exponents of the boundaryless company on both sides of the Atlantic.

So corporations began to turn work space into communal space devoted to leisure, sports' and catering facilities – public space with an aesthetic more closely resembling that of a hotel lobby than an industrial sweatshop. The idea was to sweep away rigidly hierarchical styles of management, and make staff productive, motivated and loyal. High-technology companies, in particular, adopted the new thinking. An early management motivation experiment at the Helsinki headquarters of Digital, for example, replaced conventional office desking with large comfortable chairs, padded cushions and low coffee tables. Computers descended from artificial trees like mango fruit on branches. Executives reclined and chatted as if in a hotel lounge. The picture conformed to what Dr Francis Duffy regards as his model for the office of the future: a large Pall Mall club – 'a place where you could meet friend, eat, relax and work; it was a brilliant idea'.[18]

But the best-known example of this new approach to office space was the new headquarters of Scandinavian Airline System (SAS) at Frosundavik, just outside Stockholm. Designed by Norwegian architect Niels Torp and opened in January 1988, this building refashioned entirely the traditional notion of office life by creating a giant complex with shops, restaurants and coffee bars lining a solar-heated internal 'main street' running through the spine of the building. The idea, as explained by company president Jan Carlzon, was for senior SAS managers to promenade up and down 'the street', meeting staff informally in a social context to generate and monitor projects. Carlzon championed the new approach with a vigorous defence of multi-purpose public space:

> A service company cannot be a hierarchy, and it would be absurd for us to have a chateau with rampart and towers for our head office ... Good ideas are rarely created when you are sitting at you desk feeling alone and tense, but during creative encounters between human beings ... Meeting a colleague from another department for a coffee is not the same as shirking your duties.[19]

Light, open and airy beneath its glass roof, the SAS headquarters, with its working population of 1,400 staff, moved as far away from Taylorism in aesthetic and organisational terms as one could get. It presented itself as a city on the outskirts of Stockholm, complete with swimming pool, medical centre, gym, waterside café and conference centre. It reflected the importance of providing every kind of social amenity for large numbers of workers no longer based in city centres and having to be transported to edge-of-town business parks.

Architects from all over the world closely studied Niels Torp's building, and several of his innovations gradually worked their way into, in particular, British, German and American offices. A decade after Frosundavik, Torp was invited by British Airways (BA), SAS's rival, to design a new building close to Heathrow Airport that would bring together for the first time in one workplace 2,500 BA business strategists from fourteen locations. Not surprisingly, Torp reprised his greatest hit: Waterside.

Completed in June 1998 at a cost of £200 million, Waterside has at its centre a spectacular glass-covered 175-metre street (see figure 28), with fountains, specially grown trees and an Andy Goldsworthy sculpture. A library extends into the space, with a sweeping terrace and balcony over-looking an 'olive grove' that provides a place for contemplation. The street also features a café, expresso bar, supermarket, florist and library, and terminates at a circular restaurant with views over the gardens, lakes and Japanese bridges.

The entire Waterside scheme, in redressing the balance between workspace and public space, was designed both to facilitate a change in the way BA staff behave at work and to support a more customer-led culture. A similar purpose was behind the development of another

28 Waterside
office for British
Airways at
Heathrow Airport

British workplace inspired by Niels Torp: the Ministry of Defence Procurement Executive campus at Abbey Wood in Bristol, master-planned by DEGW and completed in June 1996 at a cost of £245 million. The Ministry of Defence wanted to bring together within a single organisation the defence equipment buyers who had once served one only of the British Army, the Royal Navy or the Royal Air Force, as part of readjustment following the end of the Cold War. Building a sense of community and social cohesion was therefore an essential part of the project.

The workplace architecture – accommodating 6,000 people in 1.3 million sq. ft of space in thirteen energy-efficient buildings, clustered in four green neighbourhoods – was central to this mission. Within the plan of the pleasantly open landscaped complex, there were sited piazzas, cafés, atria, internal glazed streets, village squares, water features, a fitness centre, a nursery, an international conference centre and a circular drum library in the tradition of Gunnar Asplund or Alvar Aalto.

Whether such a setting has created the single-organisation clarity the Ministry of Defence desired is hard to assess, just as it is difficult to evaluate the effect on BA's culture of the Waterside design.[20] Such *public* environments have their critics (Taylorism dies hard). Justification of a non-hierarchical division of space also depends on economic and employment trends that consistently point to the need to attract and retain staff, as well as a level of technology sufficient to service free-flowing interdepartmental communication. In this, a fresh conflict arises – that between the fixed and the flexible office.

The fixed v. the flexible office

For most of the twentieth century, offices were fixed in place. Staff traditionally defined their status in terms of the territory they occupied, with each worker seated at his or her own desk and, as technology developed, increasingly surrounded by the mass of cabling connecting telephones and computers to workstations. But against a background of new technologies and management theories, the fixity of the office was diminishing. More flexible hours and home working started to come to the fore. Organisations began to weigh up the advantages of centralised organisational control against the cost of heating and lighting large corporate facilities, usually in city centre locations, and paying for staff to spend many hours of the day commuting long distances to and from work. The result has been a more diverse use of the office, with new notions converging on the idea of flexibility in all its forms. The most arresting technological vision is that of the 'cable-less office' which aims to radically reduce the proliferation of wires in the office interior and so enable more spatial variety. Before 1990, all office communications ran through the physical medium of a cable, either a copper wire or optical fibre. The office worker was literally tied to the workstation by a tangle of power, data and telecommunications cables. Office planning was restricted by the narrow dictates of wire management. But over the past decade and more the new technologies of wire-free working have started to liberate office environments, enabling new workspaces to emerge.

Advanced technology was integrated with the building's design at BA's Waterside, for example, to support new ways of working: internal cordless telephones allow people to make and receive calls anywhere in the building or the surrounding gardens; and radio links for portable computers allow people to connect from a café table on the central street. New cordless technology was also central to the informal and relaxed culture of the advertising agency St Luke's, in London, the first workplace (launched in 1995) to feature branded client rooms and chill-out dens. The idea behind St Luke's was that no one would have his or her own desk: 'The three things you need to work at St Luke's [are] your locker, satchel and mobile phone', explained marketing director David Abraham.[21]

Another much-discussed model of flexibility is the 'virtual office' which does at the organisational level what the wire-free office does on the technological plane. Also termed 'free address' in Japan and 'hot desking' in Europe, the virtual office has nothing to do with 'virtual reality'. It is a sophisticated name for a simple low-tech principle: desk sharing. It sacrifices the traditional practice of one worker–one desk in the interests of lower property costs. Professional and sales staff who spend up to 50 per cent of their time outside the office are not allocated their own workstations; instead they share with up to five or six others, taking whichever desks are available at a given time, relying for their accommodation on the absence of others.

IBM and other multinationals were early adopters of the idea. The savings on cost to companies were immediate – as also was the onset of headaches for office designers. In January 1996 Andersen Consulting, in France, relocated 1,200 employees from La Defense to a new office with 30 per cent less space, closer to the centre of Paris, a move that saved the company $1 million a year in property costs. This was achieved only by designing a 'smart', if austerely depersonalised, office in which no one 'owns' a desk and space is 'booked' according to a strict system. The facility's smart-card entry system tells employees who of their fellow staff are 'in' and which spaces are available for use. A sophisticated concierge system books space on each of the four main consultants' practice floors.

The virtual, non-territorial, office requires that internal communications improve, as people are no longer located in fixed spaces but take whichever workstations are free when they arrive at the office. (Here cordless communication assumes a special relevance.) It also calls for specific innovations to the furniture. Individual workstations need higher performance specifications to cope with the relentless traffic of anonymous users (the workstations lack the 'softening' influence that comes with personal ownership). For their personal effects staff need mobile storage facilities that can be wheeled to the workstations allocated to them.

But all the concerns over internal communications and workstation design in the virtual office are as nothing compared to the psychological barrier of professional status that is linked to the fixed location and ownership of a desk. This has been management's carrot since the offices first came out of the home into its own distinct environment soon after the invention of the telephone, typewriter and electric lightbulb in the 1880s. Promotion for hard work and efficiency has invariably involved more space, better furnishings, a private office. Without such blandishments, what could organisations do to motivate their executives? Even so, the cost advantages of intensifying the use of space through sharing outweighed all other considerations. As Dr Francis Duffy observed: 'Once companies have discovered it, the concept has the logic of double-entry bookkeeping. It just drives them on. The iconography for things shared is different from things owned, so the design challenge is to develop equipment which is easy to share, adapt and modify.' 22

The virtual or cable-less office provides valuable scenarios of flexibility, but perhaps the clearest illustration of the erosion of the fixed office,

and of the gradual deconstruction of the old-fashioned monolithic cor-
poration is the growth of home working, which takes work outside of the
office altogether. The home office has developed as technology has
advanced and office machines have slimmed in size and price. In a sense
it takes office work full circle: back to the farmhouse table at which pre-
industrial business deals used to be struck, back to the private residences
of colonial traders and shipping magnates who converted the ground
floors of their homes into the earliest offices.

But this time there are crucial differences, most notably in the ability
to communicate globally via e-mail, the internet, facsimile, and so on.
People can work from home and still belong to large organisations. This
means that office designers must create a landscape for those who might
spend a large proportion of the working week in the home environment
and who have not a job but, in Professor Charles Handy's term, 'a portfolio of work'.[23] Working from home has become one of the key social
change trends of our time – a shift driven by changing business practices,
new technologies and evolving social attitudes.[24] In Britain today, at least
one employer in ten makes use of some form of home-based working
and an estimated 2 million people now work wholly or partially at
home. This includes 1.2 million professional teleworkers who work via
computer and telephone, and a 'hidden' force up to 800,000 home workers doing mainly clerical, assembly and manual work on piecework rates.
According to the Henley Centre for Forecasting, by 2006 more than 30
per cent of Britain's workforce will work from home.[25]

Home working is the logical – some would say the ultimate – extension of the flexible office. Trusting your employees to get on with it at
home to suit their life–work balance is as far removed from the supervisory culture of the fixed office as one can go. It also reunites the spheres
of work and home severed by mid-nineteenth-century industrialisation
when men went off to work in offices and factories, leaving women
behind as guardians and beautifiers of the home. With paid labour now
re-entering the domestic sphere, considerable design and aesthetic re-
adjustments are required. But if 'working from home' is one trend,
another, ironically, is 'living at work' – due to the long-hours' culture and
management stress of the typical UK or US company. To alleviate this,
during the 1990s some office interiors and furnishings became
progressively feminised and domesticated.

Architecture v. design

The fourth and final conflict characteristic of the office after modernism concerns the tensions between architecture and design. The building has traditionally housed the infrastructure and servicing for the office – and architecture has been the dominant discipline in creating the aesthetic of the workplace. An especially clear illustration of this is Frank Lloyd Wright's Larkin Building, Buffalo, New York (1904), with one large space proclaiming the unity of the organisation and the power of the business owner. The USA's early skyscraper buildings also reflected both the need to maximise real-estate values by building *upwards* in such cities as New York and Chicago and the corporates' mastery of the skyline.

By the early 1990s, however, architectural domination was under challenge. There was what Duffy described as 'a massive emigration of problem-solving from the realms of architecture into that of office furnishings'.[26] His argument was that because organisations were having to adapt continuously to market changes at a time of economic flux, economically it made better sense to invest in autonomous elements that could be reconfigured rather than in the fixed building shell that could not changed:

> Far more money is now being spent on the relatively short-life interiors of offices. It is in these interiors that restlessness is most easily accommodated. Conversely, the shell and the exterior of the office building are dwindling in both architectural and economic significance. Architecture, in this financial sense at least, is rapidly becoming a branch of interior design – the neutral shell within which the real dramas are played out.[27]

Architects, it is true, made attempts to create flexibility and variation within office buildings in the late twentieth century, reacting against the system approach while still remaining within the modernist tradition. The most successful and highly publicised of these was the Centraal Beheer insurance building in Appeldorn, Holland, designed in 1973 by Dutch architect Herman Hertzberger. He created a complex interlocking interior with an ambiguously mounting series of concrete block 'work islands'. Each unit housed sixteen workers who were free to decorate the space as they wished. Hertzberger's achievement was hailed as intellectual modernism with a human face, a solution which gave staff both privacy and a sense of belonging to the communal office. Nevertheless it was still architecture – hard concrete, fixed in time, space and place.

Interior and furniture design, especially of furniture incorporating new technology and building services, promised greater versatility in solving the problems of work at a time of rapid organisational and market change. By the 1990s this was where new investment was mainly routed – especially as the 1980s' building boom had left a glut of unlet office buildings in most of the major cities of Europe and America. New offices also began to explore micro-architectural elements independent of the building shell: the Nickelodeon scheme, for example, housed its meeting rooms in autonomous vertical wooden structures punched casually through the floor slabs of the 1970s' high-rise tower in which the company is based.

Gradually, office designers could contemplate even such ideas as the autonomous worker pod, a prefabricated building component, plugged into the bigger shell of the building, as an expression of the swing in the balance of power from architecture to design. When in December 1998 architect Clive Wilkinson unveiled his new office for American advertising agency TBWA–Chiat–Day in Los Angeles, the decision to

29 'Advertising city', Los Angeles: office of TBWA–Chiat–Day

accommodate key employees in prefabricated 'cliff dwellings' – stacked steel office boxes painted bright yellow – attracted much attention for the way it created an autonomous 'city skyline' within the giant neutral shell of a large warehouse [28] (see figure 29). But then so many of the characteristics of the TBWA–Chiat–Day office encapsulated the post-modern office, with its convincing stage-set scenery of the Greenwich Village neighbourhood of the 1960s (green park, main street, basketball court and café space) nurturing the individual within the corporate organisation, creating public areas for social interaction and providing a high degree of workplace flexibility.

Modernism's crowning glories were largely on the USA's east coast, the Seagram Building in New York marking the mid-twentieth-century zenith of the art of the machine for working in. Today, however, the spiritual home of the contemporary office, reflecting a far wider range of cultural references, is the west coast of the USA. TBWA–Chiat–Day's Los Angeles is the new movement's headquarters. After all, the slogan it dreamt up for its client Apple Computer was 'Think different'.

Notes

1 F. Duffy, *The Responsive Office: People and Change* (Streatley-on-Thames: Steelcase–Polymath, 1990), p. 7.

2 *Ibid.*

3 A. Forty, *Objects of Desire: Design and Society 1750–1980* (London: Thames & Hudson, 1986), p. 115.

4 Le Corbusier, *Towards A New Architecture* (New York: Brewer, Warren & Putnam, 1946), p. 87.

5 T. Wolfe, *From Bauhaus to Our House* (London: Jonathan Cape, 1981), p. 29.

6 *Ibid.*, p. 47.

7 *Ibid.*, pp. 64–8.

8 L. Knobel, *Office Furniture* (London: Unwin Hyman, 1987), p. 43.

9 Duffy, *The Responsive Office*, p. 8.

10 Forty, *Objects of Design and Society*, p. 126.

11 J. Woudhuysen, 'Tayloring people for production', *Design* (August 1984), 34–7.

12 *Ibid.*

13   F. Taylor, *State of the Art of Industrial Management* (1912), quoted in *Design* (August 1984), 37.

14   Woudhysen, 'Tayloring people for production', 34–7.

15   J. Myerson, *International Interiors 5* (London: Lawrence King, 1995), p. 12.

16   J. Myerson, *International Interiors 6* (London: Lawrence King, 1997), p. 12.

17   J. Merkle, *Management and Ideology: The Legacy of the International Scientific Management Movement* (Berkeley: University of California, 1980).

18   F. Duffy, quoted in *The Organisation Man*, Blueprint Orgatec supplement (October 1990), 13.

19   J. Carlzon quoted in 'Togetherness', SAS Frosundavik corporate brochure pp. 4–5.

20   See J. Myerson and P. Ross, *The Creative Office* (London: Lawrence King, 1999), for examples of new workforces influencing social change.

21   J. Myerson, and G. Turner, *New Workspace, New Culture: Office Design as Catalyst for Change* (Aldershot: Gower, 1998), p. 120.

22   F. Duffy, quoted in Jeremy Myerson (ed.), *Working it Out: Office Furniture Symposium* (London: Design Council, 1992), p. 13.

23   C. Handy, *The Age of Unreason* (London: Arrow Books, 1990), p. 146.

24   See J. Myerson (ed.), *Work at Home: The Proceedings of the Thinktank on Home-Working at the Royal College of Art* (London: Helen Hamlyn Research Centre, RCA, 1999).

25   Henley Centre, Newspaper Society Homeworking Survey (1998).

26   F. Duffy quoted in *Architectural Review* (January 1979), 54–8.

27   Duffy, *The Responsive Office*, p. 8.

28   J. Myerson, *International Interiors 7* (London: Lawrence King, 2000), p. 12.

Select bibliography

Andrews, J., Briggs, A., Porter, R., Tucker, P. and Waddington, K. *A History of Bethlem Hospital, 1247–1997* (London: Routledge, 1997)

Banham, M. and Hillier, B. (eds) *A Tonic to the Nation* (London: Thames & Hudson, 1976)

Barrett, H. and Phillips, J. *Suburban Style: The British Home, 1840–1960* (London: Macdonald & Co., 1987)

Battersby, M. *The Decorative Thirties* (London, Studio Vista, 1969)

Baudrillard, J. 'The system of objects', in J. Thackara (ed.), *Design After Modernism: Beyond the Object* (London: Thames & Hudson, 1988)

Betjeman, J. *Ghastly Good Taste*, rev. Anthony Blond (London: Chapman & Hall, 1970 [1933])

Bowlby, R. *Just Looking: Consumer Culture in Dreiser, Gissing and Zola* (London: Methuen, 1985)

Boxshall, I. *Good Housekeeping, Every Home Should Have One: Seventy-Five Years of Change in the Home* (London: Ebury Press, 1997)

Brooks, C. 'The amateur mechanic and the modern movement', in Design Council, *Leisure in the Twentieth Century* (London: Design Council, 1977)

Calloway, S. and Jones, S. *Traditional Style* (London: Pyramid Books, 1990)

Cannadine, D. *The Pleasures of the Past* (London: Fontana Press, 1990)

Cornforth, J. *The Inspiration of the Past: Country House Taste in the Twentieth Century* (Harmondsworth: Viking–Country Life, 1985)

Curran, C. P. *Dublin Decorative Plasterwork of the Seventeenth and Eighteenth Centuries* (London: Alec Tiranti, 1967)

Delgado, A. *The Enormous File: A Social History of the Office* (Norwich: Chaucer Press, 1979)

De Wolfe, E. *The House in Good Taste* (New York: Harpers & Brothers, 1935; 1st edn, New York: Century, 1913)

Digby, A. *Madness, Morality and Medicine: A Study of the York Retreat, 1796–1914* (Cambridge: Cambridge University Press, 1985)

Douglas, M. and Isherwood, B. *The World of Goods: Towards an Anthropology of Consumption*, 2nd edn (London: Routledge, 1996 [1975])

Duffy, F. *Office Landscaping: A New Approach to Office Planning* (London: Anbar Publications, 1966)

Forty, A. *Objects of Desire: Design and Society since 1750* (London: Thames & Hudson, 1995)

Greenhalgh, P. (ed.) *Modernism in Design* (London: Reaktion Books, 1990)

Hampton, M. 'On decorating: chintz charming', *House & Garden* (USA), 156 (December 1984), 62ff.

Hayden, R. *Mrs Delaney, Her Life and Her Flowers* (London: British Museum Press, 2000)

Hewison, R. *The Heritage Industry: Britain in a Climate of Decline* (London: Methuen, 1987)

Impey, O. and MacGregor, A. (eds) *The Origins of Museums: The Cabinet of Curiosities in Sixteenth- and Seventeenth-Century Europe* (Oxford: Oxford University Press, 1985)

Johnson, D. 'The history and development of do-it-yourself', in Design Council, *Leisure in the Twentieth Century* (London: Design Council, 1977)

Jones, C. *Colefax and Fowler: The Best in Decoration* (London: Barrie & Jenkins, 1989)

Kinchin, J. 'Interiors: nineteenth-century essays on the "masculine" and the "feminine" room', in P. Kirkham (ed.), *The Gendered Object* (Manchester: Manchester University Press, 1996)

Kron, J. *Home-Psych: The Social Psychology of Home and Decoration* (New York: Clarkson Potter, 1983)

Le Corbusier *Towards a New Architecture* (London: Architectural Press, 1978 [1923])

Leslie, F. *Designs for Twentieth-Century Interiors* (London: V&A Publications, 2000).

Light, A. *Forever England: Femininity, Literature and Conservatism between the Wars* (London: Routledge, 1991)

Lupton, E. and Miller, J. A. *The Bathroom, the Kitchen and the Aesthetics of Waste* (Princeton, NJ: Princeton Architectural Press, 1992)

McNeil, P. 'Designing women: gender, sexuality and the interior decorator, 1890–1940', *Art History*, 17 (December 1994), 631–57

Massey, A. *Interior Design of the Twentieth Century* (London: Thames & Hudson, 1990

Metcalf, P. C. *Ogden Codman and the Decoration of Houses* (Boston, MA: Boston Atheneum, 1988)

Miller, W. *Great Luxury Liners 1927–1954* (New York: Dover Publications, 1991)

Putnam, T. and Newton, C. *Household Choices* (London: Futures Publications, 1990)

Scull, A. *The Most Solitary of Afflictions – Madness and Society in Britain, 1700–1900* (New Haven, CT: Yale University Press, 1993)

Seebohm, C. and Sykes, C. S. *English Country: Living in England's Private Houses* (New York: Clarkson Potter, 1987)

Slesin, S. and Cliff, S. *English Style* (New York: Clarkson Potter, 1984)

Smith, J. *Elsie de Wolfe: A Life in the High Style* (New York: Atheneum, 1982)

Sparke, P. *An Introduction to Design and Culture in the Twentieth Century* (London: Routledge, 1986)

Sparke, P. *As Long as It's Pink: The Sexual Politics of Taste* (London: Pandora, 1995)

Sparke, P. (ed.) *Did Britain Make It?* (London: Design Council, 1986)

Steele, J. *The Queen Mary* (London: Phaidon, 1995)

Thornton, P. *Authentic Décor: The Domestic Interior, 1620–1920* (London: Weidenfeld & Nicholson, 1984)

Tinniswood, A. *The Polite Tourist: A History of Country House Visiting* (London: National Trust, 1998)

Tomlinson, A. (ed.) *Consumption, Identity and Style* (London: Routledge, 1990)

Wharton, E. and Codman, O., Jr *The Decoration of Houses* (New York: W. W. Norton, 1978 [1897])

Williams, R. *Dream Worlds: Mass Consumption in late Nineteenth-Century France* (Berkeley: University of California Press, 1982)

Index

Lightning Source UK Ltd.
Milton Keynes UK
UKHW020054131220
374812UK00018B/606

9 780719 067297